Tiziana

Holt Spanish

D1227155

¡Ven conmigo!®

Grammar Tutor
for Students of Spanish

Levels 1, 2, and 3

HOLT, RINEHART AND WINSTON

A Harcourt Education Company

Austin • Orlando • Chicago • New York • Toronto • London • San Diego

Copyright © by Holt, Rinehart and Winston

All rights reserved. No part of this publication may be reproduced or transmitted in any form or by any means, electronic or mechanical, including photocopy, recording, or any information storage and retrieval system, without permission in writing from the publisher.

Photography Credits

Cover
(t) © Dana White/PhotoEdit/Picture Quest; (b) Digital Imagery ® © 2003 PhotoDisc, Inc.

Teachers using ¡VEN CONMIGO! may photocopy blackline masters in complete pages in sufficient quantities for classroom use only and not for resale.

¡VEN CONMIGO! is a trademark licensed to Holt, Rinehart and Winston, registered in the United States of America and/or other jurisdictions.

Printed in the United States of America

ISBN 0-03-065893-4

3 4 5 6 7   095   05 04 03

Table of Contents

Spanish 1

Copyright © by Holt, Rinehart and Winston. All rights reserved.

Table of Contents continued

Spanish 2

Copyright © by Holt, Rinehart and Winston. All rights reserved.

Table of Contents *continued*

Spanish 3

Copyright © by Holt, Rinehart and Winston. All rights reserved.

To the Teacher

Many students do not have a clear understanding of their own language and cannot, therefore, build on that understanding as they learn a second language. The intention of this *Grammar Tutor* is to explain the basic grammar concepts introduced and practiced in *¡Ven conmigo!* first in English, with English examples and activities, and then in Spanish. Students can then relate the targeted grammar concept to something they do every day in English and thereby gain insights about how the grammar works before they attempt to learn it in the context of an entirely new language.

The Grammar Tutor presents in sequential order the main grammar points introduced in *¡Ven conmigo!*, Levels 1, 2, and 3. These grammar points are compared to English as appropriate, so that students can readily see the many similarities between the two languages. In some cases, they will, of course, see differences; however, as they compare and contrast the structures of Spanish and English, they will no doubt accomplish one goal: they will increase their understanding of language in general and become better able to use it to communicate.

The explanation of each grammar concept is accompanied by examples, and each presentation is followed by an activity that allows students to verify that they have understood the explanation of the grammar concept. The concepts are presented first in English and then in Spanish; the activity immediately following each presentation has the same format in both languages, to enable students to quickly see the comparison between the two languages. Following this basic introduction, students are asked to apply the grammar concept to simple, structured activities in Spanish. The final activity on each Activity Master encourages students to think about both the target language and their own.

On the following pages is a glossary of the grammar terms that are covered in this book. This "Grammar at a Glance" can serve as a quick reference to the more detailed material covered in the body of the *Grammar Tutor*.

Copyright © by Holt, Rinehart and Winston. All rights reserved.

Grammar at a Glance

adjective An adjective modifies a noun or a pronoun. (See also **demonstrative adjective**, **interrogative adjective**, and **possessive adjective**.)

EXAMPLES   The Garcias have a **beautiful**, **red** car.
*Los García tienen un **bonito** carro **rojo**.*

adjective agreement (See **agreement**.)

adverb An adverb modifies a verb, an adjective, or another adverb.

EXAMPLES   We walked **slowly** to class.
*Caminamos **lentamente** a clase.*

agreement Agreement is the correspondence, or match, between grammatical forms. Grammatical forms agree when they have the same number or gender.

subject-verb agreement Subject-verb agreement refers to the form of a verb that goes with its subject.

EXAMPLES   **This package is** a gift for my mother.
***Este paquete es** un regalo para mi madre.*

adjective agreement Adjective agreement refers to the form of an adjective that matches the number and gender of the noun it modifies. English has no adjective agreement, but Spanish adjectives must match the nouns they modify.

EXAMPLES   **My sister** is **tall**. **My brother** is **tall**, too.
***Mi hermana** es **alta**. **Mi hermano** es **alto** también.*

article An article refers to a noun. Articles are the most frequently used type of adjectives.

definite article A definite article refers to a specific noun.

EXAMPLES   **The** book is in **the** backpack.
***El** libro está en **la** mochila.*

indefinite article An indefinite article refers to a noun that is not specific.

EXAMPLES   He ordered **a** cookie and **a** glass of milk.
*Él pidió **una** galleta y **un** vaso de leche.*

command (See **imperative mood**.)

conditional The conditional verb form is used to tell what you would or would not do under certain conditions.

EXAMPLES   If I had the money, I **would buy** this book.
*Si tuviera el dinero, **compraría** este libro.*

conjunction A conjunction is a word that joins words or groups of words.

EXAMPLES   I want to dance, **but** I am very tired.
*Quiero bailar, **pero** estoy muy cansada.*

Copyright © by Holt, Rinehart and Winston. All rights reserved.

subordinating conjunction Subordinating conjunctions are adverbs or adverbial phrases that connect clauses.

 EXAMPLES We are going to eat *before* Alberto leaves.
     Vamos a comer antes de que salga Alberto.

definite article (See article.)

demonstrative adjective A demonstrative adjective points out a specific person, place, thing, or idea.

 EXAMPLES Do you prefer *this* coat or *that* vest?
     ¿Prefieres este abrigo o esa chaqueta?

direct object A direct object is a word or word group that receives the action of the verb or shows the result of the action. A direct object answers the question *Whom?* or *What?* after a verb of action.

 EXAMPLES My parents don't watch *television*.
     Mis padres no miran la televisión.

direct object pronoun (See pronoun.)

imperative mood A sentence in the imperative gives a command or makes a request.

 EXAMPLES *Do* your homework! And then, *let's go* to the movies.
     ¡Haz la tarea! Y luego vayamos al cine.

imperfect The imperfect tense in Spanish refers to actions or conditions in the past that were ongoing, that occurred regularly, or that were going on when another event occurred. The Spanish imperfect is similar to the English present perfect.

 EXAMPLES I *was watching* T.V. when the phone rang.
     Yo estaba mirando la televisión cuando sonó el teléfono.

indefinite article (See article.)

indirect object An indirect object is a word or word group that tells *to whom* or *to what* or *for whom* or *for what* the action of the verb is done.

 EXAMPLES Silvia gave *the girl* a toy.
     Silvia le regaló un jugete a la niña.

indirect object pronoun (See pronoun.)

infinitive The infinitive is the base form of the verb. In English the infinitive is preceded by the word *to*, and in Spanish the infinitive is one word with an *-er, -ir,* or *-ar* ending.

 EXAMPLES I want *to sing* with you.
     Quiero cantar contigo.

interrogative adjective An interrogative adjective is an adjective that introduces a question.

 EXAMPLES *Which* class do you like?
     ¿Cuál clase te gusta?

interrogative sentence An interrogative sentence asks a question and is followed by a question mark. In Spanish, it is also preceded by an upside-down question mark.

Copyright © by Holt, Rinehart and Winston. All rights reserved.

EXAMPLES   Are you coming with us?
¿ Tú vienes con nosotros?

irregular verb An irregular verb is a verb whose forms do not follow a regular, predictable pattern.

mood Mood is the form a verb takes to indicate the attitude of the speaker. (See also **imperative mood, conditional mood,** and **subjunctive mood.**)

noun A noun names a person, place, thing, or idea.
EXAMPLES   **Laura** brought the **music** to the **party**.
Laura trajo la música a la fiesta.

number Number is the form a word takes to indicate whether it is singular or plural.
EXAMPLES   The **children** ate some **strawberries**.
Los niños comieron algunas fresas.

placement Placement refers to the position of words in a sentence or phrase in relation to other words in the sentence or phrase.

possessive adjective A possessive adjective is an adjective that indicates to whom or what something belongs.
EXAMPLES   This is **my** pencil. These are **their** books.
Éste es mi lápiz. Éstos son sus libros.

preposition A preposition shows the relationship of a noun or a pronoun to another word in a sentence.
EXAMPLES   Luis is going **to** the swimming pool **with** Paola.
Luis va a la piscina con Paola.

pronoun A pronoun is used in place of one or more nouns.
EXAMPLES   Marta is going with her cousins. **She** called **them** this morning.
Marta va con sus primos. Ella los llamó esta mañana.

direct object pronoun A direct object pronoun is a pronoun that stands for the direct object of a sentence.
EXAMPLES   María is at school. I saw **her** in math class.
María está en la escuela. La vi en la clase de matemáticas.

indirect object pronoun An indirect object pronoun is a word that stands for the indirect object of a sentence.
EXAMPLES   Lisa sent **us** a letter.
Lisa nos mandó una carta.

subject pronoun A subject pronoun stands for the person or thing that performs the action of the verb.
EXAMPLES   **They** (Ana and José) are going to the mall.
Ellos (Ana y José) van al centro comercial.

Copyright © by Holt, Rinehart and Winston. All rights reserved.

reciprocal pronoun A reciprocal pronoun expresses a mutual action or relationship.

    EXAMPLES   Rosa and Manuel see *each other* at the beach.
                     Rosa y Manuel se ven en la playa.

reflexive pronoun A reflexive pronoun reflects the action of the verb back onto the subject.

    EXAMPLES   I hurt *myself* playing basketball.
                     Me hice daño jugando al baloncesto.

reflexive verb A reflexive verb indicates that the action of the verb is done to, for, or by oneself. It is accompanied by a reflexive pronoun. In English, we do not have reflexive verbs, only reflexive pronouns.

    EXAMPLES   The cat bathes *itself*.
                     El gato se baña.

regular verb A regular verb is a verb whose forms follow a regular, predictable pattern.

    EXAMPLES   Pablo *studies* Spanish.
                     Pablo estudia español.

subject A subject is a word, phrase, or clause that performs the action of the verb.

    EXAMPLES   *The students* eat lunch.
                     Los estudiantes almuerzan.

subject pronoun (See **pronoun**.)

subject-verb agreement (See **agreement**.)

subjunctive mood The subjunctive mood is used to express a suggestion, a necessity, a condition contrary to fact, or a wish.

    EXAMPLES   I wish you *were* older.
                     Ojalá fueras mayor.

subordinating conjunction (See **conjunction**.)

tense The tense of verbs indicates the time of the action or state of being that is expressed by the verb.

    EXAMPLES   She *is singing*. She *sang*. She *will sing*.
                     Ella está cantando. Ella cantó. Ella cantará.

verb A verb expresses an action or a state of being. (See also **conditional**, **infinitive**, **irregular verb**, **reflexive verb**, and **regular verb**.)

    EXAMPLES   Eduardo *plays* soccer. He *is* Spanish.
                     Eduardo juega al fútbol. Él es español.

Copyright © by Holt, Rinehart and Winston. All rights reserved.

Grammar Tutor Activities
¡Ven conmigo!
Spanish 1

■ PUNCTUATION MARKS AND ACCENTS

¡Ven conmigo! Level 1, p. 23
Adelante, p. 30

C A P Í T U L O   1

> **In English** Question marks **(?)** and exclamation points **(!)** are placed at the *end* of sentences that are questions or exclamations.
>
> What is your name**?**   Nice to meet you **!**

A Write the appropriate punctuation mark at the end of each sentence: (?) for questions and (!) for exclamations.

1. Where are you from **?**

2. Thank you ___

3. What do you like to do ___

4. Hi, Mr. Núñez ___

5. How are you ___

6. What is your name ___

7. See you tomorrow ___

8. Delighted to meet you ___

> **In Spanish** Question marks **(?)** and exclamation points **(!)** are used at the end of sentences in Spanish, too. However, you must also put an upside-down question mark **(¿)** or exclamation point **(¡)** at the *beginning* of the sentence.
>
> **¿**Cómo te llamas**?**   **¡**Mucho gusto **!**

B Below you will find the sentences from Activity A written in Spanish. Write question marks (¿...?) and exclamation points (¡...!) where necessary according to the Spanish punctuation.

1. __¿__De dónde eres_**?**

2. ___Gracias___

3. ___Qué te gusta hacer___

4. ___Hola, Sr. Núñez___

5. ___Cómo estás___

6. ___Cómo te llamas___

7. ___Hasta mañana___

8. ___Encantado de conocerte___

Spanish 1 ¡Ven conmigo!, Chapter 1

Grammar Tutor **1**

Copyright © by Holt, Rinehart and Winston. All rights reserved.

Spanish has other special marks, too. The mark found over the **o** in **cómo** is known as an **accent** and the mark over the **n** in **mañana** is a **tilde**.

An **accent mark (á, é, í, ó, ú)** often tells the reader which syllable to emphasize when pronouncing the word. Sometimes accent marks can even change the meaning of the word, so be sure to note the accent when learning new vocabulary.

The tilde (~) is also used as a guide to pronunciation. The **ñ** is pronounced like the sound *ny* as in the word *canyon*.

C Look again at Activity B. Count how many accent marks and how many tildes you can find in sentences 1-8.

Accent marks _____   Tildes _____

D Use the phrases in the box below to create a dialogue between you and a new friend. Don't forget question marks (¿...?) and exclamation points (¡...!).

Tengo que irme	Cómo te llamas	Hola
Me llamo…	Encantado/Encantada	Y tú
Yo soy…	Adiós	Hasta mañana

_____

_____

_____

_____

_____

_____

_____

_____

_____

E Why might it be useful to have an upside-down question mark or exclamation point at the beginning of a sentence in Spanish?

_____

_____

_____

_____

_____

Copyright © by Holt, Rinehart and Winston. All rights reserved.

■ SUBJECT PRONOUNS: *YOU* AND *I*

In English Every sentence has a subject. You can tell who or what the subject is by asking yourself who is doing something or what is being described. The subject may be a noun or a pronoun. In the following sentences, the subject is highlighted:

Francisco is fifteen.   (*Francisco* is a noun.)
You are from Ecuador.   (*You* is a pronoun.)

When the subject of a sentence is a noun, it can be replaced by a **subject pronoun.** Two subject pronouns in English are **I** and **you**. Use the pronoun **I** to refer to yourself and **you** when referring to someone with whom you are talking.

I like ice cream.   **You** prefer cookies.

A Circle the subject pronouns. Then check the appropriate column to tell which person the pronoun refers to.

	AMY	LUIS
AMY Hello. (I) am Amy.	✓	
LUIS Hi. I am Luis.		
Where are you from?		
AMY I am from the United States.		
Are you from Madrid?		
LUIS No, I am from Barcelona.		
I am studying at the Universidad Autónoma.		
Would you like to be pen pals?		
AMY I think that's a great idea.		
I could practice my Spanish!		

In Spanish When the subject of a sentence is a proper noun or a noun, it can also be replaced by a **subject pronoun**. Two subject pronouns in Spanish are **yo** and **tú**. **Yo**, like *I* in English, is used to refer to yourself and **tú**, like *you*, is used when talking to someone else. Remember that the pronoun **tú** always has an accent.

Yo me llamo Carla, ¿y **tú**?   **Tú** estás bien y **yo** también.

Note that, unlike *I* in English, **yo** is not capitalized, except at the beginning of a sentence. Another difference is that, while in English the pronoun is always used, in Spanish the pronoun is often omitted.

How are **you**?   ¿Cómo estás?

I am American.   Soy americana.

Copyright © by Holt, Rinehart and Winston. All rights reserved.

B Circle the subject pronouns. Then check the appropiate column to tell which person the pronouns refer to.

	JUAN	PILAR
JUAN Hola. (Yo) me llamo Juan.	✓	
JUAN ¿Y tú?		
PILAR Yo soy Pilar. ¿Qué tal?		
JUAN Regular. ¿Y tú?		
PILAR Yo estoy muy bien.		
JUAN Estupendo. Bueno, yo tengo que irme.		
PILAR Sí, yo también. ¡Hasta luego!		

C Complete the following sentences with the correct subject pronoun.

1. __Yo__ soy Luis Miguel.

2. ¿Y _____? ¿Cómo te llamas?

3. _____ me llamo Selena.

4. ¿Cómo estás _____?

5. _____ estoy bien, gracias.

6. Selena, ¿_____ tienes clase?

7. Sí _____ tengo clase ahora.

8. _____ tengo clase también. ¡Adiós!

D Compare these sentences in Spanish and in English. Why do you think in Spanish one does not always have to use a subject pronoun? What would sentences be like in English if you removed the subject pronoun?

Spanish: Soy alta. **English:** I am tall.
Eres guapa. You are good-looking.
Tengo clase. I have class.

_____

_____

_____

_____

_____

Copyright © by Holt, Rinehart and Winston. All rights reserved.

THE VERB *TO BE* TO EXPRESS ORIGIN

¡Ven conmigo! Level 1, p. 28
Adelante, p. 38

C
A
P
Í
T
U
L
O

1

In English The verb **to be** is used to describe where someone is from.

I **am** from Caracas, Venezuela.
Where **are** you from?
María **is** from Guatemala.

Notice that in every example the verb **to be** is followed by the preposition **from**.

A Circle the form of the verb **to be** in the following sentences. Then underline the preposition common to all of the sentences.

1. Juan (is) from Puerto Rico.

2. I am from Valencia, Spain.

3. You are from La Paz, Bolivia.

4. Anne Marie is from Boston, Massachusetts.

5. Laura is from Managua, Nicaragua.

6. You are from Los Angeles, California.

7. He is from Amarillo, Texas.

8. I am from Santiago, Chile.

In Spanish The verb **ser** (*to be*) is also used to describe where someone is from. As in English, the preposition **de** (*from*) also must be used.

Soy de Caracas, Venezuela.
¿De dónde **eres**?
Ramona **es** de Guatemala.

Soy, **eres**, and **es** are forms of the verb **ser**.

yo **soy**   *I am*
tú **eres**   *you are*
él, ella **es** *he, she is*

B Circle the form of **ser** in the following sentences. Then underline the preposition common to all of the sentences.

1. Ella (es) de Montevideo, Uruguay.

2. Yo soy de Phoenix, Arizona.

3. Él es de San José, Costa Rica.

4. Ricardo es de Monterrey, México.

Copyright © by Holt, Rinehart and Winston. All rights reserved.

5. Tú eres de Denver, Colorado.

6. Marta es de Santafé de Bogotá, Colombia.

7. Isabel es de Quito, Ecuador.

8. Casey es de West Palm Beach, Florida.

C Circle the correct form of **ser** in the following sentences.

1. Isabel Allende (soy/eres/es) de Chile.

2. Yo (soy/eres/es) de España.

3. Fidel Castro (soy/eres/es) de Cuba.

4. Pedro Martínez (soy/eres/es) de la República Dominicana.

5. Tú (soy/eres/es) de Estados Unidos.

6. Shakira (soy/eres/es) de Colombia.

7. Laura Esquivel (soy/eres/es) de México.

8. Jorge Luis Borges (soy/eres/es) de Argentina.

D Complete the following dialogue with **soy**, **eres**, or **es**.

FRIDA   David, ¿de dónde __eres__? ¿De Honduras?

DAVID   ¡Yo no _____ de Honduras! _____ de Nicaragua.

FRIDA   Mi amiga Blanca _____ de Nicaragua también. Ella _____ de Managua. ¿_____ tú de Managua?

DAVID   No. Yo _____ de Granada. ¿Y tú, Frida? ¿De dónde _____?

FRIDA   Yo _____ de Veracruz, México.

E What are the similarities in English and Spanish when describing where you are from?

_____

_____

_____

_____

_____

Copyright © by Holt, Rinehart and Winston. All rights reserved.

■ QUESTION WORDS

In English Some questions are formed by putting a question word such as **how**, **where**, or **what** at the beginning of a sentence, and a question mark at the end.

> **How** old are you?
>
> **Where** are you from?
>
> **What** is your name?

A Circle the correct question word to complete the following sentences.

1. (Where/What) do you live?

2. (Where/How) are you feeling today?

3. (How/What) is your favorite color?

4. (How/What) language do you speak?

5. (Where/How) do you spell your name?

6. (Where/What) were you born?

7. (How/What) is your nationality?

8. (Where/How) is the nearest post office?

In Spanish Question words are also used to form questions. Some question words in Spanish are **cómo**, **cuántos**, and **dónde**. Note that all Spanish question words have accents.

> **¿Cómo** estás?   *How are you?*
> **¿Cómo** te llamas?   *What is your name?*
> **¿Cuántos** años tienes? *How old are you?*
> **¿De dónde** eres?   *Where are you from?*

Remember that when talking about where someone is from, you must use the preposition **de** *(from)*. When you are asking where someone is from, **de** is placed before the question word.

B Circle the correct question word to complete the following sentences.

1. ¿(Cuántos/Cómo) años tienes?

2. ¿(Cuántos/De dónde) eres?

3. ¿(Cuántos/Cómo) te llamas?

4. ¿(Cuántos/De dónde) es Octavio Paz?

Copyright © by Holt, Rinehart and Winston. All rights reserved.

5. ¿(Cómo/De dónde) estás?

6. ¿(De dónde/Cuántos) años tiene Pedro?

7. ¿(Cuántos/De dónde) es la señora Martínez?

8. ¿(Cómo/Cuántos) está Miguel?

C   Write an appropriate question for each answer.

1. **¿De dónde eres?**

Soy de San Juan, Puerto Rico.

2. _____

Me llamo Carlos Andrade.

3. _____

Muy bien, gracias.

4. _____

Ella es de Nueva York.

5. _____

Tengo quince años.

D   Why do you think question words in Spanish have accents? Do you suppose the same words exist without accents?

_____

_____

_____

_____

_____

Copyright © by Holt, Rinehart and Winston. All rights reserved.

¡Ven Conmigo! Level 1, p. 33
Adelante, p. 46

C A P Í T U L O 1

DEFINITE ARTICLES AND GENDER

In English Words used to name people, places, and things are called nouns. Often a noun is introduced by the definite article **the**.

Cristina listens to **the** radio.   (*radio* is a noun)
The boy plays football.   (*boy* is a noun)
The Mexican restaurant is great.   (*restaurant* is a noun)

The is used with all nouns: nouns that refer to the masculine gender (like *boy*), the feminine gender (like *actress*), and those that have no gender (like *radio*, *restaurant*, and most nouns in English).

A Circle the definite articles in the following sentences, and underline the noun each article goes with.

1. The musician plays jazz.

2. My brother took the football.

3. She ate all the pizza.

4. The homework was easy.

5. We won the volleyball game.

6. My mom dropped the salad.

7. The CD is scratched.

8. The soccer ball is missing.

In Spanish All nouns have a gender, that is, they are either masculine or feminine. The word **fruta** *(fruit)*, for instance, is feminine; the word **chocolate** is masculine.

As in English, Spanish nouns can be introduced by definite articles. Two definite articles are **el** and **la**.

El is used with masculine nouns: **el** béisbol, **el** tenis.
La is used with feminine nouns: **la** música, **la** clase.

A good way to remember the gender of a noun is to learn the noun with its definite article: **el fútbol** (masculine), **la natación** (feminine).

B Circle the definite articles in the following sentences, and underline the noun each article goes with. Then check the appropriate column to tell whether the noun is masculine (M) or feminine (F).

	M	F
1. Me gusta el fútbol norteamericano.	✓	
2. ¿Te gusta la música pop?		

Copyright © by Holt, Rinehart and Winston. All rights reserved.

	M	F
3. No me gusta la natación.	_____	_____
4. A mí me gusta el baloncesto.	_____	_____
5. Te gusta mucho la comida italiana.	_____	_____
6. No, no me gusta la pizza.	_____	_____
7. Te gusta la clase de español.	_____	_____
8. ¿Te gusta el jazz?	_____	_____

C Complete the following sentences with the correct definite article.

1. ¿Te gusta _el_ fútbol?

2. Me gusta _____ pizza.

3. Te gusta mucho _____ música clásica.

4. _____ fruta me gusta mucho.

5. A ti te gusta _____ tenis.

6. No, no me gusta mucho _____ tenis.

7. Me gusta _____ español.

8. Te gusta _____ baloncesto.

D Write five sentences telling what you or your friend likes, using **me gusta** or **te gusta**. Circle the definite article, then underline the noun and tell whether it is masculine or feminine.

1. Me gusta (la) pizza. Pizza is feminine. _____

2. _____

3. _____

4. _____

5. _____

E Look at the following list of vocabulary words. Is there any similarity among the masculine nouns or among the feminine nouns? If so, how might this help you in the future when learning new nouns and their definite articles?

_____

_____

_____

_____

_____

el chico	la chica
el piano	la música
el amigo	la amiga
el queso	la mermelada
el año	la semana

Copyright © by Holt, Rinehart and Winston. All rights reserved.

CAPÍTULO 2

▇ PLURAL NOUNS

¡Ven conmigo! Level I, p. 52
Adelante, p. 67

In English When a noun refers to more than one thing, the plural is used. There are basic rules for making nouns plural.

1. The plural of most nouns is formed by adding an **-s** to the end of the word.

notebook	⟹	notebook**s**
folder	⟹	folder**s**

2. When a noun ends in **-s**, **-sh**, **-x**, or **-z**, add **-es** to the end of the word.

fox	⟹	fox**es**
bus	⟹	bus**es**

3. When a noun ends in **-y** preceded by a consonant, change the **y** to **i** and add **-es**.

family	⟹	famil**ies**

A In the following sentences, write the plural of the underlined words.

PLURAL

1. Claudia needs a <u>box</u> of pencils.   **boxes**

2. Pilar has a <u>calculator</u>.   _____

3. Manuel goes to the <u>library</u>.   _____

4. I found a backpack in the <u>bush</u>.   _____

5. Isabel needs a new <u>binder</u>.   _____

6. Paco has an English <u>textbook</u>.   _____

7. Susana is having a pizza <u>party</u>.   _____

8. Juan wants to buy a new <u>supply</u> of pens. _____

In Spanish There are also basic rules for making nouns plural.

1. When a noun ends in a vowel (a, e, i, o, u), add **-s**.

diccionario	⟹	diccionario**s**
pintura	⟹	pintura**s**

2. When a noun ends in a consonant (any letter except a, e, i, o, u) add **-es**.

marcador	⟹	marcador**es**
papel	⟹	papel**es**

3. When a noun ends in **-z**, change the **z** to **c** and add **-es**.

lápiz	⟹	lapi**ces**
cruz	⟹	cru**ces**

Copyright © by Holt, Rinehart and Winston. All rights reserved.

B In the following sentences, write the plural of the underlined words.

PLURAL

1. Ella tiene un <u>marcador</u>.   marcadores
2. Maribel quiere una <u>pintura</u>.   _____
3. José necesita un <u>lápiz</u>.   _____
4. Tú quieres un <u>cuaderno</u> nuevo.   _____
5. Carolina tiene un <u>pincel</u>.   _____
6. Sara necesita <u>luz</u> en su cuarto.   _____
7. Quiero más <u>papel</u>.   _____
8. Tengo una <u>clase</u>.   _____

C Your friends tell you what they need for their classes. Respond by telling them that you need *two* of each of these items.

1. Gustavo necesita un cuaderno.   Yo necesito dos cuadernos.
2. Carmen necesita una mochila.   _____
3. Luis Miguel necesita un lápiz.   _____
4. Tania necesita una calculadora.   _____
5. Margarita necesita una hoja de papel.   _____
6. Elí necesita una luz.   _____
7. Maripaz necesita un pincel.   _____
8. Antonia necesita un bolígrafo.   _____

D Write the plural of the following words, first in English, and then in Spanish.

	ENGLISH PLURAL	SPANISH PLURAL
club	_____	_____
radio	_____	_____
conductor	_____	_____
bus	_____	_____
fax	_____	_____

What kinds of words are made plural the same way in both English and Spanish?

_____

_____

Copyright © by Holt, Rinehart and Winston. All rights reserved.

■ INDEFINITE ARTICLES

¡Ven conmigo! Level I, p. 53
Adelante, p. 68

CAPÍTULO 2

In English **Indefinite articles** are used to introduce unspecified nouns. The indefinite articles in English are **a** and **an**.

> I need **a** backpack for school.   María brings **an** eraser to class.

When talking about unspecified plural nouns, **some** and **a few** are used.

> I found **some** books.   I still have **a few** exams left.

A Circle each indefinite article in the following sentences and underline the noun it introduces.

1. Ricardo has a colored pencil.

2. Ana María needs a new backpack.

3. Lisa wants a black marker.

4. Andy has an eraser on his desk.

5. Isabel wants a fancy notebook.

6. Sheila needs a folder for each class.

7. Rachel has an exam tomorrow.

8. Miguel wants a set of paintbrushes.

In Spanish **Indefinite articles** are also used to introduce unspecified nouns. There are four forms in Spanish: **un, una, unos,** and **unas** The form used depends on the number and gender of the noun.

Un and **una** are used to introduce singular nouns. **Un** is used before masculine nouns and **una** before feminine nouns.

> **un** bolígrafo   *a pen*
> **una** calculadora   *a calculator*

The indefinite articles **unos** and **unas** are used to introduce plural nouns. **Unos** and **unas** mean *some* or *a few*. **Unos** is used before masculine nouns and **unas** before feminine nouns.

> **unos** bolígrafos   *some/a few pens*
> **unas** calculadoras   *some/a few calculators*

When referring to a group of people that includes *both* males and females, **unos** is used to introduce the noun.

> **unos** estudiantes   *some/a few students*
> **unos** niños   *some/a few children*

Copyright © by Holt, Rinehart and Winston. All rights reserved.

B Circle each indefinite article in the following sentences and underline the noun that it introduces. Then check the appropriate columns to indicate whether each underlined noun is
singular (S) or plural (P), masculine (M) or feminine (F).

	S	P	M	F
1. Marta necesita (una) calculadora.	✓			✓
2. Brigid quiere unos cuadernos azules.				
3. Jimena tiene unas carpetas nuevas.				
4. Fabiola quiere una regla.				
5. Paulina necesita unos lápices de colores.				
6. Ricardo tiene unas gomas de borrar.				
7. Ángel no quiere una mochila verde.				
8. Juan Manuel necesita un libro de gramática.				

C Complete the following sentences with **un**, **una**, **unos**, or **unas**.

1. Ana tiene _____**unos**_____ marcadores para la clase de arte.

2. Yo quiero _____ libro bueno.

3. Clarisa necesita _____ cuadernos de actividades.

4. Fernando tiene _____ diccionario para la clase de inglés.

5. Margarita quiere _____ carpetas para su clase.

6. Elvira necesita _____ lápices de colores.

7. Tú tienes _____ reglas para la clase de matemáticas.

8. Marcos quiere _____ lección fácil.

E Read the following sentences. Why is **el** used in the first sentence and **un** in the second? How
would the meaning change if the second sentence used **el** instead of **un**?

       El bolígrafo es de mi amigo. *(The pen belongs to my friend.)*

       Necesito **un** bolígrafo. *(I need a pen.)*

_____

_____

_____

_____

_____

_____

Copyright © by Holt, Rinehart and Winston. All rights reserved.

CAPÍTULO 2

In English When the subject of a sentence is a noun, it can be replaced by a pronoun. Two subject pronouns in English are **he** and **she**.

Larry is handsome.   **He** is handsome.

Sarah has two cats.   **She** has two cats.

A Underline the subject in each sentence. Then write the corresponding subject pronoun (**he** or **she**) in the space to the right.

1. Francisco has to buy a math book.   He

2. Juana needs two pencils for her class.   _____

3. Patricio wants to buy a new backpack.   _____

4. Miguel needs a binder and two folders.   _____

5. Donald has three Spanish dictionaries.   _____

6. María wants a new computer.   _____

7. Ana María has to borrow a book from the library.   _____

8. Brian needs to buy school supplies.   _____

In Spanish Nouns can also be replaced by pronouns. Two subject pronouns in Spanish are **él** *(he)* and **ella** *(she)*.

María es de México.   **Ella** es de México.

Lorenzo tiene un diccionario.   **Él** tiene un diccionario.

B Underline the subject in each sentence. Then write the corresponding subject pronoun (**él** or **ella**) in the space to the right.

1. Paco es mi amigo.   Él

2. Luisa necesita estudiar.   _____

3. Carmen tiene que ir a clase.   _____

4. Manolo quiere comprar el libro.   _____

5. Sergio es inteligente.   _____

6. María es profesora de historia.   _____

7. Roberto tiene seis cuadernos.   _____

8. Eugenia necesita la goma de borrar.   _____

Copyright © by Holt, Rinehart and Winston. All rights reserved.

C Answer the following questions about what your friends need for the first day of school. Use the correct subject pronouns and the clues in parentheses.

1. ¿Qué necesita Elena? (una calculadora)

   Ella necesita una calculadora.

2. ¿Qué quiere Tomás? (un diccionario)

   _____

3. ¿Qué necesita Mercedes? (un pincel)

   _____

4. ¿Qué necesita Ángela? (una calculadora)

   _____

5. ¿Qué quiere Enrique? (unos cuadernos)

   _____

6. ¿Qué necesita Miguel? (una goma de borrar)

   _____

7. ¿Qué necesita Álvaro? (un libro)

   _____

8. ¿Qué quiere Juana? (una mochila)

   _____

D Can you think of a reason why subject pronouns are used? How would a conversation sound if you repeated the subject noun in every sentence instead of replacing it with a pronoun?

   _____

   _____

   _____

Copyright © by Holt, Rinehart and Winston. All rights reserved.

 **QUANTITY**

¡Ven conmigo! Level I, p. 58
Adelante, p. 78

C A P Í T U L O   2

In English Two ways of asking about quantity are **how much** and **how many.**

> **How many** cats are in the kitchen?   **How much** milk is in their bowl?

When responding to questions regarding quantity, the indefinite adjectives **many** or **much** are often used.

> There are **many** cats in the kitchen.   There is not **much** milk in the bowl.

The phrase **a lot** may be used to express a large quantity. This phrase is often followed by the preposition **of**.

> There is **a lot of** milk in the bowl.

A Underline the quantity words and phrases that appear in the following sentences. Then check the appropriate columns to tell whether each noun described is singular (S) or plural (P).

	S	P
1. How many books are on the shelf?		✓
2. There is a lot of noise in the hallway.		
3. How much paper is left in the copy machine?		
4. There are many students in this class.		
5. There is too much material to study.		
6. How much time will it take to complete the exam?		
7. How many workbooks are from last year?		
8. I learned a lot of new words in Spanish class.		

In Spanish There are four ways to ask *how much* or *how many*: **cuánto, cuánta, cuántos,** and **cuántas.** The ending of the word changes because, like many adjectives in Spanish, **cuánto** must agree in number and gender with the noun it describes.

¿**Cuánto** papel tienes?	(*papel* is masculine and singular)
¿**Cuánta** tarea tienes?	(*tarea* is feminine and singular)
¿**Cuántos** cuadernos tienes?	(*cuadernos* is masculine and plural)
¿**Cuántas** calculadoras tienes?	(*calculadoras* is feminine and plural)

The word **mucho** means *a lot*, *much*, or *many*. Like **cuánto**, **mucho** must agree in number and gender with the noun it describes.

Tengo **mucho** trabajo.	(*trabajo* is masculine and singular)
Isabel no tiene **mucha** tarea.	(*tarea* is feminine and singular)
Ana tiene **muchos** diccionarios.	(*diccionarios* is masculine and plural)
Tienes **muchas** clases.	(*clases* is feminine and plural)

Copyright © by Holt, Rinehart and Winston. All rights reserved.

B Underline the forms of **cuánto** and **mucho** that appear in the following sentences. Then check the appropriate columns to tell whether each noun described is singular (S) or plural (P), masculine (M) or feminine (F).

	S	P	M	F
1. ¿<u>Cuántas</u> clases tienes?		✓		✓
2. Alejandro tiene muchos amigos.				
3. No tengo mucho papel.				
4. ¿Cuánta pizza hay?				
5. ¿Cuánto papel hay en tu cuaderno?				
6. ¿Tienes mucha tarea?				
7. ¿Cuántos profesores están aquí?				
8. Hay muchas revistas en la mesa.				

C Complete the following sentences with the correct form of **cuánto** or **mucho**.

1. ¿ **Cuántas** camas tienes en tu cuarto?

2. Hay _____ computadoras en mi escuela.

3. Tienes _____ libros en tu estante.

4. ¿_____ carteles hay en el cuarto de tu amigo?

5. Hay _____ plantas en el cuarto de Miguel.

6. ¿_____ tarea tienes para la clase de historia?

7. ¿_____ discos compactos tienes?

8. Hay _____ espacio en tu cuarto.

D Study the following questions:

¿Tienes **mucha** tarea?

¿**Cuánta** tarea tienes?

Mucha and **cuánta** are both used in a question. What similarities and differences do you see between the two? Which word can <u>only</u> be used in questions?

_____

_____

_____

_____

_____

_____

Copyright © by Holt, Rinehart and Winston. All rights reserved.

 INFINITIVES

¡Ven conmigo! Level I, p. 61
Adelante, p. 86

C A P Í T U L O 2

> **In English** Verbs express actions (like *dance* and *read*) or states of being (like *become*). The **infinitive** is the base form of the verb. It is the form found in the dictionary. In English, the infinitive is often preceded by the word **to**.
>
> **to be, to study, to find**

A Circle the infinitive forms in the following sentences.

1. I have to buy school supplies.
2. We are trying to find colored pencils.
3. I like to study Spanish.
4. Luisa hopes to learn about new places.
5. Manolo wants to be a professor.
6. The students decide to eat lunch.
7. Elena agrees to help me with my homework.
8. Rosa and Teresa sign up to play soccer.

> **In Spanish** The **infinitive** is also the base form of the verb. In Spanish, the infinitive is one word and can be recognized by its endings: **-ar, -er,** or **-ir**.
>
> **comprar, ir, poner**

B Circle the infinitive forms in the following sentences.

1. Necesito comprar una mochila.
2. ¿Quieres conocer a mi amiga?
3. ¿Dónde quieres poner los lápices?
4. Quiero comprar papel.
5. Eduardo necesita ir a la escuela.
6. ¿Quieres hacer la tarea?
7. Virginia necesita encontrar la goma de borrar.
8. Nosotros necesitamos organizar la clase.

Copyright © by Holt, Rinehart and Winston. All rights reserved.

C Look at the infinitive forms you underlined in Activity B. Categorize them by writing each verb under the appropriate column.

-AR VERBS	-ER VERBS	-IR VERBS
comprar		

D Complete the following sentences with the appropriate infinitives from the box. One of the infinitives is used twice.

comprar	conocer	ir	encontrar	organizar	poner	hacer

1. Yo quiero _____ conocer _____ a la nueva chica.

2. Ella no puede _____ sus libros. ¿Dónde están?

3. La chica necesita _____ su cuarto.

4. Nosotros queremos _____ a la librería.

5. Vamos a _____ un libro nuevo.

6. Yo necesito _____ la tarea.

7. Elena necesita _____ el libro en su mochila.

8. Quiero _____ el dinero.

E Read the sentences in Activity D again. What kind of words do infinitives follow?

_____

_____

F Now write five sentences in Spanish using verbs in the infinitive.

1. _____

2. _____

3. _____

4. _____

5. _____

Copyright © by Holt, Rinehart and Winston. All rights reserved.

CAPÍTULO 3

■ DEFINITE ARTICLES

¡Ven conmigo! Level 1, p. 83
Adelante, p. 109

In English Nouns may be introduced by the definite article **the**. Its form remains the same whether the noun it introduces is singular or plural.

Gabriella goes to **the** lunch room.   (*lunch room* is a singular noun)
Lauren has **the** history books.   (*books* is a plural noun)

A In each of the following sentences, circle the definite article and underline the noun it modifies. Then check the appropriate column to indicate whether the noun is singular (S) or plural (P).

	S	P
1. Constance has (the) first class.	✓	
2. The students always arrive on time.		
3. The art class meets at 9 A.M.		
4. Vanesa brings the calculators to geometry class.		
5. I think the teachers at my school are nice.		
6. We have the history exam tomorrow.		
7. At 7:30 A.M. the school bus arrives.		
8. Manuel always gets the highest grades.		

In Spanish There are four different forms for the definite article *the*: **el**, **la**, **los**, and **las**. The form used depends on the number and gender of the noun it introduces.

El introduces singular, masculine nouns: Me gusta **el** francés.

La introduces singular, feminine nouns: Necesito **la** goma de borrar.

Los introduces plural, masculine nouns: Tengo **los** cuadernos.

Los is also used when referring to a group of people that includes both males and females: **Los** estudiantes son de Arizona.

Las introduces plural, feminine nouns: Te gustaron **las** clases.

C
A
P
Í
T
U
L
O

3

Spanish 1 ¡Ven conmigo!, Chapter 3

Grammar Tutor **21**

Copyright © by Holt, Rinehart and Winston. All rights reserved.

B In each of the following sentences, circle the definite article and underline the noun it modifies. Then check the appropriate columns to indicate whether the noun is singular (S) or plural (P), masculine (M) or feminine (F).

	S	P	M	F
1. Sí, tengo (la) <u>clase</u> de biología.	✓			✓
2. ¿Tienes los libros de ciencias?				
3. Quiero conocer a los profesores.				
4. Me gusta el arte.				
5. Quiero ir a la pizzería.				
6. ¿Estudias las ciencias?				
7. Los estudiantes son excelentes.				
8. Tengo que hacer las tareas.				

C Complete the following sentences with the correct form of the definite article.

1. __La__ clase de español es estupenda.

2. No me gusta _____ tarea de español.

3. ¿Tienes _____ libros para la clase de geografía?

4. ¿Qué hay en _____ armario?

5. Necesito _____ dinero.

6. _____ diccionarios están en la librería.

7. El profesor tiene _____ gomas de borrar.

8. _____ calculadoras son para la clase de matemáticas.

D Can you think of an advantage of having different forms in Spanish for the definite article **the**? Think of the sentence:

Las estudiantes son de México. (*The students are from Mexico.*)

_____

_____

_____

_____

_____

_____

Copyright © by Holt, Rinehart and Winston. All rights reserved.

■ POSSESSION

¡Ven conmigo! Level 1, p. 89
Adelante, p. 121

C A P Í T U L O 3

In English An **apostrophe s** ('s) is added to a singular noun to show possession, that is, that something belongs to someone.

Monica's backpack is black and yellow.
Tommy's classes are interesting.

An **apostrophe** alone (') is added after the **-s** of most plural nouns to show possession by more than one person.

Those boys' backpacks are blue.
The teachers' lounge is empty.

A Complete the following sentences with the possessive forms of the nouns in parentheses.

1. The _____student's_____ grades are excellent. (*student*)

2. _____ French lesson ends at 7 o'clock. (*Paco*)

3. The _____ hat is black. (*bus driver*)

4. My _____ homework is difficult. (*classmates*)

5. _____ class starts at one o'clock. (*Gabriella*)

6. The _____ bindings are breaking. (*books*)

In Spanish The word **de** is used to show that something belongs to one or more than one person.

El libro es **de** Amelia.   *The book is Amelia's.*
Los carteles son **de** mis amigos.   *The posters are my friends'.*

When **de** is followed by the word **el**, the two words are combined to form the contraction **del**.

El disco compacto es **del** profesor.   (de + el profesor)
Las revistas son **del** señor.   (de + el señor)

B Complete the following sentences with the possessive forms of the nouns in parentheses.

1. Los libros son _____de Rebecca_____. (*Rebecca*)

2. La guitarra es _____. (*la profesora*)

3. La goma de borrar es _____. (*Sara*)

4. El lápiz es _____. (*el señor*)

5. Las calculadoras son _____. (*Luis*)

6. El marcador es _____. (*el profesor*)

Copyright © by Holt, Rinehart and Winston. All rights reserved.

C Use the clues provided to write complete sentences telling to whom the items belong.

1. el libro / Ángela

   El libro es de Ángela.

2. los pinceles / Alfonso

   _____

3. las revistas / el profesor Ruiz

   _____

4. la calculadora nueva / Miguel

   _____

5. el cuaderno / el estudiante nuevo

   _____

6. los papeles / los señores

   _____

D Compare the following sentences. Read each one aloud, first with the contraction and then without.

The book **isn't** mine.   El libro es **del** chico.
(*contraction: is+not=isn't*)   (*contraction: de+el=del*)

Think about the difference you heard with and without the contraction. Then explain why you think contractions are used in English and in Spanish.

_____

_____

_____

_____

Copyright © by Holt, Rinehart and Winston. All rights reserved.

ADJECTIVE AGREEMENT

¡Ven conmigo! Level 1, p. 93
Adelante, p. 127

C A P Í T U L O 3

In English **Adjectives** are words used to describe nouns.

> a **good** movie (*Movie* is a noun and *good* is an adjective.)
> a **pretty** girl (*Girl* is a noun and *pretty* is an adjective.)

The spelling of an adjective does not change when describing masculine and feminine nouns, or singular and plural nouns.

> Gabriella is **tall**.   (*Gabriella* is feminine and singular.)
> The trees are **tall**.   (*Trees* has no gender and is plural.)
> My husband is **tall**.   (*Husband* is masculine and singular.)

A Circle each adjective and underline the noun it describes. Then check the appropriate column to indicate whether the noun described is singular (S) or plural (P).

	S	P
1. Larry is handsome.	✓	
2. Their exams are not difficult.		
3. The teacher is dark-haired.		
4. The topics are interesting.		
5. The boys are funny.		
6. My classmate is short.		
7. The school lunches are bad.		
8. She is beautiful.		

In Spanish **Adjectives** are also used to describe nouns. However, unlike in English, adjectives change endings to match the nouns they modify.

For adjectives that end in **-o**, change the **-o** to **-a** to describe feminine nouns. To make a feminine or masculine adjective plural, add **-s**

> un chico **guapo**   una chica **guapa**
> unos chicos **guapos**   unas chicas **guapas**

For adjectives that end in **-e** or a consonant like **-l**, **-r**, or **-n**, the ending *does not* change to match the gender (masculine or feminine) of the noun. It does change, however, to match the number (singular or plural) of the noun.

> El hombre es **fuerte**   La mujer es **fuerte**   Los hombres son **fuertes**
> El examen es **difícil**   La tarea es **difícil**   Los exámenes son **difíciles**

To describe a group of males and females, a masculine plural adjective is used.

> Los estudiantes son **simpáticos**

Copyright © by Holt, Rinehart and Winston. All rights reserved.

B Circle each adjective and underline the noun it describes. Then check the appropriate column to tell whether the noun described is singular (S) or plural (P), masculine (M) or feminine (F).

	S	P	M	F
1. El <u>libro</u> de historia es (nuevo)	✓		✓	
2. Los conciertos son divertidos.				
3. Miguel es alto.				
4. Susana es bonita.				
5. Las ventanas son pequeñas.				
6. Mis amigos son cómicos.				
7. La compañera de clase es buena.				
8. Las señoritas son guapas.				

C Circle the appropriate adjective to complete each sentence.

1. Ellos son ((bajos)/bajo).

2. Marisa es (alto/alta).

3. Los libros son (interesante/interesantes).

4. Paco es (rubia/rubio).

5. Mis amigas son (simpáticas/simpática).

6. Los exámenes son (difícil/difíciles).

7. Mi profesora es (buena/bueno).

8. El compañero de clase es (divertidos/divertido).

D 1. Rewrite the following sentences so the subject is plural.

   a. The room is big.

   _____

   b. El cuarto es grande.

   _____

2. What words needed changing in the English sentence? In the Spanish sentence? What generalization can you make about articles and adjectives in Spanish?

   _____

   _____

   _____

   _____

Spanish 1 ¡Ven conmigo!, Chapter 3

Copyright © by Holt, Rinehart and Winston. All rights reserved.

■ TAG QUESTIONS

¡Ven conmigo! Level 1, p. 96
Adelante, p. 131

C A P Í T U L O 3

In English Certain words or phrases may be added at the end of a sentence to make it a question. These words or phrases, called **tag questions**, include **isn't it**, **right**, and **don't you**.

He is going to the concert tonight, **right?**
The score is 12 to 7, **isn't it?**
You have class now, **don't you?**

A Circle the tag questions in the following sentences.

1. Your birthday party is next week, (isn't it?)

2. Our Spanish exam is this Friday, right?

3. You have a date for the dance, right?

4. The video game is yours, isn't it?

5. You like the novel, don't you?

6. The film festival is next month, isn't it?

7. That's the truth, right?

8. You have tickets for the game, don't you?

In Spanish **Tag questions** may also be added at the end of a sentence. The most common tag questions are **¿no?** (*isn't it?* or *right?*) and **¿verdad?** (*right?* or *don't you?*)

La clase de arte es interesante, **¿no?**   *The art class is interesting, isn't it?*
Te gustan los conciertos, **¿verdad?**   *You like concerts, don't you?*

B Circle the tag questions in the following sentences.

1. Te gusta la novela, (¿verdad?)

2. La fiesta es divertida, ¿no?

3. Los videojuegos son interesantes, ¿no?

4. Tienes la clase a la una, ¿verdad?

5. El perro es feo, ¿no?

6. Tienes la clase de historia, ¿verdad?

7. Te gustan las mochilas grandes, ¿verdad?

8. El cuaderno es nuevo, ¿no?

Copyright © by Holt, Rinehart and Winston. All rights reserved.

C Change the following sentences to questions using tag questions.

1. Maribel tiene dos entradas para el concierto.

   Maribel tiene dos entradas para el concierto, ¿verdad?

2. La clase de geometría es muy difícil.

   _____

3. Las fiestas son divertidas.

   _____

4. Te gusta la natación.

   _____

5. Son divertidos los bailes.

   _____

6. No te gusta el baloncesto.

   _____

7. Las clases de ciencias son tus favoritas.

   _____

8. Tienes la clase de historia a las ocho.

   _____

D Consider the pairs of sentences below. Do tag questions change the tone of the question? Explain why or why not.

¿Los maestros son simpáticos?   _Are the teachers nice?_
Los maestros son simpáticos, ¿verdad?   _The teachers are nice, right?_

_____

_____

_____

_____

_____

Copyright © by Holt, Rinehart and Winston. All rights reserved.

CAPÍTULO 4

■ VERB ENDINGS

In English Verbs are words that express actions or states of being. The endings of most verbs in English change only when the subject, or doer of the action, is *he, she, it,* or a *proper name* like Rosa. With these subjects, an **-s** is added at the end of the verb.

I	sing		*we*	sing
you	sing		*you*	sing
he, she, it	sing**s**		*they*	sing

A Draw one line under the subject and two lines under the verb in each sentence. Then circle the ending of each verb. Not all verbs have an ending.

1. Carlos sings well.
2. They walk home.
3. Sara listens to music.
4. I dance at parties.
5. You talk to Juan.
6. Luis plays every day.
7. We work hard.
8. Claudia rides her bicycle.

In Spanish Like English, verb endings change according to the subject. However, in Spanish there are six different verb endings. Changing the endings is called *conjugating the verb.*

The unchanged form of the verb, or *infinitive,* can end in **-ar**, **-er**, or **-ir**. To conjugate a regular **-ar** verb like **cantar**, remove the **-ar** ending (**cant-**) and attach these endings:

yo	cant**o**		*nosotros(as)*	cant**amos**
tú	cant**as**		*vosotros(as)*	cant**áis**
él, ella, Ud.	cant**a**		*ellos, ellas, Uds.*	cant**an**

To use other **-ar** verbs, just remove **-ar** and add endings like those above. Remember that the ending changes according to the subject!

Copyright © by Holt, Rinehart and Winston. All rights reserved.

B Draw one line under the subject and two lines under the verb in each sentence. Then circle the ending of each verb.

1. Carlos canta bien.

2. Ellos caminan a casa.

3. Sara escucha la música.

4. Yo bailo en las fiestas.

5. Tú hablas con Juan.

6. Luis estudia computación.

7. Nosotros trabajamos mucho.

8. Claudia monta en bicicleta.

C Complete the following sentences with the correct form of the verb **hablar**.

1. Ellos ____hablan____ y descansan.

2. José _____ inglés.

3. Yo _____ español.

4. Nosotros _____ por teléfono.

5. Ellos _____ en clase.

6. Tú _____ muy bien.

7. El profesor _____ mucho.

8. Sergio y Berta _____ con sus amigos.

D 1. Go back and look at the endings you circled in Activities A and B. Fill in the table below and then answer the questions that follow.

ACTIVITY A		ACTIVITY B	
Verb	Ending	Verb	Ending
1. to sing	s	1. cantar	a
2.		2.	
3.		3.	
4.		4.	
5.		5.	
6.		6.	
7.		7.	
8.		8.	

2. How do the endings of verbs in English differ from those in Spanish? How can you figure out the endings of unfamiliar verbs in Spanish? Use verbs from the table as examples.

_____

_____

Copyright © by Holt, Rinehart and Winston. All rights reserved.

THE VERB *TO BE* TO STATE LOCATION

¡Ven conmigo! Level 1, p. 118
Adelante, p. 162

CAPÍTULO 4

In English The verb **to be** can be used to talk about location.

I **am** in the city.

The verb **to be** has different forms depending on the subject.

I	am	we	are
you	are	you (plural)	are
he, she, it	is	they	are

A Circle the verb in each sentence. Then write the subject in the blank.

1. They (are) at home. _____They_____
2. The dog is outside. _____
3. We are in class. _____
4. I am in the bookstore. _____
5. You are with your family. _____
6. She is in the kitchen. _____
7. Ana is at the supermarket. _____
8. Geraldo is at the gym. _____

In Spanish The verb **estar** *(to be)* can be used to talk about location.

Yo **estoy** en la ciudad.

As in English, the verb endings change depending on the subject.

yo	estoy	nosotros(as)	estamos
tú	estás	vosotros(as)	estáis
él, ella, Ud.	está	ellos, ellas, Uds.	están

B Circle the verb in each sentence. Then write the subject in the blank.

1. (Estoy) en el cine. _____Yo_____
2. María está en casa de Pilar. _____
3. Estás en la tienda de deportes. _____
4. Estamos en la ciudad de México. _____
5. El correo está en la calle principal. _____
6. Elena y Ricardo están en la plaza. _____

Copyright © by Holt, Rinehart and Winston. All rights reserved.

7. Lucía está en la piscina. _____

8. Mi papá está en casa. _____

C Answer the following questions by filling in the correct form of the verb **estar**.

1. ¿Dónde estás? _____**Estoy**_____ en la clase.

2. ¿Dónde está Luis? _____ en el centro.

3. ¿Dónde estamos ahora? _____ en la ciudad.

4. ¿Dónde están ellos? _____ en la librería.

5. ¿Dónde está la casa de Carmela? _____ en la calle ocho.

6. ¿Dónde está el mural? _____ en la Universidad.

7. ¿Dónde estoy ahora? _____ en el Museo de Bellas Artes.

8. ¿Dónde está mi hermano? _____ en casa.

D Look at your answers for Activity C. Write the subject (**yo**, **tú**, **él**, **ella**, **nosotros**, or **ellos**) that corresponds to each verb you wrote.

1. _____

2. _____

3. _____

4. _____

5. _____

6. _____

7. _____

8. _____

E Explain how you can know what the subject of a verb is in Spanish when it is not mentioned in the sentence. Why must you include the subject in sentences in English?

_____

_____

_____

_____

_____

Copyright © by Holt, Rinehart and Winston. All rights reserved.

■ MORE SUBJECT PRONOUNS

¡Ven conmigo! Level 1, p. 121
Adelante, p. 166

In English The subject of a sentence is the person or thing that is doing something or is being described. It can be a noun or a pronoun.

> **Amelia** eats lunch. (*Amelia* is a noun.)

Pronouns are words that stand for nouns. The subject pronouns in English are **I**, **you**, **he**, **she**, **it**, **we**, and **they**.

> **I** walk to school every day.
> **You** walk with your friends.
> **We** walk very fast.

A Circle the subject pronoun in each sentence.

1. (I) walk to school.

2. You buy lunch.

3. He dances well.

4. We sing in class.

5. They need books.

6. It scurried across the floor.

7. She found a penny.

8. You are my favorite students.

In Spanish The subject of a sentence can also be a noun or a pronoun.

> **Teresa** camina a la escuela. (*Teresa* is a noun.)

The subject pronouns in Spanish are **yo** *(I)*, **tú** *(informal you)*, **usted** *(formal you)* **él** *(he)*, **ella** *(she)*, **nosotros/as** *(we)*, **vosotros/as** *(you plural)*, **ustedes** *(you plural)*, **ellos/as** *(they)*.

> **Yo** hablo con una amiga.
> **Tú** ves tu casa.
> **Nosotros** jugamos al fútbol.

- The subject pronoun **tú** is generally used to speak to friends and family members, and **usted** is generally used to speak to adults and people in authority.

- In Spain, **vosotros/as** is the plural of **tú** and **ustedes** is the plural of **usted**. In the Americas, **ustedes** is the plural of both **tú** and **usted**.

- The masculine forms (**nosotros** and **vosotros**) are used for groups of males or groups of males and females. The feminine forms (**nosotras** and **vosotras**) are used for groups of females only.

Copyright © by Holt, Rinehart and Winston. All rights reserved.

B Circle the subject pronoun in each sentence. If the subject pronoun is implied, write it on the line to the right of the sentence.

1. Soy de Texas. _____yo_____

2. ¿Dónde está usted? _____

3. ¿Ella canta contigo? _____

4. Tienes un examen hoy. _____

5. Él quiere ser artista. _____

6. Pintamos un mural. _____

7. Hablo con mi amigo en clase. _____

8. Él compra revistas en español. _____

C Write complete sentences by combining a subject pronoun from the first box with a verb from the second box. Remember, you do not always have to write the subject pronoun in Spanish.

yo	usted	ellas
tú	nosotros	él

cantar	hablar	estudiar
comparar	estar	bailar

1. (Yo) bailo con mis amigos. _____

2. _____

3. _____

4. _____

5. _____

6. _____

7. _____

8. _____

D Think of specific situations in which it would be useful to use the subject pronoun in Spanish. Write some examples below.

_____

_____

_____

_____

_____

Copyright © by Holt, Rinehart and Winston. All rights reserved.

THE IRREGULAR VERB *TO GO*

In English Most verbs follow a regular pattern: an **-s** is added in the third person singular, and for all other subjects the base form of the verb is used.

> I <u>eat</u> lunch.   Melissa <u>eat**s**</u> lunch.

The verb **to go** follows a slightly different pattern. An **-es** is added in the third person singular.

I	**go**	*we*	**go**
you	**go**	*you*	**go**
he, she, it	**goes**	*they*	**go**

A Complete the following sentences with an appropriate subject from the box. Use each subject once.

Verónica	Uncle Joe	We	He	They	I	You	Antonio

1. _____**They**_____ go to the park.

2. _____ goes fishing.

3. _____ go to their cousin's house.

4. _____ go to our classroom.

5. _____ goes to her room.

6. _____ go home.

7. _____ goes to the concert with friends.

8. _____ go to the basketball game.

In Spanish Most verbs follow a regular pattern. The ending is removed and the appropriate ending is added based on the subject. The verb **ir** (*to go*) is irregular because it does not follow this pattern.

yo	**voy**	*nosotros(as)*	**vamos**
tú	**vas**	*vosotros(as)*	**vais**
él, ella, usted	**va**	*ellos, ellas, ustedes*	**van**

Copyright © by Holt, Rinehart and Winston. All rights reserved.

B Complete the following sentences with an appropriate subject from the box. Use each subject once

| Claudia y Luis | Vosotros | Tú | Nosotros | Mis hermanos | Ella | Yo | Sr. Navarro |

1. _____Yo_____ voy a clase.

2. _____ vas al gimnasio.

3. _____ va al baile.

4. _____ vamos al cine.

5. _____ vais al centro.

6. _____ van a casa.

7. _____ va a una conferencia.

8. _____ van al concierto.

> To ask where someone is going, use the question word **adónde**.
>
> ¿**Adónde** va Carmen? (*Where is Carmen going?*)

C Write a question using the word **adónde** to find out where each person is going.

1. Luis   **¿Adónde va Luis?** _____

2. Celia   _____

3. tú   _____

4. ellos   _____

5. nosotros   _____

6. yo   _____

7. ustedes   _____

8. mis padres   _____

D Explain how you know what the hidden subject pronoun is in an irregular verb like **ir**.

_____

_____

_____

_____

_____

Copyright © by Holt, Rinehart and Winston. All rights reserved.

CAPÍTULO 5

■ NEGATIVE WORDS

¡Ven conmigo! Level 1, p. 145
Adelante, p. 196

In English Several different words can be used to make negative sentences, such as, **no**, **not**, **never**, **nobody**, **nothing**, **none**, **no one**, etc.

> I **never** eat chocolate.
> **Nobody** comes to my party.
> **Nothing** exciting happens to me.
> I am **not** going to do anything.

Two negative words cannot be combined to form a negation in English.

INCORRECT: *Not nobody called today*.   CORRECT: **Nobody** called today.

A Circle the negative words in each sentence.

1. I (never) watch television in the morning.

2. Yesterday nobody wanted to play tennis with me.

3. I do not want to arrive late to class.

4. I am so tired I am not going to do anything.

5. Samuel is never late.

6. Sundays are boring because there is nothing to do.

7. Nobody expected Aunt Ana to come to visit.

8. Manolito will not eat his string beans.

In Spanish Several different words can also be used to make negative sentences: **no** (*no*), **nunca** (*never*), **nadie** (*nobody*), **nada** (*nothing*).

> **Nunca** como chocolate.
> **Nadie** toca un instrumento.
> **Nada** hay en la televisión.
> **No** voy a tomar **nada**.

In Spanish, unlike English, two negative words are often used together to form a negative sentence. Look at the last sentence above. In this case, **no** is written before the verb and the other negative word is written after the verb.

> **No** cuido a mi hermano **nunca**.   OR   **Nunca** cuido a mi hermano.
> **No** sabe cocinar **nadie**.   OR   **Nadie** sabe cocinar.

Spanish 1 ¡Ven conmigo!, Chapter 5

Copyright © by Holt, Rinehart and Winston. All rights reserved.

B Circle the negative words in each sentence.

1. David (nunca) va a la playa.

2. Andrés no conoce a nadie en la fiesta.

3. No quiero comer nada.

4. Marta no baila nunca en las fiestas.

5. ¿Nunca vas a la Fiesta de la Calle Ocho?

6. Nadie quiere ir conmigo a Miami.

7. No desayuno cereal nunca.

8. Alejandro no ve a nadie alto y moreno.

C Rewrite the following sentences using the word **no**.

1. Nunca ayudo en casa.

   No ayudo nunca en casa.

2. Nadie va a la biblioteca para estudiar.

   _____

3. Nunca descansamos después de clases.

   _____

4. Nada necesito para la clase de inglés.

   _____

5. Nadie quiere más pizza.

   _____

6. José nunca va al centro comercial.

   _____

7. Nadie sabe tocar el saxofón.

   _____

8. Nada quiero para el postre.

   _____

D What is the biggest difference between making a negative statement in English and in Spanish? What happens in English when two negative words are combined in a sentence?

_____

_____

_____

_____

Copyright © by Holt, Rinehart and Winston. All rights reserved.

■ THE VERB *TO LIKE*

> **In English** The verb **to like** usually comes after a word that tells *who* likes something. This word is the *subject*.
>
> Sometimes the subject is a *pronoun* like *we* or *I*.
>
> > *We* **like** orange juice.   *I* **like** horror movies.
>
> Sometimes the subject is a *noun* like *Enrique* or *girl*.
>
> > *Enrique* **likes** chocolate ice cream.   The *girl* **likes** strawberry shortcake.

A Circle the word that tells who likes each activity. Then write the word in the appropriate column to indicate whether it is a noun or a pronoun.

	NOUN	PRONOUN
1. (Benito) likes surfing.	Benito	_____
2. Adolfo likes fishing.	_____	_____
3. Rita likes riding her bike.	_____	_____
4. They like eating at the Cuban restaurant.	_____	_____
5. My friends like to ski.	_____	_____
6. You like to play the guitar.	_____	_____
7. I like to play in the park.	_____	_____
8. Margarita likes to play volleyball at the beach.	_____	_____

> **In Spanish** The verb **gustar** (*to like*) also comes after a word that tells *who* likes something. This word is a type of *pronoun* because it stands for a noun. These pronouns are *me, te, le, les*, and *nos*.
>
> > *Me* **gusta** la música.   *Les* **gusta** el juego.
>
> The structure of a sentence using the verb **gustar** is different from the structure of a sentence using the verb **to like**. The Spanish verb **gustar** works like the English verb *to be pleasing*. Compare the following English translations of the above sentences.
>
> > The music **is pleasing** *to me*.   The game **is pleasing** *to them*.
> > (*I* **like** the music.)   (*They* **like** the game.)
>
> To clarify *who* likes it, the phrase **a** + *subject pronoun* or **a** + *noun* is used.
>
> > **A Manuel** le gusta bucear.   **A los estudiantes** les gusta hacer ejercicio.

Copyright © by Holt, Rinehart and Winston. All rights reserved.

B Circle the words that tell who likes each activity. Then write each word in the appropriate column to indicate whether it is a noun or a pronoun.

	NOUN	PRONOUN
1. A (Benito) (le) gusta hacer surfing.	Benito	le
2. A Adolfo le gusta pescar.	_____	_____
3. A Rita le gusta montar en bicicleta.	_____	_____
4. Les gusta comer en el restaurante cubano.	_____	_____
5. A mis amigos les gusta esquiar.	_____	_____
6. Te gusta tocar la guitarra.	_____	_____
7. Me gusta jugar en el parque.	_____	_____
8. A Margarita le gusta jugar al voleibol en la playa.	_____	_____

C You are being interviewed about yourself and your friends. Answer the following questions using the correct form of the verb **gustar**.

1. ¿Te gusta leer libros o mirar la televisión?

   _____

2. ¿A tus amigos les gusta la comida italiana o la comida mexicana?

   _____

3. ¿A tu mejor amigo (*best friend*) le gusta bailar o cantar?

   _____

4. ¿A tus amigos les gusta leer el periódico o las revistas?

   _____

5. ¿Te gusta el béisbol o el fútbol?

   _____

D Which of the following sentences need a phrase added for clarification? Explain your answer.

   Nos gusta comer hamburguesas.

   Les gusta leer las tiras cómicas.

   Me gusta pescar y bucear.

   _____

   _____

   _____

   _____

Copyright © by Holt, Rinehart and Winston. All rights reserved.

■ MORE VERB ENDINGS

¡Ven conmigo! Level 1, p. 150
Adelante, p. 207

C A P Í T U L O   5

> **In English** Regular present tense verbs add the ending **-s** only in the third person singular.
>
> *I* **write** letters.
> *We* **see** the rainbow.
>
>   BUT
>
> *Sam* **eats** dinner.
> The *truck* **delivers** spring water.

A Circle the correct verb form in each sentence.

1. Alligators (live/lives) in the Everglades wetlands.

2. A scuba diver (explore/explores) the Biscayne Bay.

3. People (dance/dances) to Caribbean music at the festival.

4. Several men (play/plays) chess at a park in Little Havana.

5. Raúl (listen/listens) to music under the bright sun.

6. The girls (swim/swims) at the neighborhood pool.

7. Artists (sell/sells) paintings near Miami Beach.

8. Many people (speak/speaks) Spanish in southern Florida.

> **In Spanish** Verb endings always change to match the subject pronoun or the doer of the action. With regular verbs whose basic forms end in **-er** or **-ir**, you remove the **-er** or the **-ir** and attach these endings:
>
> | **CORRER** | | **RECIBIR** | |
> |---|---|---|---|
> | yo | corr**o** | yo | recib**o** |
> | tú | corr**es** | tú | recib**es** |
> | él, ella, usted | corr**e** | él, ella, usted | recib**e** |
> | nosotros(as) | corr**emos** | nosotros(as) | recib**imos** |
> | vosotros(as) | corr**éis** | vosotros(as) | recib**ís** |
> | ellos, ellas, ustedes | corr**en** | ellos, ellas, ustedes | recib**en** |

B Circle the correct verb form in each sentence.

1. Los turistas (come/comen) pizza en el café.

2. Mi amiga (escribe/escribes) una carta de amor.

3. Yo (corres/corro) por la playa.

4. Gustavo (asiste/asista) a una escuela secundaria en Miami.

Copyright © by Holt, Rinehart and Winston. All rights reserved.

5. Gloria (ves/**ve**) a su madre en el jardín.

6. Tú (**recibes**/reciben) muchas cartas de tu familia.

7. Nosotros (beben/**bebemos**) refrescos.

8. Mimi (**lee**/lea) el periódico en el patio.

C Use the verbs in the box to write about what each of these people do during their summer vacation.

asistir a	comer	leer	beber	correr	escribir	recibir

1. Raquel y Anita

   Raquel y Anita escriben cartas.

2. Diana

   _____

3. mis amigos

   _____

4. nosotros

   _____

5. el profesor

   _____

6. tú

   _____

7. yo

   _____

D Which endings are not identical for **-er** and **-ir** verbs?

_____

_____

_____

_____

Copyright © by Holt, Rinehart and Winston. All rights reserved.

CAPÍTULO 6

▮ POSSESSIVE ADJECTIVES

¡Ven conmigo! Level 1, p. 174
Adelante, p. 237

In English Possessive adjectives include **my, your, his, her, our**, and **their**. As their title suggests, possessive adjectives show possession or ownership.

Our family is very small.
Your sister looks just like you both!
Their father works at the train station.

Our cousins live in Texas.
Your brothers are very funny.
Their grandparents are visiting.

Possessive adjectives in English do not change forms whether they modify plural or singular nouns.

A Underline the possessive adjective and circle the noun it describes in each sentence. Then check the appropriate column to tell whether it is singular (S) or plural (P).

	S	P
1. Elena and Isabel, your dog is very friendly!	✓	
2. Have you ever seen my kittens?		
3. Their mother is very protective.		
4. Our neighbors want two kittens.		
5. Their parents will only let them have one.		
6. Will your parents let you take one?		
7. Rita will give you directions to our house.		
8. You are going to love your new kitten!		

In Spanish Possessive adjectives include **mi(s), tu(s), su(s), vuestro/a(s)**, and **nuestro/a(s)**. The same word **su(s)** is used to mean *your (plural)* and *their*.

Nuestra familia es muy pequeña.
Su hermana se parece a ustedes.
Su padre trabaja en la estación de tren.

Nuestros primos viven en Texas.
Sus hermanos son muy chistosos.
Sus abuelos están de visita.

Unlike English, **possessive adjectives** in Spanish must agree in *number* and *gender* with the nouns they describe.

su hermana/su**s** herman**as**   nuestr**o** herman**o**/nuestr**a** herman**a**

*In Spain, the possessive adjective **vuestro/a(s)** *is used for the plural familiar form of you. Like* **nuestro/a(s)** *it must agree in number and gender with the noun it describes.*

Copyright © by Holt, Rinehart and Winston. All rights reserved.

B Underline the possessive adjective and circle the noun it describes. Then check the appropriate column to tell whether it is singular (S) or plural (P), masculine (M) or feminine (F).

	S	P	M	F
1. Vamos a la boda de <u>nuestra</u> (prima)	✓			✓
2. Rafael y Manuel bailan con sus amigas.				
3. Nuestros hermanos son altos.				
4. ¿Ustedes ven a sus abuelos?				
5. Los abuelos hablan con sus nietos.				
6. Hay mucha comida en nuestra mesa.				
7. Los padres encuentran a sus hijos.				
8. ¿Preparan ustedes su desayuno?				

C Write a sentence using the possessive adjectives **su(s)** and **nuestro/a(s)** to describe each of the following people. You may use the words from the box or you may think of your own.

bonito	simpático	alto	rubio	inteligente
cómico	moreno	serio	guapo	cariñoso

1. *la esposa de Paco*

   Su esposa es muy guapa.

2. *el padrastro de Roberto y Diego*

   _____

3. *los padres de nosotros*

   _____

4. *la nieta de Ramón y Celia*

   _____

5. *el abuelo de nosotros*

   _____

D Compare these sentences:

ENGLISH	SPANISH
Your mother is very nice.	**Su** madre es muy simpática.
Their father is tall.	**Su** padre es alto.

When might you have to clarify who the possessive adjective refers to in *English*?
When might you have to clarify who the possessive adjective refers to in *Spanish*? Explain.

_____

_____

_____

Copyright © by Holt, Rinehart and Winston. All rights reserved.

CAPÍTULO 7

■ SPELLING OF VERB STEMS

¡Ven conmigo! Level 1, p. 209
En camino, p. 52

In English The stem is the part of the verb that remains when the ending is removed. For example, the stem of the verb **prefers** is **prefer**. In English, the spelling of the stem remains the same even if the ending changes.

I	**want**	*we*	**want**
you	**want**	*you*	**want**
he, she, it	**wants**	*they*	**want**

A Circle the conjugated verb and underline the subject in each sentence. Then write the stem of the verb on the line to the right of the sentence.

1. She (prefers) tennis. _____ **prefer** _____

2. You want to dance with your friend. _____

3. We start the course in August. _____

4. My friend prefers to watch thrillers. _____

5. I want to visit my grandmother. _____

6. The movie starts at seven o'clock. _____

7. They want to have dinner at their place. _____

8. Luisa prefers to invite them to the restaurant. _____

In Spanish Some verbs have a spelling change in the stem, the part of the verb without the ending. **Querer** (*to want*) is a **stem-changing verb**. Its ending follows the pattern of regular verbs, but the **e** in the stem (**quer**) changes to **ie** (**quier**) in all forms except the *nosotros* and *vosotros* forms.

yo	qu**ie**ro	*nosotros(as)*	queremos
tú	qu**ie**res	*vosotros(as)*	**queréis**
él, ella, Ud.	qu**ie**re	*ellos, ellas, Uds.*	qu**ie**ren

Other examples of **e → ie stem-changing verbs** are **preferir** (*to prefer*), **empezar** (*to start*), **venir** (*to come*), and **tener** (*to have*).

The verbs **venir** and **tener**, in addition to having a stem change, have an irregular ending in the **yo** form, like **hacer** and **salir**.

Yo **vengo** de la playa.   Yo **tengo** mucho trabajo.

Copyright © by Holt, Rinehart and Winston. All rights reserved.

B Circle the conjugated verb and underline the subject in each sentence. Then write the stem of the verb on the line to the right of the sentence.

1. <u>Yo</u> (tengo) un libro en casa.   **ten-**

2. Tú prefieres ir a la playa este verano.   _____

3. La película empieza a las cinco y media.   _____

4. Cristina no quiere invitar a Diego a su fiesta.   _____

5. Sus amigos prefieren ir a un concierto de guitarra.   _____

6. Ellos vienen a mi fiesta.   _____

7. Ellos quieren bailar con sus amigas.   _____

8. Tú tienes dos hermanos.   _____

C Combine the elements to write complete sentences saying what the people want or prefer to do in their free time.

1. Hoy / yo / querer / ir al cine

   Hoy yo quiero ir al cine. _____

2. Esta tarde / tú / preferir / mirar la televisión

   _____

3. Mi madre / querer / salir al campo

   _____

4. Mis amigos y yo / querer / ir a la playa

   _____

5. Los domingos / mis abuelos / preferir / cenar en casa

   _____

6. Mi familia y yo / preferir / la comida italiana

   _____

D How are e ➞ ie stem-changing verbs different from the regular -ar, -er, and -ir verbs that you have learned before? Are there any similarities?

DIFFERENCES: _____

_____

_____

SIMILARITIES: _____

_____

_____

Copyright © by Holt, Rinehart and Winston. All rights reserved.

¡Ven conmigo! Level 1, p. 214
En camino, p. 64

C A P Í T U L O 7

REFLEXIVE VERBS AND PRONOUNS

In English **Reflexive pronouns** are used to show that an action "reflects" back on the subject. The reflexive pronouns are **myself, yourself, himself, herself, ourselves**, and **themselves**.

He bathes **himself.**
The cat cleans **itself.**
The children dress **themselves** for school.

A Circle the verb and underline the subject in each sentence. Then write the reflexive pronoun on the line to the right.

REFLEXIVE PRONOUN

1. I clean myself up before dinner.   _____myself_____

2. Luisa dresses herself quickly.   _____

3. You buy yourself a razor at the store.   _____

4. We admire ourselves in the mirror.   _____

5. You prepare yourself to go out.   _____

6. I make myself a new dress.   _____

7. The babies cannot feed themselves.   _____

8. The dog finds itself a new stick.   _____

In Spanish **Reflexive verbs** are used when the same person performs and receives the action of the verb. The pronoun **–se** attached to the infinitive identifies the verb as reflexive (**ducharse, peinarse**). Unlike English, reflexive verbs in Spanish always use reflexive pronouns.

The reflexive pronoun changes according to the subject of the verb.

Yo necesito duchar **me.**   Tú necesitas lavar **te.**
Juan necesita afeitar **se.**   Ellas necesitan maquillar **se.**
Nosotros necesitamos bañar **nos.** Usted necesita lavar **se** los dientes.

When a **body part** is mentioned in Spanish, it comes after a **definite article,** unlike **English,** where it comes after a **possessive.**

Ella necesita peinarse **el** pelo.   *She needs to comb her hair.*

Copyright © by Holt, Rinehart and Winston. All rights reserved.

B Circle the reflexive verb and underline the subject in each sentence. Then write the reflexive pronoun on the line to the right. If a reflexive pronoun is not used, write "none."

REFLEXIVE PRONOUN

1. <u>Yo</u> voy a (lavarme) la cara.   _____ me _____

2. Luisa necesita peinarse el pelo.   _____

3. Tú necesitas afeitarte la barba (*beard*).   _____

4. Paco va a lavarse los dientes antes de salir.   _____

5. Tú vas a prepararte para salir.   _____

6. Yo voy a maquillarme la cara.   _____

7. Ana va a lavarse el pelo antes de la fiesta.   _____

8. Él necesita afeitarse antes de salir.   _____

C Translate the following sentences into Spanish.

1. Are you going to shave today?

   ¿Vas a afeitarte hoy? _____

2. I need to brush my teeth everyday.

   _____

3. Are you going to put some makeup on for the party?

   _____

4. Does he need to shower in the morning?

   _____

5. I sometimes need to bathe in the evening.

   _____

6. Are you going to wash your hands?

   _____

D Is the reflexive pronoun ever implied in English or in Spanish? Give examples.

_____

_____

_____

_____

_____

     Spanish 1 ¡Ven conmigo!, Chapter 7

Copyright © by Holt, Rinehart and Winston. All rights reserved.

CAPÍTULO 8

■ INDIRECT OBJECT PRONOUNS

¡Ven conmigo! Level 1, p. 236
En camino, p. 89

CAPÍTULO 8

In English **Indirect object pronouns** take the place of nouns that tell *to whom* or *for whom* an action is done.

Ana and her mother made **us** enchiladas.
(The pronoun **us** tells for whom Ana prepared the enchiladas.)

You can ask yourself *to whom* or *for whom* the action occurs in order to determine whether or not it is an indirect object. Verbs such as **to send** and **to give** often have indirect objects.

I sent **them** a thank you note.
To whom did I send a thank you note? *To* **them**.

A Underline the indirect object pronoun in each sentence. Then check the appropriate column to tell whether it is singular (S) or plural (P).

	S	P
1. My sister sent me a recipe for paella.	✓	
2. My grandmother used to make us seafood paella.		
3. Juan served him flan for dessert.		
4. You told them your secret ingredient.		
5. Lisa, I would like to make you dinner tonight.		
6. Could you give me directions to your house?		
7. I will tell you my secret when I arrive.		
8. Then you can make them dessert!		

In Spanish **Indirect object pronouns** are also used to tell *to whom* or *for whom* an action is done. Like English, these pronouns can replace nouns. Unlike English, they can be used in combination with the nouns they refer to.

The verbs **gustar** (*to like*) and **encantar** (*to love*) take indirect object pronouns in Spanish. When used in conjunction with these verbs, the indirect object pronouns tell *to whom* something is pleasing.

Me encantan los chiles rellenos.
A Elena y Gustavo **les** gusta el flan.

Spanish 1 ¡Ven conmigo!, Chapter 8

Grammar Tutor **49**

Copyright © by Holt, Rinehart and Winston. All rights reserved.

B Underline the indirect object pronoun in each sentence. Then check the appropriate column to tell whether it is singular (S) or plural (P).

	S	P
1. <u>Me</u> encantan las uvas.	✓	
2. ¿Te gusta la piña?		
3. A mis padres les encantan las frutas del Caribe.		
4. A Luisa y a mí nos encanta el café con leche.		
5. A mi hermano le gusta el jugo de manzana.		
6. A Susana le encantan las ensaladas.		
7. Me gusta el helado de chocolate.		
8. A Ricardo y a Juan les encantan los plátanos.		

- The verbs **encantar** and **gustar** must agree in number with the subject.

    Me encant**an** *las uvas.*   (*uvas* is the subject and is plural)
    ¿Te gust**a** *la piña?*   (*piña* is the subject and is singular)

- The definite article **el**, **la**, **los**, or **las** must be used with these verbs.

    A Luis y a mí nos encanta **el** café con leche.

- The phrase **a** + *noun* can be used to clarify *to whom* the pronoun refers.

    A mis padres les encantan las frutas del Caribe.

C Use the verb **encantar** and the correct indirect object pronoun to tell who likes what.

1. a mi abuela / las papitas

    A mi abuela le encantan las papitas.

2. a ti / la crema de maní

    _____

3. a mí / la sopa

    _____

4. a Laura y a mí / el pollo

    _____

5. a los niños / los pasteles

    _____

6. a Olga y a Luisa / el pescado

    _____

Copyright © by Holt, Rinehart and Winston. All rights reserved.

STEM-CHANGING VERBS

¡Ven conmigo! Level 1, p. 238
En camino, p. 92

C A P Í T U L O   8

> **In English** The endings of present tense verbs vary with the subject in the third person singular. The spelling of the **stem**, or part of the verb without the ending, remains the same for regular verbs.
>
> | | | | |
> |---|---|---|---|
> | *I* | **eat** | *we* | **eat** |
> | *you* | **eat** | *you (plural)* | **eat** |
> | *he, she, it* | **eats** | *they* | **eat** |

A Circle the form of the verb **to eat** and underline the subject in each sentence.

1. I (eat) a sandwich for lunch.

2. José eats tamales at his grandmother's house.

3. We eat lunch in the school cafeteria during the week.

4. The cooks eat lunch later.

5. You eat chicken tacos at the Mexican restaurant.

6. Luisa eats a salad with her meal.

7. Our parents eat dinner early.

8. The professors eat Spanish custard.

> **In Spanish** The ending of a verb also varies with its subject. Unlike English, Spanish has several cases of verbs in which the spelling of the stem, or part of the verb without the ending, changes. One type is called an **o ➡ue stem-changing verb.**
>
> **Almorzar** is an **o ➡ ue stem-changing verb**. The **o** in the stem (**almorz-**) changes to **ue**. All forms of the verb have a stem-change except the *vosotros* and *nosotros* forms.
>
> | | | | |
> |---|---|---|---|
> | *yo* | **almuerzo** | *nosotros(as)* | **almorzamos** |
> | *tú* | **almuerzas** | *vosotros(as)* | **almorzáis** |
> | *él, ella, Ud.* | **almuerza** | *ellos, ellas, ustedes* | **almuerzan** |
>
> Another example of an **o ➡ ue** stem-changing verb is **poder**.

B Circle the form of **poder** or **almorzar** in each sentence and underline the subject.

1. Diana (almuerza) una sopa de pollo.

2. Cristina y yo almorzamos quesadillas.

3. Yo almuerzo en mi casa los miércoles.

4. Tú puedes comer conmigo.

Copyright © by Holt, Rinehart and Winston. All rights reserved.

5. ¿Almuerza Carmen con nosotros hoy?

6. Juan y Mario almuerzan perros calientes.

7. Ellos pueden comer el postre.

8. Nosotros almorzamos huevos con tocino.

C Use the verb **almorzar** and foods from the box to write complete sentences about what everyone has for lunch.

ensalada mixta	sándwich de crema de maní
arroz	pollo asado
huevos fritos	legumbres

1. Julia

   Julia almuerza un sándwich de crema de maní.

2. Lorenzo y Cristina

   _____

3. Tú

   _____

4. Yo

   _____

5. Nosotros

   _____

D Why do the **nosotros** and **vosotros** forms not have a stem-change? Look at the forms of **almorzar** and **poder** divided into syllables and with marks showing where the stress falls. Can you think of a rule for when the stem changes spelling? Write the rule on the lines below.

ALMORZAR	PODER
al-muer´-zo	pue´-do
al-muer´-zas	pue´-des
al-muer´-za	pue´-de
al-mor-za´-mos	po-de´-mos
al-mor-zais´	po-deis´
al-muer´-zan	pue´-den

_____

_____

_____

_____

_____

Copyright © by Holt, Rinehart and Winston. All rights reserved.

¡Ven conmigo! Level 1, p. 240
En camino, p. 98

CAPÍTULO 8

THE VERB *TO BE* TO DESCRIBE THINGS

In English There is only one verb that means **to be**.

• The verb **to be** is used to describe specific qualities of particular items, such as how they taste, look, or feel.

This sofrito **is** very spicy.

• The verb **to be** is also used to describe the general nature of things.

Sofrito **is** a spicy Cuban dish.

• The form of the verb **to be** changes depending on the subject.

The <u>tacos</u> **are** delicious.
The <u>salsa</u> **is** made with tomatoes.

A Circle the form of the verb **to be** in each sentence. Then check the appropriate column to tell whether it describes a specific quality (S) or the general nature (G) of something.

	S	G
1. Gazpacho (is) a cold soup served in Spain.	_____	✓
2. Maria's gazpacho is chunky.	_____	_____
3. Plantains are a traditional side dish in Latin America.	_____	_____
4. These plantains are ripe.	_____	_____
5. Red snapper is my favorite fish.	_____	_____
6. Red snapper is a mild fish.	_____	_____
7. Arepas are like pancakes.	_____	_____
8. These arepas are warm.	_____	_____

In Spanish There are two Spanish verbs that mean *to be*: **ser** and **estar**.

• The verb **estar** is used to describe variable qualities, such as how a specific item looks, tastes, or feels.

El pollo con mole de José **está** riquísimo.

• The verb **ser** is used to describe permanent characteristics or the general nature of things.

El pollo con mole **es** una comida de México.

• Like English, the form of the verb changes depending on the subject.

El <u>gazpacho</u> **es** una sopa.   Este <u>tocino</u> **está** delicioso.
Las <u>uvas</u> **son** frutas.   Las <u>papitas</u> **están** saladas.

Copyright © by Holt, Rinehart and Winston. All rights reserved.

B Circle the form of **ser** or **estar** in each sentence. Then check the appropriate column to tell whether it describes a specific quality (S) or the general nature (G) of something.

	S	G
1. La sopa (es) mi comida favorita.	___	✓
2. Tu sopa está caliente.	___	___
3. La limonada de Ana está fría.	___	___
4. La limonada no es un refresco.	___	___
5. El arroz con frijoles es un plato popular.	___	___
6. El arroz con frijoles está picante.	___	___
7. La toronja es una fruta.	___	___
8. Mi toronja está muy dulce.	___	___

C For each of the following situations, decide whether you use **ser** or **estar**. Write a complete sentence using the correct form of the verb.

1. to tell Ana that Mexican food is spicy (la comida mexicana/picante)

   La comida mexicana es picante. _____

2. to tell your grandmother that the sweet roll is delicious (el pan dulce/delicioso)

   _____

3. to say that lorco is an Ecuadorean dish (lorco/plato del Ecuador)

   _____

4. to say that the soup is hot (la sopa/caliente)

   _____

5. to say that your ham is very salty (el jamón/salado)

   _____

D Re-read the sentences you wrote for Activity C. In the chart below, write the verbs you used in the left-hand column and your reasons for choosing the verbs in the right column.

	VERB	REASON
1.		
2.		
3.		
4.		
5.		

Spanish 1 ¡Ven conmigo!, Chapter 8

Copyright © by Holt, Rinehart and Winston. All rights reserved.

CAPÍTULO 9

■ MORE INDIRECT OBJECT PRONOUNS

¡Ven conmigo! Level 1, p. 270
En camino, p. 133

> **In English** Indirect objects are used to tell *to whom* and *for whom* an action is done. **Indirect object pronouns** take the place of nouns that tell *to whom* and *for whom*. These pronouns are **me**, **you**, **him**, **her**, **us**, and **them**.
>
> > Enrique and Monse gave **them** some guavas.
> > Nicky wrote **her** a letter.
>
> In English, indirect object pronouns usually come after the verb and before the noun that answers the question, *what*?
>
> > *Tell* **us** a story. (*Tell* is the verb. *Story* is what is told. *Us* is to whom it is told.)

A Circle the indirect object pronouns and underline the verbs in the following sentences.

1. Alexandra showed them her first film yesterday.

2. Tim cooked him some cheeseburgers.

3. He wrote her a letter about the party.

4. Give him his lucky charm immediately!

5. Their grandmother gave them the country house.

6. Did Jaime tell her the story?

7. We should give her the ring.

8. Did you give them the present?

> **In Spanish** **Indirect object pronouns** also take the place of nouns used to tell *to whom* or *for whom* an action is done. These pronouns are **me**, **te**, **le**, **les**, and **nos**.
>
> - **Le** can mean (to/for) *him*, *her*, or *you (formal)*.
>
>   > **Le** podemos dar flores a Ana.
>   > **Le** voy a regalar un libro a Manolo.
>
> - **Les** can mean (to/for) *them* or *you (plural)*.
>
>   > **Les** quiero regalar flores a mis amigos.
>   > **Les** vamos a comprar un cartel a ustedes.
>
> In Spanish, indirect object pronouns can either precede a conjugated verb or be attached to an infinitive.
>
> > **Le** quiero regalar algo útil a Marcos.
> > Quiero regalar**le** algo útil a Marcos.

Copyright © by Holt, Rinehart and Winston. All rights reserved.

B Circle the indirect object pronouns and underline the verbs in the following sentences.

1. (Le) regalo un disco compacto a Miguel.

2. Les quiere regalar juguetes a sus niños.

3. Quiere regalarte un collar.

4. Tienes que regalarnos camisas.

5. Le doy una cartera a mi abuelo.

6. Les quiero dar dulces a mis hermanas.

7. Vamos a darle un libro a Juan.

8. Ustedes nos dan regalos a nosotros.

C Complete the sentence with the appropriate indirect object pronoun. Then underline the phrase that the pronoun represents.

1. A Juana ___le___ voy a regalar una planta.

2. _____ quiero dar refrescos a mis primos.

3. A usted yo _____ voy a dar el libro de matemáticas.

4. A ustedes voy a dar_____ mis zapatos viejos.

5. Tienes que dar_____ las llaves a Mauricio.

6. _____ voy a regalar mis discos a Julia y Lourdes.

7. Yo _____ doy a usted la tarea.

8. Tengo que dar_____ papel a mis estudiantes.

D In English, the indirect object and the person it represents can not be included together in the same sentence. For example, in English you cannot say

> *I gave _him_ the present _to Mark_.

In Spanish, however, you can say

> _Le di el regalo a Marcos_.

Think about when it is useful to include both the indirect object pronoun and **the person it** represents in Spanish, and when it is not necessary. Give some examples.

_____

_____

_____

_____

_____

Spanish 1 ¡Ven conmigo!, Chapter 9

Copyright © by Holt, Rinehart and Winston. All rights reserved.

MAKING COMPARISONS

¡Ven conmigo! Level 1, p. 277
En camino, p. 145

C A P Í T U L O 9

In English The following formulas are used to make comparisons with adjectives:

> **more** + *adjective* + **than**
> **less** + *adjective* + **than**
> **as** + *adjective* + **as**

> He is **more** *intelligent* **than** Norman.
> María is **less** *cautious* **than** Wanda.
> That maple tree is **as** *strong* **as** the pine tree.

When the adjective is one syllable, the formula **more** + *adjective* + **than** is changed to (*adjective* + **-er**) + **than**.

> My shirt is **whiter than** yours.
> Nick is **taller than** Rafael.

A In the following sentences, underline the phrase that expresses the comparison.

1. Raúl is heavier than Reynaldo.

2. Your grass is greener than mine.

3. Tito is as talented as his brother.

4. Her second movie was less interesting than her first.

5. Your speech was less boring than mine.

6. The dessert was as delicious as the main course.

7. That poem is more inspiring than this one.

8. My dog is prettier than any other.

In Spanish The following formulas are used to make comparisons with adjectives:

> **más** + *adjective* + **que**
> **menos** + *adjective* + **que**
> **tan** + *adjective* + **como**

> Tere es **más** *alta* **que** Clara.
> José es **menos** *aplicado* **que** Juan.
> Janet es **tan** *apasionada* **como** Lucy.

Note that the adjective agrees in number and gender with the word it describes.

> La azucena es más aromática que el lirio.
> Los automóviles son menos económicos que las bicicletas.
> Esas bufandas son tan caras como los sombreros.

B In the following sentences, underline the phrase that expresses the comparison.

1. Lupe es más divertida que Francisca.

2. Eva es más alta que Gabriela.

3. La falda es menos cara que el vestido.

Copyright © by Holt, Rinehart and Winston. All rights reserved.

4. Tus hijas son tan simpáticas como mis hijos.

5. La blusa es más barata que los pantalones.

6. Mi libro es más interesante que tu libro.

7. Ramón es más grande que Rosita.

8. Las sandalias son tan baratas como los zapatos.

C Using the different comparison formulas, construct sentences with the words provided.

1. color verde / bonito / color azul

   El color verde es más bonito que el color azul.

2. el profesor de ciencias / estricto / el profesor de matemáticas

   _____

3. camisa blanca / bonito / camisa de rayas

   _____

4. falda de seda / caro / falda de algodón

   _____

5. fiesta / divertido / clase

   _____

6. sandalias / cómodo / zapatos

   _____

7. profesores / serio / estudiantes

   _____

8. aretes / barato / collar

   _____

D Imagine you are a Spanish teacher and have to teach your students the three comparison formulas: **más**+*adj.*+**que**, **menos**+*adj.*+**que**, **tan**+*adj.*+**como**. Remember that there are three formulas in English too: **more**+*adj.*+**than**, **less**+*adj.*+**than**, **as**+*adj.*+**as**. Come up with a "catchy" strategy for your students to memorize the comparison formulas in Spanish.

_____

_____

_____

_____

_____

Copyright © by Holt, Rinehart and Winston. All rights reserved.

■ DEMONSTRATIVE ADJECTIVES

¡Ven conmigo! Level 1, p. 279
En camino, p. 150

CAPÍTULO 9

> **In English** **Demonstrative adjectives** point out people and things. They must agree in number with the nouns they describe.
>
> | Singular | | Plural | |
> |---|---|---|---|
> | **this** | I like **this** dress. | **these** | Do you like **these** dresses? |
> | **that** | I need **that** pencil. | **those** | She wants **those** notebooks. |

A In the following sentences, underline the demonstrative adjective and circle the noun it modifies. Then check the appropriate column to tell if it is singular (S) or plural (P).

	S	P
1. Myrna prefers this dress to the one I gave her.	✓	
2. Johanna selected these ties for her husband.		
3. What did Inés say about those flowers?		
4. I gave him one dollar for this mango.		
5. That tree looks quite old.		
6. I love this beach more than any other.		
7. Would you rather have these decorations?		
8. This car is very clean.		

> **In Spanish** **Demonstrative adjectives** also point out people and things. Like other adjectives in Spanish, they agree in number and gender with the nouns they describe.
>
> **MASCULINE:**
>
> | Singular | | Plural | |
> |---|---|---|---|
> | **este** (*this*) | Me gusta **este** vestido. | **estos** (*these*) | ¿Te gustan **estos** vestidos? |
> | **ese** (*that*) | Necesito **ese** lápiz. | **esos** (*those*) | Ella quiere **esos** cuadernos. |
>
> **FEMININE:**
>
> | | | | |
> |---|---|---|---|
> | **esta** (*this*) | Quiero **esta** corbata. | **estas** (*these*) | Nesesito **estas** sandalias. |
> | **esa** (*that*) | Te regalo **esa** camisa. | **esas** (*those*) | Me gustan **esas** botas. |

Copyright © by Holt, Rinehart and Winston. All rights reserved.

B In the following sentences, underline the demonstrative adjective and circle the noun it modifies. Then check the appropriate column to tell whether it is singular (S) or plural (P), feminine (F) or masculine (M).

	S	P	M	F
1. Esta casa es bonita.	✓			✓
2. Me gusta esa cartera.				
3. Voy a comprar ese diccionario.				
4. Esos chicos son simpáticos.				
5. ¿Te gusta este plato rojo?				
6. Estas niñas son muy inteligentes.				
7. Estos discos compactos son mis favoritos.				
8. Julián me va a regalar este libro.				

C Using the following words, construct sentences using the different demonstrative adjectives.

1. chicas / alto   _**Esas chicas son altas.**_

2. niña / bonito   _____

3. sancocho / delicioso   _____

4. muchachos / guapo   _____

5. computadora / lento   _____

6. escuelas / excelente   _____

7. libro / interesante   _____

8. señoras / simpático   _____

D Explain the difference in meaning between the following sentences:

Este zapato es de cuero.
Ese zapato es de cuero.

_____

_____

_____

_____

_____

_____

Copyright © by Holt, Rinehart and Winston. All rights reserved.

CAPÍTULO 10

■ PRESENT PROGRESSIVE

¡Ven conmigo! Level 1, p. 299
En camino, p. 172

C
A
P
Í
T
U
L
O

1
0

> **In English** The **present progressive** is the verb tense used to talk about what is happening right now. It is formed by combining the verb **to be** in the present tense with the **-ing** form, or **present participle**, of the action verb.
>
> You **are reading**. It **is raining**.

A Rewrite the following sentences from the present tense to the present progressive.

1. I write. _____I am writing._____

2. Luis eats. _____

3. We sing. _____

4. You watch the birds. _____

5. The sun shines. _____

6. They tell stories. _____

7. It snows. _____

8. He plays guitar. _____

> **In Spanish** The **present progressive** also tells what is happening right now. It is formed by combining the verb **estar** in the present tense with the **present participle** of the action verb.
>
> Yo **estoy pensando**. Alex **está corriendo**.
>
> While in English the present participle always ends in *-ing*, in Spanish, it can have two different endings, depending on the type of verb.
>
> • For **-ar** verbs, like *cantar* or *bailar*, remove **-ar** and add **-ando** to the stem.
>
> Tú estás cant**ando**. Nosotros estamos bail**ando**.
>
> • For **-er** and **-ir** verbs, like *comer* or *escribir*, remove **-er** or **-ir** and add **-iendo** to the stem.
>
> Ellos están com**iendo**. Usted está escrib**iendo**.
>
> • For verbs whose stem ends in a vowel, like *leer*, **-iendo** changes to **-yendo**.
>
> ¿Está le**yendo** Pedro?

Spanish 1 ¡Ven conmigo!, Chapter 10

Grammar Tutor **61**

Copyright © by Holt, Rinehart and Winston. All rights reserved.

B Rewrite the following sentences from the present tense to the present progressive.

1. Yo escribo.   <u>Yo estoy escribiendo.</u>

2. Luis come.   _____

3. Nosotros cantamos.   _____

4. Tú sales.   _____

5. Yolanda pinta.   _____

6. Ellos nadan.   _____

7. Nieva.   _____

8. ¿Qué hace él?   _____

C Imagine you are spending a week at the beach with your friends. Your parents call, and you tell them what everyone is doing. Use the verbs in the box to write six sentences describing what everyone is doing.

bucear	comer	bailar
nadar	beber (limonada)	mirar (la televisión)
cantar	correr	pescar

_____

_____

_____

_____

_____

_____

_____

_____

D What is the difference in meaning between the present tense and the present progressive? Think of two sentences such as:

Yo como carne.   *I eat meat.*
Yo estoy comiendo carne.   *I am eating meat.*

_____

_____

_____

_____

_____

Copyright © by Holt, Rinehart and Winston. All rights reserved.

COMMANDS

¡Ven conmigo! Level 1, p. 304
En camino, p. 181

C A P Í T U L O   1 0

> **In English Commands** are used when you want to give advice or instruct someone to do something. Commands are formed by using the infinitive form of the verb without the word **to**. The subject (you) is usually not stated when giving a command.
>
> **Do** your homework.   **Be** quiet!

A Underline only the sentences that express a command.

1. <u>Read the directions carefully.</u>

2. He listens to his parents.

3. Speak clearly when you give a presentation.

4. Smell the roses!

5. I go to my appointment.

6. Take some medicine.

7. They drink plenty of orange juice.

8. Please mow the lawn.

> **In Spanish Informal commands** are used with people you would address as **tú**. To state an informal command in Spanish, take the **tú** form of the present tense and drop the **-s**. For example, **escuchas** becomes **escucha** and **lees** becomes **lee**. Like in English, the subject pronoun is usually omitted.
>
> **Escucha** bien a Lorena.   **Lee** todo dos veces.
>
> Several command forms are irregular and should be memorized because they don't follow a single pattern. Verbs that are irregular in the command form include:
>
> | | | |
> |---|---|---|
> | hacer: **haz** | ir: **ve** | poner: **pon** |
> | venir: **ven** | salir: **sal** | |

B In each of the following sentences, the subject is **tú**. Underline only the sentences that express a command.

1. <u>Come todo el arroz.</u>

2. Dibujas muy bien.

3. Bebes mucha agua.

4. Corta el césped.

Copyright © by Holt, Rinehart and Winston. All rights reserved.

5. Limpia la sala.

6. Escuchas con atención.

7. Pon la mesa.

8. Haz la tarea.

C Your best friend wants to have a dinner party. Use the clues to write commands telling her what she must remember to do.

1. llamar a los invitados

   Llama a los invitados.

2. poner la mesa

3. preparar la cena

4. hacer un postre

5. lavar los platos

6. mandar las invitaciones

7. inflar los globos

D Commands can be used to request a favor, give instructions, or express an order. Read the following sentences and indicate what each one does.

Pon dos cucharas de azúcar.

¡Vete!

Ven aquí, por favor.

What is the difference in the choice of words between an order and a favor? Is it the same in English? Give examples.

Copyright © by Holt, Rinehart and Winston. All rights reserved.

¡Ven conmigo! Level 1, p. 307
En camino, p. 187

C A P Í T U L O 1 0

■ THE PAST TENSE

In English The simple **past** tense expresses an action or process that already took place. For regular verbs in English, the past tense is formed by adding **-ed** to the verb.

Ariel **played** soccer yesterday.   I **cooked** the pasta.

A Underline the verb in each sentence. Then check the appropriate column to tell whether the verb is in the present or past tense.

	PRESENT	PAST
1. Yolanda <u>worked</u> at the ice cream stand.	_____	✓
2. They talk all night.	_____	_____
3. You play tennis.	_____	_____
4. Ana lived in Boston for two years.	_____	_____
5. Luisa and Juan visited your grandmother.	_____	_____
6. I finished the book on Monday.	_____	_____
7. He cleans his room.	_____	_____
8. They planted a lot of pretty flowers.	_____	_____

In Spanish The **preterite tense**, like the simple *past tense* in English, is used to talk about events that have already taken place. For regular **-ar** verbs in Spanish, the preterite is formed by removing the **-ar** and attaching these endings:

yo	prepar**é**	*nosotros(as)*	prepar**amos**
tú	prepar**aste**	*vosotros(as)*	prepar**asteis**
él, ella, usted	prepar**ó**	*ellos, ellas, ustedes*	prepar**aron**

Notice the accent marks in **preparé** and **preparó**. The accent points to the syllable which should be stressed.

B Underline the verb in each sentence. Then check the appropriate column to tell whether the verb is in the present or preterite tense.

	PRESENT	PRETERITE
1. María <u>habló</u> mucho en la reunión.	_____	✓
2. Pedro y Luis cantan bien.	_____	_____
3. Ustedes bailaron con gracia.	_____	_____

Copyright © by Holt, Rinehart and Winston. All rights reserved.

	PRESENT	PRETERITE
4. Rolando lavó la ropa ayer.	_____	_____
5. Tú inflaste los globos, ¿no?	_____	_____
6. Ellas organizan los papeles.	_____	_____
7. Preparo la cena.	_____	_____
8. Nosotros pasamos la aspiradora ayer.	_____	_____

C Carlos asks Pilar about several activities, and she tells him that they were done yesterday. Write Pilar's answers.

1. CARLOS   ¿Tú caminas a casa hoy?

    PILAR   **No, caminé a casa ayer.** _____

2. CARLOS   ¿María plancha la ropa hoy?

    PILAR   _____

3. CARLOS   ¿Elena monta en bicicleta hoy?

    PILAR   _____

4. CARLOS   ¿Ellos hablan por teléfono hoy?

    PILAR   _____

5. CARLOS   ¿Organizamos la casa hoy?

    PILAR   _____

6. CARLOS   ¿Isabel corta el césped hoy?

    PILAR   _____

7. CARLOS   ¿Alejandra prepara la cena hoy?

    PILAR   _____

8. CARLOS   ¿Trabajo hoy?

    PILAR   _____

D In English and in Spanish, the ending of the verb usually tells the tense (whether it is present or past/preterite). What form of the verb in Spanish requires more information to tell the tense? Give an example.

_____

_____

_____

_____

Copyright © by Holt, Rinehart and Winston. All rights reserved.

■ DIRECT OBJECT PRONOUNS

In English A **direct object** is the person or thing in a sentence that receives the action of the verb. It answers the question *whom*? or *what*?

> I gave him the book. (*The book* answers the question, "What did I give him?")

> I introduced Peter to Mary. (*Peter* answers the question, "Whom did I introduce to Mary?")

Direct object pronouns can be used instead of nouns. Three singular forms for these pronouns in English are **him**, **her**, and **it**.

> I gave him <u>the book.</u> He read **it** immediately.
> I introduced <u>Peter</u> to Mary. But she had already met **him**.

A Circle the direct object pronoun and underline the noun it refers to in the following sentences.

1. I saw the <u>film</u> and enjoyed (it) immensely.

2. David thought the cake was delicious, so he ate it.

3. I met Liliana at the party, but I knew her from before.

4. You want to meet Julián, so I will introduce him to you.

5. They finished their mural, and they love it.

6. If you are interested in Nick's game, I can lend it to you.

7. We knew Raquel was going to come, but we didn't think we would see her here.

8. I saw José at the beach yesterday and gave him my phone number.

In Spanish **Direct object pronouns** are also used to refer to someone or something that receives the action of the verb. The singular forms of these pronouns are **lo** and **la**.

Lo is used to refer to a masculine noun: <u>Juan</u> está aquí pero no **lo** veo.
La is used to refer to a feminine noun: <u>La cartera</u> no es cara; **la** compro.

In Spanish, the direct object pronoun is placed before the verb.

> Marina **lo** probó.   **La** compramos.

B Circle the direct object pronoun and underline the noun it refers to in the following sentences.

1. Tengo que hablar con <u>María.</u> (La) llamo por teléfono.

2. La torta está deliciosa. La quiero comer.

3. Quiero jamón. Lo necesito para hacer un sándwich.

Copyright © by Holt, Rinehart and Winston. All rights reserved.

4. ¿Cuándo compró el regalo Eva? Lo compró ayer.

5. Juan está en la playa. Lo veo nadando.

6. ¿Me puede traer un cuchillo? Lo necesito para cortar la carne.

7. ¿Tienes la tarea? La necesito hoy.

8. ¡Ése libro es de Nacho! ¿Dónde lo encontraste?

C Answer the following questions using direct object pronouns.

1. ¿Quieres ver la película de Almodóvar?

   Sí, la quiero ver.
   _____

2. ¿Lees el periódico?

   _____

3. ¿Laila toma el autobús?

   _____

4. ¿Alejandro va a cuidar el gato?

   _____

5. ¿Dónde compras la comida?

   _____

6. ¿Tienes este libro?

   _____

7. ¿Quieres leer este libro de Laura Esquivel?

   _____

D Fill in the following chart with the direct object pronouns, in English and in Spanish, that you would use instead of the nouns in the first column.

	ENGLISH	SPANISH
Mario		
Andrea		
book / libro		
party / fiesta		

What is the main difference between direct object pronouns in English and in Spanish? In Spanish, what do you need to know and keep in mind when writing direct object pronouns?

_____

_____

_____

Copyright © by Holt, Rinehart and Winston. All rights reserved.

CAPÍTULO 11

■ THE VERB *TO PLAY* IN THE PAST

¡Ven conmigo! Level 1, p. 340
En camino, p. 229

> **In English** The verb **to play** is a regular verb. The past tense conjugation is the same for all persons.
>
> | | | | |
> |---|---|---|---|
> | *I* | play**ed** | *we* | play**ed** |
> | *you* | play**ed** | *you* | play**ed** |
> | *he, she, it* | play**ed** | *they* | play**ed** |

A Circle the subject and underline the verb in each sentence. Then check the appropriate column to indicate whether the verb is in the past or present tense.

	PAST	PRESENT
1. (He) played raquetball yesterday.	✓	
2. Emma plays with her friends in the yard.	_____	_____
3. Lucía and Jaime played dominoes last night.	_____	_____
4. We played basketball this morning.	_____	_____
5. They play volleyball at the beach.	_____	_____
6. You played water polo the night before last.	_____	_____
7. I play tennis with my brother.	_____	_____
8. You played soccer with the champions.	_____	_____

> **In Spanish** The verb **jugar** (*to play*) has a regular conjugation in the preterite in all forms except the *yo* form.
>
> | | | | |
> |---|---|---|---|
> | *yo* | jug**ué** | *nosotros(as)* | jug**amos** |
> | *tú* | jug**aste** | *vosotros(as)* | jug**asteis** |
> | *él, ella, Ud.* | jug**ó** | *ellos, ellas, Uds.* | jug**aron** |

B Circle the subject and underline the verb in each sentence. Then check the appropriate column to indicate whether the verb is in the preterite or present tense.

	PRETERITE	PRESENT
1. (Elías) jugó al tenis conmigo.	✓	
2. Emilia y Modesto juegan en la casa.	_____	_____
3. Nosotros jugamos al béisbol ayer por la tarde.	_____	_____
4. ¿Tú jugaste al jai alai con Reinaldo?	_____	_____

Copyright © by Holt, Rinehart and Winston. All rights reserved.

5. Yo juego al voleibol en la escuela.   _____   _____

6. Ellos jugaron al baloncesto muy bien anoche.   _____   _____

7. Ustedes juegan al dominó con Inés y Nico.   _____   _____

8. Elena jugó con Pepe ayer.   _____   _____

C Look back at the sentences in Activity B. How did you know if each was in the present or preterite tense? Were there any cases where the verb alone would not indicate the tense? Explain.

_____

_____

_____

_____

D Complete the following sentences with the correct form of jugar in the preterite tense.

1. Yo _____ **jugué** _____ al tenis ayer.

2. Mario _____ al golf con sus amigos la semana pasada.

3. Nosotros _____ con el perro anoche.

4. Tú _____ al baloncesto.

5. Julia y Francisco _____ a las cartas anteanoche.

6. Rigo y yo _____ con los niños.

7. Nancy y Kristen _____ al dominó con los chicos.

E Why do you think a u is added in the yo form of jugar in the preterite? Think about how the verb would be pronounced if the u was not added. Then write a rule that you can apply for conjugating unknown -ar verbs in the preterite tense.

_____

_____

_____

_____

_____

_____

Copyright © by Holt, Rinehart and Winston. All rights reserved.

THE VERB *TO GO* IN THE PAST

¡Ven conmigo! Level 1, p. 342
En camino, p. 232

C A P Í T U L O 1 1

In English The verb **to go** is irregular in the past tense.

I	**went**	we	**went**
you	**went**	you	**went**
he, she, it	**went**	they	**went**

A Circle the subject and underline the verb in each sentence. Then check the appropriate column to indicate whether the verb is in the past or present tense.

	PAST	PRESENT
1. (I) went to the theater yesterday.	✓	
2. You go to the movies with Roger.		
3. We went to a restaurant for dinner last night.		
4. You went to yoga class this morning.		
5. Rogelio went to the concert with his friends.		
6. Mimi and Rolando go to a writing workshop.		
7. Sylma goes to San Juan to see the soccer game.		
8. You go to New York to study.		

In Spanish The verb **ir** (*to go*) is irregular in the preterite tense because the root changes.

yo	**fui**	nosotros(as)	**fuimos**
tú	**fuiste**	vosotros(as)	**fuisteis**
él, ella, Ud.	**fue**	ellos, ellas, Uds.	**fueron**

B Circle the subject and underline the verb in each sentence. Then check the appropriate column to indicate whether the verb is in the preterite or present tense.

	PRETERITE	PRESENT
1. (Antonia) va a la Puerta de San Juan.		✓
2. Pedro y Benjamín fueron al Viejo San Juan.		
3. Carmela va a la playa.		
4. Ignacio y yo fuimos al Castillo del Morro.		
5. Tú fuiste al Museo de Pablo Casals.		

Spanish 1 ¡Ven conmigo!, Chapter 11

Grammar Tutor **71**

Copyright © by Holt, Rinehart and Winston. All rights reserved.

6. Usted fue a la Plaza de Hostos. _____ _____

7. Yo fui a casa de mis amigos. _____ _____

8. El profesor va a la universidad. _____ _____

C Complete the following sentences using the correct form of **ir** in the preterite tense.

1. Yo _____fui_____ a la Plaza de Hostos ayer.

2. ¿Tú _____ a la universidad ayer?

3. Nosotros _____ al concierto el jueves por la noche.

4. Ellos _____ a la casa de Sergio para jugar al dominó.

5. ¿Sabes si Julián _____ al estadio de fútbol?

6. ¿Ustedes _____ al partido de béisbol el sábado?

7. María _____ al mercado ayer.

D Answer the following questions negatively. Use the preterite tense of **ir** and **anoche**.

1. ¿Vas a casa de los abuelos?

   _**No, fui anoche.**_____

2. ¿Van Juana y Ramón al cine?

   _____

3. ¿Voy al parque?

   _____

4. ¿Van ustedes al concierto?

   _____

5. ¿Vas tú al Yunque?

   _____

6. ¿Va Paulina al gimnasio?

   _____

E Imagine that you and three of your friends each went on your dream vacations. Tell where each person went, using the preterite tense of the verb **ir**.

_____

_____

_____

_____

_____

Spanish 1 ¡Ven conmigo!, Chapter 11

Copyright © by Holt, Rinehart and Winston. All rights reserved.

CAPÍTULO 12

■ VERBS + INFINITIVES

> **In English** There are a number of verbs that may be followed by an infinitive. This means that the second verb is not conjugated and is usually preceded by the word *to*.
>
> I **want** *to go* to that concert.
> You **need** *to exercise* more.
> They **ought** *to listen* to their mother.
>
> She **hopes** *to travel* this summer.
> We **prefer** *to eat* at home.
> I **have** *to talk* to Inés today.

A Complete the sentences by adding an infinitive and the rest of the predicate.

1. I prefer __to eat outside._____

2. You have _____

3. They want _____

4. Elisa needs _____

5. Nicholas ought _____

6. You prefer _____

7. Enrique and Yoli need _____

8. I really hope _____

> **In Spanish** There are also a number of verbs that may be followed by an infinitive. This means that the second verb is not conjugated.
>
> Yo **quiero** *ir* al mercado.
> Ella **necesita** *comprar* un traje.
> Nosotros **pensamos** *preparar* una sopa.
>
> Ustedes **deben** *hacer* ejercicios.
> Tú **esperas** *tener* suerte.
> Él **puede** *comer* con nosotros.
>
> Sometimes adding a preposition or conjunction to a verb creates a verbal phrase with a meaning slightly different than that of the original verb. Some verbal phrases are also followed by an infinitive.
>
> Tú **tienes que** *hacer* la tarea.
> Yo **voy a** *salir*.

B Complete the sentences by adding an infinitive and the rest of the predicate.

1. Yo quiero __jugar con mis amigos._____

2. ¿Tú vas a _____

3. Él necesita _____

4. Marisa piensa _____

Copyright © by Holt, Rinehart and Winston. All rights reserved.

5. Marisol y Joaquín prefieren _____

6. Juliana debe_____

7. Nosotros podemos_____

8. Ustedes tienen que_____

C Manolo has a problem and a group of his friends gets together to discuss it. Using the verbs in parentheses, complete the following sentences to show what the conversation was like. The first person states Manolo's problem and the rest offer suggestions.

DORA   Tengo que decirles que Manolo ____*piensa hacer algo muy drástico.*____(pensar)

Verán, la situación es que Manolo _____

_____(querer)

JULIA   Yo creo que él _____

_____(necesitar)

CARMEN   En mi opinión, él _____

_____(deber)

TOMÁS   Pero él también _____

_____(poder)

ELENA   A mí me parece que Manolo _____

_____(ir a)

MARISOL   Bueno, tal vez él _____(esperar)

D Explain the difference in meaning between the verb **ir** and the verbal phrase **ir a** as well as the difference between **tener** and **tener que**. Which can be followed by an infinitive and which can not?

_____

_____

_____

_____

E Think about the Spanish verbs that are often followed by an infinitive: **querer** (*to want*), **necesitar** (*to need*), **deber** (*should*), **pensar** (*to think*), **esperar** (*to hope*), **poder** (*to be able to*). Which of these verbs are not followed by an infinitive in English?

_____

_____

Spanish 1 ¡Ven conmigo!, Chapter 12

Copyright © by Holt, Rinehart and Winston. All rights reserved.

THE VERB *TO BE*: SUMMARY

En camino, p. 264

In English There is only one verb that means **to be**. This verb can be used:

1. to say what someone or something is like.
2. to say where something or someone is from.
3. to define something or someone.
4. to say what something is made of.
5. to give the date or the time.
6. to talk about states and conditions.
7. to talk about location.
8. with the present participle (-ing form).

She **is** a tall girl.
They **are** from San José.
That **is** my brother Nick.
My shirt **is** cotton.
It **is** four o'clock.
I **am** happy today.
My book **is** on the chair.
You **are** playing tennis.

A Underline the form of the verb **to be** in the following sentences. Then indicate what kind of state the verb expresses by writing the number of the corresponding example above.

1. María is Luisa's sister.   3
2. The books are in bad condition.   _____
3. Julio and José are quite tall.   _____
4. I am calmer than yesterday.   _____
5. It is five o'clock.   _____
6. Ruth is from Santiago, Chile.   _____
7. They are dancing the merengue.   _____
8. My pants are wool.   _____

In Spanish There are two verbs that mean *to be*: **ser** and **estar**. In general, the difference between them is that **ser** usually expresses permanent, essential, non-changing states, whereas **estar** expresses changing states.

Use **ser**:

1. to say what someone or something is like.
2. to say where something or someone is from.
3. to define something or someone.
4. to say what something is made of.
5. to give the date or the time.

Carmela **es** inteligente.
Soy de San Juan, Puerto Rico.
Pablo **es** estudiante de ingeniería.
Los zapatos **son** de cuero.
Son las seis menos cuarto.

Use **estar**:

6. to talk about states and conditions.
7. to talk about location.
8. with the present participle (-ing form).

Rubén **está** de muy buen humor.
Está sobre el televisor.
Están hablando con Jorge.

Grammar Tutor **75**

Copyright © by Holt, Rinehart and Winston. All rights reserved.

B Underline the form of the verb **ser** or **estar** in the following sentences. Then indicate what kind of state the verb expresses by writing the number of the corresponding rule.

1. ¿Dónde <u>está</u> Héctor ahora?   7

2. Yolanda es muy guapa.   _____

3. Hoy es el 7 de septiembre.   _____

4. Abuela está cansada.   _____

5. El señor Ruiz es un profesor.   _____

6. Tu chaqueta es de cuero.   _____

7. Jaime está preparando la cena.   _____

8. Rita es de Buenos Aires.   _____

C Read each incomplete sentence. To the right, say if the verb is going to express a permanent or impermanent state. Then, complete each sentence using the present tense of the appropriate verb: **ser** or **estar**.

	PERMANENT	IMPERMANENT
1. Ema ___es___ una mujer elegante.	✓	
2. Juan Luis _____ un excelente cantante.	_____	_____
3. Las toallas _____ en el baño.	_____	_____
4. María Elena _____ un poco enferma.	_____	_____
5. Nosotros _____ hermanos.	_____	_____
6. Ustedes _____ muy equivocados (*mistaken*).	_____	_____

> Note that **ser** is generally used for permanent states, and **estar** is used for impermanent states. There are some states or qualities that can be expressed as permanent or impermanent, depending on whether **ser** or **estar** is used.
>
> • *Elena* **es** *muy delgada* means *Elena* **is** *very thin*. We don't expect her to change.
> • *Elena* **está** *muy delgada* means *Elena* **has become** *very thin*. There has been a change.

D Think of other examples of states or qualities that might change from permanent to impermanent by changing the verbs from **ser** to **estar**. Write two examples below and explain their meanings.

_____

_____

_____

_____

Spanish 1 ¡Ven conmigo!, Chapter 12

Copyright © by Holt, Rinehart and Winston. All rights reserved.

Grammar Tutor Activities
¡Ven conmigo!
Spanish 2

CAPÍTULO 1

ADJECTIVES: REVIEW

> **In English** **Adjectives** are words that describe nouns. English adjectives do not change their forms to match the nouns they describe.
>
> The girl is **pretty**. The **thin** boy is my brother.

A Underline the noun and circle the adjective in each sentence. Then check the appropriate columns to indicate whether the noun is singular (S) or plural (P), masculine (M) or feminine (F).

	S	P	M	F
1. My sister is (extroverted).	✓			✓
2. My nephews are athletic.				
3. Claudia always has smart ideas.				
4. Your brother is shy.				
5. Luis works in a Mexican restaurant.				
6. My grandmother is gray-haired.				
7. María is intelligent.				
8. The tall girl plays basketball.				

> **In Spanish** As in English, **adjectives** describe nouns. Unlike in English, Spanish adjectives change their forms according to the nouns they describe.
>
> • All adjectives agree with their nouns in number (singular or plural). The ending **-s** or **-es** is added to form the plural.
>
> El libro es **interesante**. Los libros son **interesantes**.
> Mi tío es **joven**. Mis tíos son **jóvenes**.
>
> • Adjectives ending in **o** or **a** agree with their nouns in gender (masculine or feminine). Adjectives ending in **e** or a consonant, however, don't change.
>
> La muchacha es **morena**. El muchacho es **moreno**.
> Conchita es **elegante**. Armando es **elegante**.
>
> • Adjectives ending in **-dor** or referring to **nationality** end in **a** in the feminine form.
>
> El chico es **hablador**. La chica es **habladora**.
> Luis es **español**. Pilar es **española**.

Copyright © by Holt, Rinehart and Winston. All rights reserved.

B Underline the noun and circle the adjective in each sentence. Then check the appropriate columns to indicate whether the noun is singular (S) or plural (P), masculine (M) or feminine (F).

	S	P	M	F
1. El <u>muchacho</u> es (rubio)	✓		✓	
2. Tu compañera está deprimida.				
3. La materia es difícil.				
4. Las casas son bonitas.				
5. Luis es argentino.				
6. Los chicos están enfadados.				
7. Me gusta la comida china.				
8. Los libros son interesantes.				

C Complete the following sentences with the correct form of the adjective in parentheses.

1. Las chicas _____jóvenes_____ bailan sevillanas. (joven)

2. Una anciana _____ camina por la Plaza de España. (canoso)

3. Los turistas _____ visitan la Plaza del Triunfo. (costarricense)

4. Un hombre _____ pasea por el Parque de María Luisa. (delgado)

5. La Giralda es una torre _____. (viejo)

6. Vivo en Sevilla, pero mis padres son _____. (venezolano)

7. Cenamos en un café _____. (pequeño)

D Use the clues to write complete sentences that tell the nationality of each person.

1. Valeria Mazza / modelo / argentino

   <u>**Valeria Mazza es una modelo argentina.**</u>

2. Frida Kahlo y Diego Rivera / artistas / mexicano

   _____

3. David Torres / cantante / cubano

   _____

4. Pedro Martínez y Sammy Sosa / atletas / dominicano

   _____

5. Rita Moreno / actriz / puertorriqueño

   _____

Copyright © by Holt, Rinehart and Winston. All rights reserved.

> **In English** All verbs express actions or states of being. **Verbs** in the **present tense** change only in the third person singular.
>
> | | | | |
> |---|---|---|---|
> | *I* | **speak** | *we* | **speak** |
> | *you* | **speak** | *you* | **speak** |
> | *he, she, it* | **speaks** | *they* | **speak** |

A Draw one line under the subject and two lines under the verb in each sentence. Then circle the ending of each verb.

1. Raúl returns from Andalucía.

2. His family throws a party.

3. Friends and neighbors help with the preparations.

4. Julia makes a cake.

5. After dinner, Raúl shows pictures of Sevilla.

6. He describes the beautiful buildings.

7. Then he tells about his adventures.

8. The guests listen intently.

> **In Spanish** **Regular verbs** are conjugated by dropping the **-ar**, **-er**, or **-ir** and adding the appropriate ending. In the present tense, each verb has six endings, which show who is doing the action.
>
> | | **HABLAR** | **COMER** | **VIVIR** |
> |---|---|---|---|
> | *yo* | habl**o** | com**o** | viv**o** |
> | *tú* | habl**as** | com**es** | viv**es** |
> | *él, ella, usted* | habl**a** | com**e** | viv**e** |
> | *nosotros(as)* | habl**amos** | com**emos** | viv**imos** |
> | *vosotros(as)* | habl**áis** | com**éis** | viv**ís** |
> | *ellos, ellas, ustedes* | habl**an** | com**en** | viv**en** |

B Draw one line under the subject and two lines under the verb in each sentence. Then circle the ending of each verb.

1. Eduardo vive en Sevilla.

2. Nosotros estudiamos juntos todos los días.

3. Yo visito a su familia.

4. Ellos leen libros españoles.

Copyright © by Holt, Rinehart and Winston. All rights reserved.

CAPÍTULO 1

5. Su madre me presta (*lends me*) un libro de Lorca.

6. Luego, comemos paella y ensalada de frutas.

7. Eduardo y su hermano aprenden inglés en la escuela.

8. Ellos practican conmigo.

C Look at the verbs you underlined in Activity B. Write them below and tell whether each is an **-ar**, **-ir**, or **-er** verb.

1. _____ _____

2. _____ _____

3. _____ _____

4. _____ _____

5. _____ _____

6. _____ _____

7. _____ _____

8. _____ _____

D Complete the following sentences with the correct present form of the verb in parentheses.

1. Ellos _____**hablan**_____ todo el día. (hablar)

2. ¿Ustedes _____ español? (leer)

3. ¿A qué hora _____ tú el cuarto? (limpiar)

4. Andrés _____ perfectamente. (nadar)

5. Nosotros _____ el baloncesto los viernes. (practicar)

6. Yo no _____ el piano. (tocar)

7. Ustedes _____ mucho en el mercado. (comprar)

8. El coro _____ música clásica. (cantar)

E Read this sentence: *Vamos mucho al parque pero no me gusta ir con Sergio porque él corre muy rápido.* Explain how the ending of the verb allows you to eliminate the subject in many cases. Why is a subject sometimes needed?

_____

_____

_____

_____

_____

Spanish 2 ¡Ven conmigo!, Chapter 1

Copyright © by Holt, Rinehart and Winston. All rights reserved.

CAPÍTULO 1

CAPÍTULO 2

■ PAST TENSE OF REGULAR VERBS

¡Ven conmigo! Level 2, p. 43

> **In English** The simple **past tense** is used to describe events that took place in the recent or distant past. The simple past tense of most regular verbs is formed by adding **-d** or **-ed** to the base form of the verb.
>
> | | | | | |
> |---|---|---|---|---|
> | *I* | walk**ed** | | *we* | walk**ed** |
> | *you* | walk**ed** | | *you* | walk**ed** |
> | *he, she, it* | walk**ed** | | *they* | walk**ed** |

A Underline the verb in each sentence and circle the ending. Then write the subject of the verb on the line to the right of the sentence.

1. He looked for his hat everywhere.   _____ He _____

2. They worked hard all day.   _____

3. We sailed all the way to Costa Rica.   _____

4. I passed the exam.   _____

5. You all expected to see him there.   _____

6. Luisa talked on the phone.   _____

7. Carlos scolded his little sister.   _____

8. The teacher assigned three pages.   _____

> **In Spanish** The **preterite tense**, like the simple past in English, can be used to describe events that happened in the past and are now finished. To form the preterite tense of any regular **-ar** verb, drop the **-ar** and add the following endings.
>
> | | | | |
> |---|---|---|---|
> | *yo* | compr**é** | *nosotros(as)* | compr**amos** |
> | *tú* | compr**aste** | *vosotros(as)* | compr**asteis** |
> | *él, ella, Ud.* | compr**ó** | *ellos, ellas, Uds.* | compr**aron** |

B Underline the verb in each sentence and circle the preterite ending. Then write the subject of the verb on the line to the right of the sentence.

1. Compré fresas ayer.   _____ Yo _____

2. Estudiamos ciencias la semana pasada.   _____

3. Mis amigos tomaron café por la tarde.   _____

Copyright © by Holt, Rinehart and Winston. All rights reserved.

4. Les gustó la película anoche. _____

5. María Luisa me regaló una blusa anteayer. _____

6. Todos los chicos regresaron a la escuela. _____

7. Luis y Teo jugaron al fútbol esta mañana. _____

8. Las muchachas cantaron en el coro. _____

C Complete each sentence with the correct preterite form of the verb in parentheses.

1. ¿Qué _____compraron_____ Andrés y Juana en el mercado? (comprar)

2. Ayer Luisa _____ canciones mexicanas. (cantar)

3. ¿Por qué tú _____ café después de cenar? (tomar)

4. La semana pasada nosotros _____ la cultura de Andalucía. (estudiar)

5. Todas las chicas _____ a clase a la una. (regresar)

6. ¿Quién _____ la lección ayer? (estudiar)

7. Carlos _____ en la piscina de su amigo. (nadar)

8. Anoche yo _____ la comida. (preparar)

D What is the *nosotros* form of **hablar** in the <u>present</u> tense? _____

What is the *nosotros* form of **hablar** in the <u>preterite</u> tense? _____

How can you know whether the action is in the present or in the past?

_____

_____

_____

_____

_____

Copyright © by Holt, Rinehart and Winston. All rights reserved.

CAPÍTULO 3

■ REFLEXIVE VERBS AND PRONOUNS

¡Ven conmigo! Level 2, p. 72

In English Sometimes the action of a verb is directed (or reflected) back on the subject. These verbs may be followed by **reflexive pronouns** which include **myself, yourself, himself, herself, itself, themselves, ourselves,** and **yourselves.**

I look at **myself.**   He bought **himself** a computer.

A Circle the reflexive pronoun and underline the verb it follows in each sentence. Then write the infinitive form of the underlined verb in the space to the right.

1. I dry myself after leaving the shower.   _____to dry_____

2. The little bird bathes himself in the pond.   _____

3. You call yourself an exceptional student?   _____

4. They prepare themselves before entering the library.   _____

5. Marta admires herself in the mirror.   _____

6. The athletes treat themselves to ice cream after the big win.   _____

7. Paola dresses herself before eating breakfast.   _____

8. The raccoon cleans itself in the stream.   _____

In Spanish **Reflexive verbs** express actions that reflect back on the subject. Reflexive verbs are easy to identify in Spanish because the infinitives have the **reflexive pronoun se** attached to them, as in **cepillarse.** The reflexive pronoun changes to **me, te, se, nos,** or **os** according to the subject of the verb.

yo	**me** cepillo	nosotros(as)	**nos** cepillamos
tú	**te** cepillas	vosotros(as)	**os** cepilláis
él, ella, Ud.	**se** cepilla	ellos, ellas, Uds.	**se** cepillan

- Reflexive pronouns are either placed before the conjugated verb or attached to the infinitive.

  Lorenzo **se** baña por la noche porque no le gusta bañar**se** por la mañana.

- When using a reflexive verb with a body part, a definite article is used.

  Nos secamos **el** pelo con la secadora y **las** manos con la toalla.

Copyright © by Holt, Rinehart and Winston. All rights reserved.

B Underline the reflexive verb and circle the reflexive pronoun. Then write the infinitive form of the reflexive verb in the space to the right.

1. María (se) pone la ropa. _____**ponerse**_____

2. Te cepillas los dientes con pasta de dientes. _____

3. Se miran en el espejo. _____

4. Nos acostamos a las diez de la noche. _____

5. Me lavo el pelo con champú. _____

6. Los hermanos se levantan a las seis de la mañana. _____

7. Mi amiga se viste de amarillo todos los días. _____

8. Nos despertamos con el despertador. _____

C Complete the following sentences using the correct form of each reflexive verb in parentheses.

1. Normalmente José _____**se levanta**_____ a las once los fines de semana. (levantarse)

2. Yo siempre _____ en el espejo antes de ir al colegio. (mirarse)

3. Iván siempre _____ los dientes después de comer. (cepillarse)

4. Nosotros _____ de ropa formal para la fiesta. (vestirse)

5. Tú _____ el pelo después de bañarte. (secarse)

6. Los estudiantes _____ a las seis por lo general. (despertarse)

7. Nosotros _____ a la medianoche casi todos los días. (acostarse)

8. Yo _____ la ropa que me gusta. (ponerse)

D Oftentimes, the meaning of reflexive verbs in Spanish may be expressed in English without a reflexive pronoun. Consider the examples below. Then write three more examples of sentences that use a reflexive pronoun in Spanish but not in English.

_____**Sam takes a shower.**_____   _____**Sam se ducha.**_____

_____   _____

_____   _____

_____   _____

_____   _____

_____   _____

Copyright © by Holt, Rinehart and Winston. All rights reserved.

CAPÍTULO 3

In English Adverbs are used to modify verbs, adjectives, or other adverbs. Adverbs are used most often to modify verbs and can be used

1. to tell *when*.	I wake up **late**.
2. to tell *where*.	I sleep **there**.
3. to tell *how much* or *how often*.	Mary studies **daily**.
4. to tell *how*.	I get out of bed **slowly**.

Adverbs that tell <u>how</u> an action is done are usually formed by adding **-ly** to the end of adjectives. In example 4 above, the adjective **slow** changes to the adverb **slowly**. Other examples include:

typical	⟹	**typically**
elegant	⟹	**elegantly**
quick	⟹	**quickly**

A Underline the verb and circle the adverb in the following sentences. In the space provided, state whether the adverb expresses **when**, **where**, or **how** an action is done.

1. Mary <u>showers</u> (quickly.)   how

2. The child looked shyly at the guests.   _____

3. Guadalupe sat here.   _____

4. I will buy new clothes tomorrow.   _____

5. Generally I get dressed after breakfast.   _____

6. The alarm clock rings softly.   _____

7. Dad bathes the baby carefully.   _____

8. Please put your toothbrush there.   _____

In Spanish Adverbs are also used to modify verbs, adjectives, or other adverbs. Adverbs are most often used to modify verbs and can be used:

1. to tell *when*.	Me despierto **tarde**.
2. to tell *where*.	Duermo **allí**.
3. to tell *how much* or *how often*.	Mary estudia **diariamente**.
4. to tell *how*.	Me levanto **lentamente**.

Adverbs that tell how an action is done are usually formed by adding **-mente** to the feminine form of adjectives. In example 4 above, the adjective **lenta** changes to the adverb **lentamente**. Other examples include:

típica	⟹	**típicamente**
elegante	⟹	**elegantemente**
cómoda	⟹	**cómodamente**

CAPÍTULO 3

Copyright © by Holt, Rinehart and Winston. All rights reserved.

B Underline the verb and circle the adverb in the following sentences. In the space provided, state whether the adverb expresses **when**, **where**, or **how** an action is done.

1. Yo me <u>baño</u> (rápidamente.)   ____**how**____

2. Ella normalmente se mira en el espejo antes de ir al colegio. _____

3. Nosotros nos vestimos elegantemente para la fiesta.   _____

4. Tú te secas el pelo lentamente.   _____

5. Mi abuela baila allí.   _____

6. La modelo se viste estupendamente.   _____

7. Ustedes típicamente se levantan a las ocho y cuarto.   _____

8. Mi tía viene mañana.   _____

C Complete the following sentences with adverbs formed from the adjectives in parentheses.

1. Plácido Domingo canta ____**estupendamente**____. (estupendo)

2. Mi amigo Tomás se viste _____. (rápido)

3. _____ voy a la escuela en bicicleta. (típico)

4. Mi hermana menor canta _____. (dulce)

5. Magda se despierta siempre _____. (fácil)

6. No me gusta bailar con Jorge porque baila _____. (cómico)

7. El estudiante contestó la pregunta _____. (inteligente)

8. Como siempre, tía Meches nos habló _____. (cariñoso)

D In English, some words that end in **-ly** are not adverbs. Look at the following five sentences and decide which **-ly** words are adverbs and which are adjectives. Then write each sentence in Spanish.

*Remember: **adjectives** modify *nouns* and **adverbs** modify *verbs*.

1. She talks slowly.   _____

2. The party is lovely.   _____

3. We should walk carefully.   _____

4. We ate quickly.   _____

5. The new student is friendly.   _____

By looking at the Spanish sentences, how can you tell which **-ly** words are adverbs in the English sentences?

_____

_____

CAPÍTULO 3

Copyright © by Holt, Rinehart and Winston. All rights reserved.

■ DIRECT OBJECT PRONOUNS

In English Direct objects answer *whom* or *what*.

Claudia dusts the lamp.	*What* does Claudia dust?	**the lamp**
Marcos invites Teresa.	*Whom* does Marcos invite?	**Teresa**
Pablo makes the beds.	*What* does Pablo make?	**the beds**

The lamp, **Teresa**, and **the beds** are all direct objects because they answer *whom* or *what*. Direct objects can be replaced by **direct object pronouns**, such as, **him**, **her**, **it**, or **them**.

Claudia dusts <u>the lamp</u>.	Claudia dusts **it**.
Marcos invites <u>Teresa.</u>	Marcos invites **her**.
Pablo makes <u>the beds.</u>	Pablo makes **them**.

A Circle the direct object in the following sentences. Then write the direct object pronoun which could be used to replace the direct object.

1. Fernando mops (the floor.) _____it_____

2. Maricarmen vacuums the rugs. _____

3. My mom pays the mechanic. _____

4. Guadalupe clears the tables. _____

5. Manuela cleans the basement. _____

6. Lorenzo´s dad calls the cleaning lady. _____

7. Mateo does the chores. _____

8. The homeowner hires the gardener. _____

C A P Í T U L O 3

In Spanish Direct objects also answer *who* or *what*. As in English, direct objects can be replaced by **direct object pronouns**. Four direct object pronouns are **lo**, **la**, **los**, and **las**. The direct object pronoun used depends on the gender and number of the direct object it replaces.

Sacudo <u>el polvo</u>.	**Lo** sacudo.
Quito <u>la mesa</u>.	**La** quito.
Hago <u>los quehaceres</u>.	**Los** hago.
Tiendo <u>las camas</u>.	**Las** tiendo.

Notice that the direct object pronoun comes right before the conjugated verb. The direct object pronoun can also be attached to the infinitive.

¿Quién tiene que lavar los platos?	Mi hermana **los** tiene que lavar.
OR	Mi hermana tiene que lavar**los**.

Copyright © by Holt, Rinehart and Winston. All rights reserved.

B Circle the direct object in the following sentences. Then write the direct object pronoun which could be used to replace the direct object.

1. Yo riego (las flores). _____ las _____

2. Su padre barre el cuarto de baño. _____

3. Tú llamas al jardinero. _____

4. Mi hermano tiende la cama. _____

5. Los niños sacuden el polvo. _____

6. Mi madre ordena los libros. _____

7. Ustedes lavan las toallas. _____

8. El abuelo ayuda a la abuela. _____

C Answer the following questions replacing the direct object with the appropriate direct object pronoun.

1. ¿Quién quita la mesa en tu casa?
   Mi hermano menor la quita. _____

2. ¿Tiendes las camas?
   _____

3. ¿Quién limpia el comedor?
   _____

4. ¿Quién hace los quehaceres?
   _____

5. ¿Quién barre el piso de la cocina?
   _____

6. ¿Quién cuida los jardines?
   _____

7. ¿Quién generalmente limpia la casa?
   _____

D Direct object pronouns cannot be used unless the direct object that they replace has already been stated. Explain why, using the sentences below as examples.

    I clean it.   *Lo limpio.*
    We cut them.   *Las cortamos.*

_____

_____

_____

Copyright © by Holt, Rinehart and Winston. All rights reserved.

CAPÍTULO 4

THE VERB *TO BE*: REVIEW

In English There is one verb that means to be. The verb to be can be used to talk about qualities that define or characterize people and things such as personality, nationality, size, or color.

The teacher is nice.	*personality*
The new students are Chilean.	*nationality*
The ball is small and blue.	*characteristics (size, color)*

The verb to be can also be used to say where something is located, to describe how someone feels, or to describe a state or condition.

The boys are in the church.	*location*
Lucas is very happy.	*how someone feels*
The tennis racket is broken.	*a state or condition*

A Circle the form of the verb to be in each sentence. Then choose the quality from the list that best describes what each verb expresses.

personality   *nationality*   *characteristics*
location   *how someone feels*   *a state or condition*

1. My little brother is sick today.   _____a state or condition_____
2. The students are responsible.   _____
3. My aunt is Ecuadorian.   _____
4. The exam is on your desk.   _____
5. The books are heavy and old.   _____
6. Guadalupe is tired.   _____
7. The computer is in the basement.   _____
8. Mary's sisters are tall and blond.   _____

In Spanish There are two verbs that mean *to be*: ser and estar.

Ser is used to talk about qualities that define or characterize people and things (personality, nationality, size, color).

El profesor es inteligente.	*personality*
Las alumnas nuevas son peruanas.	*nationality*
La pelota es roja y redonda.	*characteristics (size, color)*

Estar is used to say where something is located, to describe how someone feels, or to describe a state or condition.

Los chicos están en la playa.	*location*
Lucía está muy triste.	*how someone feels*
La cancha de tenis está ocupada.	*a state or condition*

Copyright © by Holt, Rinehart and Winston. All rights reserved.

B Circle the form of the verb **ser** or **estar** in each sentence. Then choose the quality from the list that best describes what each verb expresses.

personality   *nationality*   *characteristics*
location   *how someone feels*   *a state or condition*

1. (Estoy) en la cocina.   **location**

2. Susana es rubia y delgada. _____

3. Emilio y Eva son españoles. _____

4. Ustedes están de mal humor. _____

5. Tu padre es estricto. _____

6. El café está caliente. _____

7. Mi abuela es generosa. _____

8. Alejandro y yo estamos contentos. _____

C Andrew has to write an autobiography for his Spanish class. Help him by circling the appropriate verb to complete each sentence.

Me llamo Andrew. Tengo quince años. (Soy/Estoy) estadounidense pero mis padres (son/están) italianos. Vivo en Nueva York. Mi casa (es/está) en la avenida Washington. (Es/Está) una casa grande, de color amarillo. Yo también (soy/estoy) grande. Mido 6' 4" y peso 230 lbs. (Soy/Estoy) jugador de baloncesto. Hoy (soy/estoy) alegre porque no tengo clase. Mis clases (son/están) interesantes pero yo no (soy/estoy) un estudiante muy aplicado. Mi hermana menor se llama Matilda. Ella (es/está) en su clase de baile. Yo (soy/estoy) muy torpe y no bailo. Bueno, (soy/estoy) aburrido, así que me voy a practicar baloncesto.

D Write your own autobiography using **ser** or **estar** in each sentence.

1. _____

2. _____

3. _____

4. _____

5. _____

6. _____

Now tell whether the verb in each sentence above states *personality, nationality, characteristics, location, how someone feels, a state or condition.*

1. _____   4. _____

2. _____   5. _____

3. _____   6. _____

Copyright © by Holt, Rinehart and Winston. All rights reserved.

MORE DIRECT OBJECT PRONOUNS

¡Ven conmigo! Level 2, p. 112

In English Direct objects answer *whom* or *what*.

Andy reads the book. | *What* does Andy read? | **the book**
Carlos calls his parents. | *Whom* does Carlos call? | **his parents**

In English, direct objects can be replaced by **direct object pronouns**. You have already learned the direct object pronouns **him**, **her**, **it**, and **them**.

Fran invites your sister. | Fran invites **her**.
Patricia buys the flowers. | Patricia buys **them**.

The other direct object pronouns are **me**, **you** *(singular)*, **us**, and **you** *(plural)*.

Raúl calls **me**. | Pilar asks **us**.
Nuria invites **you**. | Teresa believes **you**.

A Circle the direct object pronouns in the following sentences.

1. Elizabeth invites (us) to the party.
2. David's brothers ask you for the address.
3. Carol calls me in the morning.
4. We invite you to the show.
5. Gabriela asks you for the homework.
6. Lauren believes me.
7. Felipe calls us every weekend.
8. I see you jogging every morning.

In Spanish Direct objects also answer *whom* or *what* and can be replaced by **direct object pronouns**. You have already learned the object pronouns **lo**, **la**, **los**, **las** *(him, her, it, them)*. The remaining direct object pronouns are **me**, **te**, **nos**, **os** *(me, you, us, you [plural])*.

Me llama Raúl. | **Nos** ayudó Pilar.
Te invita Nuria. | **Os** cree Teresa.

Remember that direct object pronouns may be placed directly before the conjugated verb or attached to the infinitive.

Emilio **me** va a invitar al baile. | Emilio va a invitar**me** al baile.

B Circle the direct object pronouns in the following sentences.

1. (Me) llama una amiga.
2. Roberto tiene que invitarnos.
3. Elena te ayuda a cocinar.
4. La profesora nos cree.
5. Voy a invitarte a mi fiesta.
6. ¿Me necesitas, mamá?
7. Nos mira el vecino.
8. Tengo que llamarlos.

C A P Í T U L O 4

Copyright © by Holt, Rinehart and Winston. All rights reserved.

C Complete the following dialogue by choosing the correct direct object pronoun.

FRANCISCO   Hola Silvia. Mira, quiero invitar(me/te) a mi fiesta el viernes.

SILVIA   ¿(Me/Os) invitas a tu fiesta?

FRANCISCO   ¡Claro que sí! Y a tu hermano también.

SILVIA   ¡Qué bien! Yo (te/nos) llamo el martes.

FRANCISCO   Tengo clase el martes. (Me/Los) llamo yo el miércoles.

SILVIA   Bueno, (te/nos) veo el viernes. Gracias por invitar(nos/te).

FRANCISCO   Adiós.

D Using the cues, write complete sentences that contain direct object pronouns.

1. Joaquín / ver / tú / en el café Mayapán

   Joaquín te ve en el café Mayapán.

2. ustedes / poder / llamar por teléfono / yo

   _____

3. Marisol / ayudar / nosotros / a hacer la tarea

   _____

4. Eulalio / visitar / tú / en el hospital

   _____

5. nosotros / esperar / Paco y Toño / por una hora

   _____

6. el profesor / presentar / ustedes / a la clase

   _____

E Write each of the following sentences in Spanish two separate ways.

1. *We are helping them.*

   _____

   _____

2. *I want to see you.*

   _____

   _____

Explain in your own words the difference of placement of direct object pronouns in English and in Spanish.

_____

_____

_____

Copyright © by Holt, Rinehart and Winston. All rights reserved.

CAPÍTULO 5

■ MORE PAST TENSE VERBS

¡Ven conmigo! Level 2, p. 136

> **In English** The **past tense** is used to talk about actions that occurred in the past. For most regular verbs, the simple past tense is formed by adding **-d** or **-ed** to the verb.
>
> They **attended** the track meet.   He **lifted** weights.

A Underline the verb and circle the subject in each sentence.

1. (They) attended the soccer game last Thursday.

2. He played on the hockey team.

3. You jumped rope last night at the gym.

4. We competed the martial arts competition last fall.

5. Gregorio performed with the band in college.

6. Amelia and Pilar missed their aerobics class this afternoon.

7. I rowed in the regatta every September.

8. She lifted weights for an hour.

> **In Spanish** The **preterite tense**, like the *simple past tense* in English, is used to talk about events completed sometime in the past. The preterite endings for regular **-er** and **-ir** verbs are:
>
> | | | | |
> |---|---|---|---|
> | *yo* | corr**í** | *nosotros(as)* | corr**imos** |
> | *tú* | corr**iste** | *vosotros(as)* | corr**isteis** |
> | *él, ella, Ud.* | corr**ió** | *ellos, ellas, Uds.* | corr**ieron** |
>
> Note the accent marks in the **yo** form and in the *third person singular.*
>
> In the preterite, the verb **dar** (*to give*) uses **-er/-ir** endings but without the accent marks.
>
> | | | | |
> |---|---|---|---|
> | *yo* | d**i** | *nosotros(as)* | d**imos** |
> | *tú* | d**iste** | *vosotros(as)* | d**isteis** |
> | *él, ella, Ud.* | d**io** | *ellos, ellas, Uds.* | d**ieron** |

B Underline the verb and circle the subject in each sentence. If the subject is implied (not stated), check the column to the right.

Subject Implied

1. (Javier) corrió el maratón de Boston.   _____

2. Asistimos al partido de voleibol ayer.   _____

Copyright © by Holt, Rinehart and Winston. All rights reserved.

3. ¿Diste la pelota a Hermán? _____

4. Margarita y Cristina asistieron a la competición de natación. _____

5. Di la receta a mi amiga. _____

6. Corriste con un equipo en el colegio. _____

7. Éric se inscribió al nuevo gimnasio. _____

8. Mi tía Teresa me dio la bicicleta. _____

C Complete the following sentences using the preterite form of the verb in parentheses.

1. Yo _____ corrí _____ a la casa de Marcos ayer. (correr)

2. Gustavo y Pedro _____ al partido de golf. (asistir)

3. El hermano de Sara _____ la pelota al jugador. (dar)

4. Nosotros _____ la carrera de ochocientos metros. (correr)

5. Tú me _____ la bicicleta a mí. (dar)

6. Ustedes _____ al gimnasio. (asistir)

7. Elisa _____ cien metros. (correr)

8. Nosotros _____ a dar un paseo. (salir)

D Look at numbers 4 and 8 from Activity C. How can you tell if these sentences are in the present or preterite tense? What kinds of context clues could you provide in order to show the tense? Give examples.

_____

_____

_____

_____

_____

CAPÍTULO 5

Copyright © by Holt, Rinehart and Winston. All rights reserved.

In English All commands are formed by using the infinitive form of the verb without the word *to*.

Eat something.   Please **stop** shouting!   **Be** nice!

To make commands negative, place the word(s) **don't** or **do not** before the command.

Don't smoke.   **Do not** step on the grass!

A Circle the verbs that express commands. Then check the appropriate column to tell whether the command is positive or negative.

	POSITIVE	NEGATIVE
1. You're so nervous. Calm down!	✓	
2. Be quiet! The teacher is talking.		
3. I'm bored. Please take me home.		
4. It is raining. Drive carefully!		
5. You are going to the gym. Don't forget your ID!		
6. I'm really hot. Please give me that fan.		
7. What a racket. Please turn off the television!		
8. You're friends. Don't fight!		

CAPÍTULO 5

In Spanish **Informal commands** are used to tell a friend or relative to do something. Positive commands are formed by using the **tú** form of the present tense and dropping the **-s**.

STATEMENT   POSITIVE COMMAND
(Tú) Habl**as**.   ¡Habl**a**!   *Speak!*

Negative commands are formed by switching the **tú** form endings of **-ar** and **-er** verbs.

STATEMENT   NEGATIVE COMMAND
(Tú) No habl**as**.   ¡No habl**es**!   *Don't speak!*
(Tú) No corr**es**.   ¡No corr**as**!   *Don't run!*

Some verbs, such as **jugar**, suffer a change in spelling in the negative command form. **Jugar** is spelled with **gu** instead of **g** to keep the hard **g** sound.

STATEMENT   NEGATIVE COMMAND
(Tú) No jue**g**as.   ¡No jue**gu**es!   *Don't play!*

Copyright © by Holt, Rinehart and Winston. All rights reserved.

B Circle the verbs that express commands. Then check the appropriate column to tell whether the command is positive or negative.

	POSITIVE	NEGATIVE
1. Te duelen los pies. ¡(Deja) de correr!	✓	
2. Eres antipático. ¡No me hables así!		
3. Mañana tenemos examen. Estudia mucho.		
4. Es muy tarde. ¡Duerme!		
5. ¡No escales montañas! Es peligroso.		
6. ¡No levantes pesas! Te puedes lastimar la espalda.		
7. Come bien. Te vas a sentir mejor.		
8. ¡No juegues en la cocina! Papá está trabajando allí.		

C Rebecca is moving into a very strict dormitory. Use the information provided to make up a list of rules that she must follow while living there.

1. no fumar

   No fumes. _____

2. sacar la basura

   _____

3. pagar el alquiler (*rent*)

   _____

4. no comer en la cama

   _____

5. cortar el césped

   _____

5. no escuchar música muy fuerte

   _____

D Look back at Activities A and B. How did you know which sentences expressed commands? What is the difference in English and in Spanish when identifying commands?

_____

_____

_____

_____

Spanish 2 ¡Ven conmigo!, Chapter 5

Copyright © by Holt, Rinehart and Winston. All rights reserved.

> **In English** Positive commands are formed by using the infinitive form of the verb without the word *to*. Negative commands are formed by placing **don´t** or **do not** before the verb.
>
> **Come** to the party!   **Have** a great day!   Please **drive** carefully!
> Please **don´t lie**.   **Do not cheat**!   **Don´t get** angry!
>
> All verbs follow this rule. There are no irregular commands in English.

A Circle the verbs that express commands. To the right, mark whether the command is positive or negative.

	POSITIVE	NEGATIVE
1. We finished school. (Celebrate!)	✓	
2. Don´t steal. Stealing is wrong.		
3. Tomás is studying. Don´t make noise.		
4. I´m trying to sleep. Don't disturb me, please.		
5. Biking can be dangerous. Always wear your helmet.		
6. Don´t be grumpy! It is Friday.		
7. It is snowing. Bring your gloves.		
8. You´re on my foot. Please move!		

> **In Spanish** There are eight irregular informal commands.
>
> | Verb | Positive Command | Negative Command |
> |---|---|---|
> | hacer | haz | no hagas |
> | poner | pon | no pongas |
> | tener | ten | no tengas |
> | ir | ve | no vayas |
> | ser | sé | no seas |
> | venir | ven | no vengas |
> | salir | sal | no salgas |
> | decir | di | no digas |

B Circle the verbs that express commands. To the right, mark whether the command is positive or negative.

	POSITIVE	NEGATIVE
1. Tu cuarto es un desastre. ¡(Haz) la cama!	✓	
2. Quiero hablar contigo. ¡Ven aquí!		

Copyright © by Holt, Rinehart and Winston. All rights reserved.

C A P Í T U L O 5

	POSITIVE	NEGATIVE

3. ¿Te gusta fumar? ¡No seas tonto! _____ _____

4. La ropa está en el piso. ¡Pon la ropa en el armario! _____ _____

5. Te quiero. ¡No te vayas! _____ _____

6. Es tarde. ¡Sal de prisa! _____ _____

7. Es un secreto. ¡No digas nada! _____ _____

8. Es un regalo. ¡Ten! _____ _____

C Use the following information to write a positive and a negative command.

1. venir aquí   <u>**Ven aquí. No vengas aquí.**</u>_____

2. ser estudioso _____

3. poner la mesa _____

4. tener calma _____

5. hacer eso _____

6. decir mentiras _____

7. salir del cuarto _____

8. ir por la leche _____

D Sometimes when you need to memorize something in English or in Spanish it is a good idea to create a phrase to help you remember it. For example, the eight irregular informal **tú** commands could be remembered by thinking of this phrase:

Silly	*Sallie*	*Puts*	*Hot*	*Tamales*	*In*	*Victor's*	*Dessert*
E	A	O	A	E	R	E	E
R	L	N	C	N		N	C
	I	E	E	E		I	I
	R	R	R	R		R	R

The first letter of each word stands for the first letter of one the eight irregular command verbs. Write your own sentence to help you remember the irregular commands in Spanish.

_____

_____

_____

Copyright © by Holt, Rinehart and Winston. All rights reserved.

CAPÍTULO 5

CAPÍTULO 6

■ THE VERB *TO KNOW*

In English There is one verb that means **to know**. It can be used to refer to facts and information, to a person or place, or to an activity (*how to do something*).

We **know** the answer.	*information*
Laura **knows** my sister.	*person*
Brad and Maika **know** the area.	*place*
I **know** how to dance.	*activity*

A Underline the form of the verb **to know**. Then state whether the verb refers to **information**, an **activity**, a **person**, or a **place**.

1. The sisters <u>know</u> the dance.   *activity*

2. I know his cousin.   _____

3. We know how to get to the town.   _____

4. The guide knows the work of art.   _____

5. You know the neighborhood.   _____

6. They know my grandmother.   _____

7. Clarisa knows the lesson.   _____

8. Bobby and Marc know the restaurant.   _____

In Spanish There are two verbs that mean *to know*: **saber** and **conocer**.

• **Saber** is used to refer to facts and information.

     Nosotros **sabemos** el vocabulario.   *information*

When followed by an infinitive, **saber** means *to know how to (do an activity)*.

     Yo **sé** bailar.   *activity*

• **Conocer** can be translated as *to know* or *to be acquainted with* and is used to refer to a person or a place.

     Brad y Maika **conocen** el área.   *place*

Use the personal **a** after the verb **conocer** when referring to a person or people.

     Laura **conoce a** mi hermana.   *person*

Copyright © by Holt, Rinehart and Winston. All rights reserved.

B Underline the form of the verb saber or conocer in each sentence. Then state whether the verb refers to **information**, an **activity**, a **person**, or a **place**.

1. Ana <u>sabe</u> usar la computadora.   <u>   activity   </u>

2. Ellos saben tocar la guitarra.   _____

3. Mi primo conoce a Britney Spears.   _____

4. Nosotros sabemos escribir la fecha en español.   _____

5. Su hermana mayor conoce la discoteca.   _____

6. Yo sé escribir en chino.   _____

7. ¿Ustedes conocen a mi madre?   _____

8. ¿Conoces este lugar?   _____

C Circle the verb that correctly completes each sentence.

1. Leann (sabe/conoce) cantar muy bien.

2. Yo (sé/conozco) a la hermana de José.

3. Nosotros (sabemos/conocemos) la casa de la profesora.

4. Emilia y Jacobo (saben/conocen) su número de teléfono.

5. Tú (sabes/conoces) a la secretaria.

6. Ustedes (saben/conocen) escribir poemas.

7. Rodrigo (sabe/conoce) el parque de atracciones.

8. Ellas (saben/conocen) cocinar pasteles de chocolate.

D Use the clues to write questions in Spanish using saber or conocer.

1. Ask your friend if she knows a good restaurant nearby.

   ¿Conoces un buen restaurante cerca de aquí?

2. Ask your friend if she knows where the restaurant is.

   _____

3. Ask the teacher if he knows the new student.

   _____

4. Ask the teacher if he knows the new student's name.

   _____

5. Ask the new students if they know how to get to the library.

   _____

6. Ask your parents if they know your classmates.

   _____

CAPÍTULO 6

Copyright © by Holt, Rinehart and Winston. All rights reserved.

In English Most verbs in the simple past tense are formed by adding **-d** or **-ed** to the verb. The verbs **to ask for** and **to serve** are regular verbs.

I **asked for** paella.   The waiter **served** tacos.

The verb **to bring**, however, is irregular.

I	**brought**	*we*	**brought**
you	**brought**	*you*	**brought**
he, she, it	**brought**	*they*	**brought**

A First circle the verb, and then use a subject from the list to complete each sentence. Each subject should only be used once.

Harold   I   The twins   We   You   You guys   Mimi   They

1. _____Harold_____ brought two notebooks.

2. _____ served ice cream to everybody.

3. _____ asked for some water.

4. _____ brought the boys to the park.

5. _____ served dessert on the patio.

6. _____ brought a camera and film.

7. _____ asked for paper and pencils.

8. _____ brought nothing.

In Spanish Several verbs are irregular in the preterite because their stems change. Some verbs, like **servir** and **pedir**, have vowel changes in their stems. Other verbs, like **traer**, have a consonant added to the stem.

SERVIR

yo	**serví**	*nosotros(as)*	**servimos**
tú	**serviste**	*vosotros(as)*	**servisteis**
él, ella, Ud.	**sirvió**	*ellos, ellas, Uds.*	**sirvieron**

PEDIR

yo	**pedí**	*nosotros(as)*	**pedimos**
tú	**pediste**	*vosotros(as)*	**pedisteis**
él, ella, Ud.	**pidió**	*ellos, ellas, Uds.*	**pidieron**

TRAER

yo	**traje**	*nosotros(as)*	**trajimos**
tú	**trajiste**	*vosotros(as)*	**trajisteis**
él, ella, Ud.	**trajo**	*ellos, ellas, Uds.*	**trajeron**

C A P Í T U L O 6

Copyright © by Holt, Rinehart and Winston. All rights reserved.

B First circle the verb and then use a subject from the list to complete each sentence. Each subject should only be used once.

Nosotros   Tú   Alicia   Ustedes   Yo   Tim y Jimmy   Ellas   Juan

1. _____Juan_____ (trajo) el menú.

2. _____ sirvieron la comida.

3. _____ pidieron la cuenta.

4. _____ traje la ensalada.

5. _____ trajo la propina.

6. _____ pedimos el postre.

7. _____ sirvieron pastas.

8. _____ trajiste un refresco.

C Tell what each individual brought to the birthday party. Use the correct form of the verb **traer**.

1. Tú / el pastel de cumpleaños

    Tú trajiste el pastel de cumpleaños.

2. Elisa / una radio

    _____

3. Nosotros / una pelota para jugar

    _____

4. Yo / refrescos

    _____

5. Los amigos / regalos

    _____

6. Tú / música salsa

    _____

D In Spanish and in English, irregular verbs may follow certain patterns. Summarize how to conjugate the verb **pedir** in the preterite. You can use this summary to help you conjugate other irregular verbs in the preterite that follow the same pattern.

_____

_____

_____

_____

Copyright © by Holt, Rinehart and Winston. All rights reserved.

CAPÍTULO 3

CAPÍTULO 7

■ THE PAST TENSE: *USED TO*

In English The past tense is used to talk about actions that took place in the past.

    Constance <u>learned</u> how to skate.   They <u>skated</u> all night long.

Habitual actions in the past can be expressed with the formula **used** + *infinitive*.

    I **used** *to play* baseball.   They **used** *to read* a lot.

A Circle *used + infinitive* in the following sentences. Then write the subjects in the space provided.

1. We used to share an apartment.   We

2. Teresa used to get scared at night.   _____

3. I used to hate beets.   _____

4. You guys used to climb trees.   _____

5. My brother used to play tricks on me.   _____

6. María used to write poetry.   _____

7. Ivan and Guy used to dream about being stars.   _____

8. Bernadette used to build snowmen.   _____

In Spanish The preterite tense is used to talk about completed actions in the past.

    La semana pasada <u>hablé</u> con mi primo de Irlanda.

The **imperfect tense** is used to talk about what people or things *used to do* or what they *used to be like* in the past.

    Yo **jugaba** al béisbol.   *I used to play baseball.*
    Ellos **leían** mucho.   *They used to read a lot.*

The imperfect endings are as follows.

	-ar verbs	-er verbs	-ir verbs
yo	jug**aba**	com**ía**	viv**ía**
tú	jug**abas**	com**ías**	viv**ías**
él, ella, Ud.	jug**aba**	com**ía**	viv**ía**
nosotros(as)	jug**ábamos**	com**íamos**	viv**íamos**
vosotros(as)	jug**abais**	com**íais**	viv**íais**
ellos, ellas, Uds.	jug**aban**	com**ían**	viv**ían**

Copyright © by Holt, Rinehart and Winston. All rights reserved.

CAPÍTULO 7

B Circle the verbs in the following sentences. Then write the subjects in the space provided.

1. Amy (peleaba) con su hermanito.   _____Amy_____

2. Trepábamos a los árboles.   _____

3. Ellos tenían dos gatos.   _____

4. Yo hacía travesuras.   _____

5. Odiabas los exámenes.   _____

6. Mi padre contaba chistes.   _____

7. Encontrabas genial las tiras cómicas.   _____

8. Elí y Dana fastidiaban al profesor.   _____

C Complete the following paragraph with the imperfect tense of the verbs in parentheses.

Cuando yo era niña siempre _____jugaba_____ (jugar) en el parque.

_____ (venir) también mi hermano. Nosotros _____

(trepar) a los árboles y _____ (construir) castillos de arena. A mi her-

mano le _____ (gustar) molestar a los pájaros en el lago del parque. Mis

padres también _____ (venir) al parque con nosotros. Ellos

_____ (traer) la comida y todos nosotros _____

(comer) juntos. Yo siempre _____ (estar) muy contenta con mi familia en

el parque. ¿Y tú? ¿_____ (visitar) el parque con tu familia?

D Depending on the context, the Spanish imperfect tense can be equivalent to the English simple past tense. Think about the following sentences. Write each in Spanish using the preterite or the imperfect tense, and explain why.

1. I wrote a letter to my grandmother yesterday.

_____

_____

2. I wrote letters to my grandmother every week.

_____

_____

3. I played soccer today.

_____

_____

4. I played soccer when I was young.

_____

_____

Spanish 2 ¡Ven conmigo!, Chapter 7

Copyright © by Holt, Rinehart and Winston. All rights reserved.

In English The following formula is used to compare the *qualities* of people or things that are the same or equal:

> **as** + *adjective* or *adverb* + **as**

Mary is **as** *smart* **as** Einstein.
Raúl runs **as** *fast* **as** Mercury.

To compare *quantities* of equal value, the following formulas are used:

> **as much** + *noun* + **as**
> **as many** + *noun* + **as**

He has **as much** *hair* **as** his dad.
You have **as many** *cousins* **as** Tomás.

A Underline the comparative phrase in each sentence. In the space provided, state whether each compares **quality** or **quantity**.

1. Your mother talks <u>as loud as</u> our teacher.   quality
2. Sheila has as much money as Bill Gates.   _____
3. Hillary is as friendly as Carmen.   _____
4. He is as stubborn as my brother.   _____
5. Michael is as strong as my father.   _____
6. Mary has as many gray hairs as her grandmother.   _____
7. My backpack is as big as the desk.   _____
8. We have as much work as the seniors.   _____

In Spanish The following formula is used to compare *qualities* of people or things that are the same or equal:

> **tan** + *adjective* or *adverb* + **como**

Mary es **tan** *inteligente* **como** Einstein.
Raúl corre **tan** *rápido* **como** Mercury.

To compare *quantities* of equal value, the following formulas are used:

> **tanto**/**tantos** + *noun* + **como**
> **tanta**/**tantas** + *noun* + **como**

Él tiene **tanto** *pelo* **como** su padre.
Tienes **tantas** *primas* **como** Tomás.

Notice that **tanto** always agrees in number and gender with the noun it precedes.

CAPÍTULO 7

Copyright © by Holt, Rinehart and Winston. All rights reserved.

B Underline the comparative phrase in each sentence. In the space provided, state whether each compares **quality** or **quantity**.

1. Soy <u>tan alta como</u> Linda.   _____quality_____

2. Ella tiene tantos vestidos como su hermana.   _____

3. Los científicos son tan interesantes como los autores. _____

4. Tenemos tanto tiempo como para ir y regresar.   _____

5. Mi hermano es tan fuerte como tu hermano.   _____

6. Escribes tan bien como un poeta.   _____

7. Tengo tantos zapatos como la tía de Ana.   _____

8. Eres tan noble como el rey.   _____

C Summarize what the following people have in common using the appropriate comparison formulas.

1. De niño, Pablo tenía muchos libros y Pedro también.

   Pablo tenía tantos libros como Pedro. _____

2. Teresa era muy delgada y Marisol también.

   _____

3. Mi abuela tomaba muchas clases de pintura y mi abuelo también.

   _____

4. Juan tiene cinco hermanas y Manolo también.

   _____

5. Rosa juega muchos deportes y Paola también.

   _____

6. Mi hermano toca muchos instrumentos y yo también.

   _____

D In both English and Spanish, comparisons can be used to form similies. Similies are poetic comparisons that are used to create vivid images when describing something or someone. For example, *My hands are as cold as ice*. Write four similies in Spanish.

_____

_____

_____

_____

Copyright © by Holt, Rinehart and Winston. All rights reserved.

CAPÍTULO 7

CAPÍTULO 8

■ SUPERLATIVES

¡Ven conmigo! Level 2, p. 227

In English **Superlatives** are used to single out something as **the most** or **the least**.

- Most adjectives of one syllable and some adjectives of two syllables form their superlative degrees by adding **-est**.

    The actress is tall.   She is the **tallest** actress in Hollywood.

- Some adjectives of two syllables and all adjectives of more than two syllables form their superlative degrees with the formula **most** + *adjective*.

    My friend José is cheerful.   José is my **most cheerful** friend.

- To indicate the least, the formula **least** + *adjective* is always used.

    Ignacio is not faithful.   Ignacio is my **least faithful** friend.

- Some adjectives are irregular in the superlative form.

    bad ➡ **worst**   good ➡ **best**   little ➡ **least***   much ➡ **most**

A Underline the superlative phrase in each sentence.

1. The snake is <u>the least attractive animal</u> I can imagine.

2. The Ferris wheel is the slowest ride in the park.

3. The zoo is the funniest place in the city.

4. This is the biggest roller coaster we have ever seen.

5. We saw the longest movie in the history of Hollywood.

6. Tom Hanks is the most famous actor of his generation.

7. Julia Roberts is the prettiest actress I know.

8. The monkey is the silliest animal in the zoo.

In Spanish **Superlatives** are also used to single out something or someone as **the most** or **the least**.

- All regular adjectives form the superlative degree with the following formula:

    el/la/los/las + *noun* + **más/menos** + *adjective*

    La actriz es cómica.   Ella es **la actriz más cómica** de Hollywood.

    La película no es graciosa.   Es **la película menos graciosa** de todas.

- Like in English, some adjectives have irregular superlative forms.

    bueno ➡ **mejor**   malo ➡ **peor**
    Ésta es la **mejor** película del festival.   Emilio es el **peor** actor.

*Littlest is also a superlative for *little*. *Least* is used to refer to quantity, while *littlest* is used to refer to size.

Copyright © by Holt, Rinehart and Winston. All rights reserved.

B Underline the superlative phrase in each sentence.

1. Harrison Ford es <u>el hombre más inteligente</u> de la película.

2. La tortuga y la serpiente son los animales menos activos de todos.

3. La montaña rusa es la atracción más divertida del parque.

4. Son las estrellas de cine menos simpáticas del mundo.

5. Jackie Chan es el mejor actor de películas de acción.

6. Ésta es la peor película de Almodóvar.

7. Penélope Cruz es la actriz más guapa de la película.

8. Los días en el parque son los mejores días de mi vida.

C Rewrite the following sentences to single out the students of the school as the most or the least.

1. Carolina es inteligente.

   <u>Carolina es la estudiante más inteligente del colegio.</u>

2. Mateo y Juan son traviesos.

   _____

3. Patricio no es estudioso.

   _____

4. Daniel es bueno.

   _____

5. Laura no es atlética.

   _____

6. María no es chismosa.

   _____

D Read the following sentences and explain why sometimes the noun in the superlative formula (el/la/los/las + *noun* + más/menos + *adjective*) can be omitted.

Luisa is the fastest runner on the team.   **Luisa is the fastest.**
Luisa es la corredora más rápida del equipo.   *Luisa es la más rápida.*

_____

_____

_____

_____

_____

Copyright © by Holt, Rinehart and Winston. All rights reserved.

■ *TO SAY/TO TELL* IN THE PAST

In English The verbs **to say** and **to tell** are irregular in the simple past tense. The stem changes spelling and **-ed** is not added.

I	said	we	said	I	told	we	told
you	said	you	said	you	told	you	told
he, she, it	said	they	said	he, she, it	told	they	told

One way to report how someone felt in the past is to use the past conjugation of **to say** or **to tell** followed by the past tense of the verb that expresses emotion or opinion.

Alejandro **said** that the parades **interested** him.
She **told** us that the party **bored** her.

A Circle the form of the verb **to say** or **to tell** in each sentence. Then underline the verb that expresses emotion or opinion.

1. I (said) that I <u>hated</u> parades.

2. We told them that the festival fascinated us.

3. The children said that they loved the costumes.

4. Josephine told me that you liked the floats.

5. You told us that you enjoyed everything.

6. Mathew and Andy said that the decorations bored them.

7. They said that the masks impressed them.

8. You told her that you disliked the festival.

In Spanish The verb **decir** (*to say, to tell*) is irregular in the preterite. The stem changes spelling, and the *ellos/ellas/ustedes* ending is **-eron** instead of **-ieron**.

yo	dije	nosotros(as)	dijimos
tú	dijiste	vosotros(as)	dijisteis
él, ella, Ud.	dijo	ellos, ellas, Uds.	dijeron

When reporting about how someone felt in the past, use **decir** in the **preterite** followed by a verb in the **imperfect** that expresses emotion or opinion.

Alex **dijo** que le **interesaban** los carnavales.
Ella nos **dijo** que le **aburría** la fiesta.

B Circle the form of the verb **decir**. Then underline the verb that expresses emotion or opinion.

1. Elisa (dijo) que le <u>interesaba</u> el desfile.

2. Dijimos que nos gustaban los disfraces.

CAPÍTULO 8

Copyright © by Holt, Rinehart and Winston. All rights reserved.

3. Yo les dije que me fastidiaba el festival.

4. Ellos nos dijeron que les gustaba la carroza.

5. Dijeron que no les interesaban las máscaras.

6. Tú le dijiste que te chocaba decorar para la fiesta.

7. Yo te dije que me interesaba diseñar disfraces.

8. Farola y Marí dijeron que todo les parecía bonito.

C Complete each sentence with the correct forms of the verbs in parentheses.

1. Yo _____dije_____ (decir) que a mí me ___gustaban___ (gustar) las máscaras.

2. Antonia _____ (decir) que a ella le _____ (fastidiar) desfilar.

3. Ellos _____ (decir) que a ellos no les _____ (gustar) los diseños.

4. Nosotros _____ (decir) que no nos _____ (interesar) el festival.

5. Tú _____ (decir) que a ti te _____ (chocar) los disfraces.

6. Los padres _____ (decir) que les _____ (encantar) las carrozas.

7. Yo _____ (decir) que me _____ (fascinar) el carnaval.

8. Pablo _____ (decir) que él _____ (pensar) disfrutar del día.

D Translate each of the following sentences into Spanish.

1. I said I liked the game.

_____

2. Elizabeth told us she was tired.

_____

3. We said the movie bored us.

_____

4. My brothers told me the idea interested them.

_____

E How do you know when the verb **decir** means *to say* and when it means *to tell*? Think about when the indirect pronoun is used in English and then write a rule to help you remember.

_____

_____

_____

_____

_____

Copyright © by Holt, Rinehart and Winston. All rights reserved.

■ FORMAL COMMANDS

¡Ven conmigo! Level 2, p. 260

> **In English** All commands are formed by using the infinitive form of the verb, without the word *to*. There is no difference between *formal* and *informal* commands, so the verb remains the same no matter whom the command is directed to.
>
> > Ángela, **help** me move this box.
> > Ms. Pérez, please **help** me with this question.

A Circle the verb in the command form. In the space provided, write the infinitive of the conjugated verb.

1. (Be) nice! _____ **to be** _____

2. Laura, stop that bus! _____

3. Walk in the hallways! _____

4. Professor Ayala, show me the new library! _____

5. Feed the dogs in the morning. _____

6. Honey, bring me my slippers please! _____

7. Write me! _____

8. Please close the door, Mr. López. _____

> **In Spanish** There are two types of commands: *informal* and *formal*. **Formal commands** are used with people you would address as **usted** and **ustedes**. Follow these rules to form **formal commands**.
>
> - For regular verbs, stem-changing verbs, and verbs with irregular **yo** forms, use the present tense **yo** form, drop the **o** and add **-e** or **-en** to **-ar** verbs, and add **-a** or **-an** to **-er** and **-ir** verbs.
>
> | | | | |
> |---|---|---|---|
> | HABLAR | *yo hablo* | ¡**Hable** Ud.! | ¡**Hablen** Uds.! |
> | CERRAR | *yo cierro* | ¡**Cierre** Ud. la caja! | ¡**Cierren** Uds. la caja! |
> | LEER | *yo leo* | ¡**Lea** Ud.! | ¡**Lean** Uds. |
> | VENIR | *yo vengo* | ¡**Venga** Ud.! | ¡**Vengan** Uds.! |
>
> - Reflexive pronouns come before negative commands or are attached to affirmative commands. An accent is added on the third-to-last syllable when the pronoun is attached to the verb.
>
>   > ¡No **se** levante sin pedir permiso!   ¡Levánte**se** cuando quiera!

Copyright © by Holt, Rinehart and Winston. All rights reserved.

B Circle the verb in the command form and underline the ending. In the space provided, write the infinitive of the conjugated verb.

1. ¡Estudie!   *estudiar*

2. ¡Sigan las instrucciones!   _____

3. ¡Duerma ya!   _____

4. ¡Suban al coche!   _____

5. ¡Lávese la cara!   _____

6. ¡Tenga cuidado!   _____

7. ¡Cierre las ventanas antes de irse!   _____

8. ¡Asistan a las clases!   _____

- Verbs ending in **-car**, **-gar**, and **-zar** have spelling changes in the command form.

buscar (**c ➞ qu**)	*yo busco*	¡Bus**que** Ud.!	¡Bus**quen** Uds.!
jugar (**g ➞ gu**)	*yo juego*	¡Jue**gue** Ud.!	¡Jue**guen** Uds.!
empezar (**z ➞ c**)	*yo empiezo*	¡Empie**ce** Ud.!	¡Empie**cen** Uds.!

- These five verbs have irregular formal commands and do not follow any previous rules:

    dar: dé, den   **saber**: sepa, sepan   **ir**: vaya, vayan
    estar: esté, estén   **ser**: sea, sean

C Complete each formal command with the correct form of the verb in parentheses.

1. ¡ _____*Cruce*_____ la avenida La Paz! (cruzar, usted)

2. ¡ _____ el nombre a su profesor! (dar, usted)

3. ¡ _____ inteligente! (ser, ustedes)

4. ¡ _____ el examen ahora! (empezar, ustedes)

5. ¡ _____ limpio! (jugar, usted)

6. ¡ _____ tranquilo! (estar, usted)

7. ¡ _____ dos cuadras más al norte! (ir, ustedes)

8. ¡ _____ protegerse de los criminales! (saber, ustedes)

D Why do you think there are there two types of commands (informal and formal) in Spanish and only one in English?

_____

_____

Copyright © by Holt, Rinehart and Winston. All rights reserved.

CAPÍTULO 10

■ PAST TENSE FORMS

¡Ven conmigo! Level 2, p. 290 and p. 296

In English To describe a situation in which one action in progress was interrupted by another action, the **past progressive** is used to express the action in progress and the simple **past tense** is used to express the interrupting event.

Paula **was waiting** for the train when the earthquake **hit**.

The **past progressive** can also be used to talk about an action that had already started and was still continuing when a particular event happened. The particular event is described with the **past**.

It **was raining** when the race **finished**.

Notice that the verbs in the simple past tense are introduced by the word **when**.

A Underline the verbs in the past progressive and circle the verbs in the simple past tense.

1. The sun was shining when the women fainted.

2. I was watching TV when the phone rang.

3. They were eating dinner when they heard the noise.

4. She was crying when they said goodbye.

5. It was snowing when the heater broke.

6. The crowd was panicking when the police arrived.

7. The guard was napping when the robbery occurred.

8. We were surfing when I saw the shark.

In Spanish When describing a situation in which one action is interrupted by another, the **imperfect** is used to express the action in progress while the **preterite** expresses the interrupting event.

Paula **esperaba** un taxi cuando **llegamos** en carro.

The **imperfect** also describes the conditions surrounding a particular event, such as the weather, the way people felt, and what was going on. The **preterite** is used to tell the completed action.

Llovía cuando **salí** para la escuela.

The action in the preterite is usually introduced by the word **cuando** (*when*).

Copyright © by Holt, Rinehart and Winston. All rights reserved.

CAPÍTULO 10

B Underline the verbs in the imperfect and circle the verbs in the preterite.

1. <u>Hacía</u> buen tiempo cuando (se casaron.)

2. Estaban en el valle cuando vieron el rayo.

3. Hablabas con los amigos cuando llegó el profesor.

4. Había una tormenta cuando ocurrió el accidente.

5. Había niebla cuando se perdieron en la montaña.

6. Miguel estaba en el sofá cuando entré en la casa.

7. Estábamos contentos cuando recibimos las notas.

8. Yo jugaba con mi hermano cuando me caí.

> When telling a story in Spanish, both the **preterite** and **imperfect** tenses are used. The imperfect is used to set the scene and to describe people, places, moods, and situations.
>
> > Las princesas **jugaban** en el jardín.   *The princesses were playing in the garden.*
> > El enano **era** bajo y de color verde.   *The dwarf was short and green.*
>
> The preterite is used to tell that something happened or occurred. Expressions like **un día** (*one day*), **de repente** (*all of a sudden*), and **fue cuando** (*it was when...*) are used to introduce a verb in the preterite.
>
> > Un día **llegó** un hombre misterioso.   *One day a mysterious man arrived.*
> > De repente, la paja **se convirtió** en oro. *All of a sudden the straw turned into gold.*

C Complete the following paragraph with either the preterite or the imperfect forms of the verbs in parentheses. Use the vocabulary box for words you don´t recognize.

un ruido espantoso – *a scary noise*	empezar a llorar – *to start to cry*
un monstruo – *a monster*	valentía – *courage*
armario – *closet*	vencer – *to defeat*
miedo – *fear*	salvar – *to save*

_____Era_____ (ser) una noche nublada y misteriosa. El príncipe Pier

_____ (estar) en su cuarto cuando, de repente, _____ (oír)

un ruido espantoso. _____ (haber) un monstruo en su armario. El príncipe

_____ (tener) mucho miedo y por eso, _____ (empezar) a

llorar. En seguida _____ (llegar) su hermana pequeña, la princesa Francesca.

La pequeña _____ (tener) mucha valentía. _____ (vencer)

al monstruo y _____ (salvar) a su hermano mayor. Y todos

_____ (vivir) felizmente.

Copyright © by Holt, Rinehart and Winston. All rights reserved.

CAPÍTULO 11

■ WE COMMANDS

In English When talking about cooperating and getting involved, the **we command** is often used (**let's** + *verb*). The verb is the same as in the you command.

YOU COMMAND:

    Work together.   **Keep** our neighborhood clean.

WE COMMAND:

    Let's work together.   **Let's keep** our neighborhood clean.

A Mark the appropriate column to indicate whether each sentence is a **we** or a **you** command.

	WE	YOU
1. Let's protect the environment.	✓	
2. Conserve energy.		
3. Exercise daily.		
4. Let's go home.		
5. Let's finish the project.		
6. Let's be friends.		
7. Respect your teachers.		
8. Follow your dreams.		

In Spanish When talking about cooperating and getting involved, the **nosotros command** form is often used. **Nosotros** commands are formed by adding **-mos** to the **Ud.** (you formal) command forms.

YOU COMMAND (familiar):

    Recicla los periódicos.   **Ayuda** a los compañeros.

YOU COMMAND (formal):

    Recicle los periódicos.   **Ayude** a los compañeros.

WE COMMAND:

    Reciclemos los periódicos.   **Ayudemos** a los compañeros.

C A P Í T U L O 1 1

Copyright © by Holt, Rinehart and Winston. All rights reserved.

B Underline the verb in each sentence. Then mark the appropriate column to indicate whether it is a we, you (familiar), or you (formal) command.

	WE	YOU (familiar)	YOU (formal)
1. <u>Hagamos</u> un viaje juntos.	✓		
2. Pida ayuda de los empleados.			
3. Limpia el cuarto.			
4. Conservemos energía.			
5. Usemos pocos recursos.			
6. Habla con tus padres.			
7. Pongamos los libros aquí.			
8. Explica la respuesta.			

C You are organizing an environmental awareness group at school. Use the phrases below to write **nosotros commands** describing what you can do together to protect the environment.

1. reciclar los periódicos

   Reciclemos los periódicos.

2. conservar los recursos naturales

   _____

3. respetar la naturaleza

   _____

4. proteger las especies en peligro de extinción

   _____

5. llevar el vidrio al centro de reciclaje

   _____

6. apagar la luz al salir de un cuarto

   _____

7. no poner las latas de aluminio en la basura

   _____

D Summarize the difference in forming **we comands** in Spanish and in English.

_____

_____

_____

_____

_____

Spanish 2 ¡Ven conmigo!, Chapter 11

Copyright © by Holt, Rinehart and Winston. All rights reserved.

CAPÍTULO 12

■ SUBJUNCTIVE MOOD

¡Ven conmigo! Level 2, p. 360

In English Verbs may be in one of three moods: **indicative**, **imperative**, or **subjunctive**. Most verbs used in writing and speaking are in the **indicative mood.**

- The **indicative mood** is used to make statements of fact: She <u>sits</u> down.
- The **imperative mood** is used for commands: <u>Sit</u> down!

The **subjunctive mood** is not used frequently in English. The only common uses of the subjunctive mood in English are to *express a condition contrary to fact* and to *express a wish*.

> She acted as though I **were** her daughter. *(condition contrary to fact)*
> I wish she **were** my sister. *(wish)*

A Indicate whether the underlined verbs are in the indicative (IND), imperative (IMP), or subjunctive (SUB) mood.

	IND	IMP	SUB
1. I wish we <u>were</u> finished with the work.	____	____	✓
2. We <u>are</u> finished with the work.	____	____	____
3. She wished they <u>were</u> done.	____	____	____
4. <u>Finish</u> the work!	____	____	____
5. Elena <u>rides</u> her bicycle.	____	____	____
6. Eduardo wishes he <u>had</u> a bicycle.	____	____	____
7. Please <u>leave</u> all bicycles outside.	____	____	____
8. I wish you <u>were</u> there.	____	____	____

In Spanish Verbs may also be in the **indicative**, **imperative**, or **subjunctive** mood.

- The **indicative mood** is used to make statements of fact.   Nosotros <u>comemos</u>.
- The **imperative mood** is used for commands.   <u>¡Come!</u>

Unlike English, the **subjunctive mood** is common in Spanish and can be applied to many situations. One common use of the subjunctive mood is to talk about events in the indefinite future. The following are frequently used expressions that use the subjunctive.

Cuando llegue mi abuela...   **Cuando vuelva** a clase...
Cuando termine el examen...   **Cuando encuentre** un empleo...
Cuando tenga dinero...

CAPÍTULO 12

Grammar Tutor **119**

Copyright © by Holt, Rinehart and Winston. All rights reserved.

B Indicate whether the underlined verbs are in the indicative (IND), imperative (IMP), or subjunctive (SUB) mood.

	IND	IMP	SUB
1. Cuando <u>llegue</u> a casa, voy a comer.	____	____	✓
2. Lorenzo y Natalia <u>nadan</u> en la piscina.	____	____	____
3. ¡<u>Mira</u> las estrellas!	____	____	____
4. Quiero comprar un carro cuando <u>tenga</u> dinero.	____	____	____
5. Cuando <u>termine</u> la clase, jugamos al fútbol.	____	____	____
6. <u>Ayúdame</u> con la tarea.	____	____	____
7. Cuando <u>tenga</u> tiempo, vamos a salir.	____	____	____
8. <u>Quiero</u> ir a un restaurante cubano.	____	____	____
9. <u>Pide</u> el arroz con pollo.	____	____	____
10. Cuando <u>vuelva</u> a casa, voy a estudiar.	____	____	____

C Circle the verb that correctly completes each sentence.

1. Cuando Teresa (llega/(llegue)) a casa, va a dormir.

2. Cuando (encuentro/encuentre) un empleo, voy a comprar un carro nuevo.

3. Cuando (terminan/terminen) las clases, todos vamos a la fiesta.

4. Cuando (tengo/tenga) más dinero, voy a visitar España.

5. Cuando (llega/llegue) mi primo, vamos a ver un partido de béisbol.

6. Cuando mi tío (tiene/tenga) un nuevo empleo, va a estar muy contento.

7. Cuando (vuelvo/vuelva) a México, voy a ir a un concierto de mariachis.

8. Cuando (encuentro/encuentre) mi tarea, la voy a entregar.

D Think about the verb endings in the subjunctive mood. What other verb form is like this one?

_____

_____

_____

Spanish 2 ¡Ven conmigo!, Chapter 12

Copyright © by Holt, Rinehart and Winston. All rights reserved.

Grammar Tutor Activities
¡Ven conmigo!
Spanish 3

CAPÍTULO 1

MORE STEM-CHANGING VERBS

In English For most verbs, the spelling of the stem (the part of the verb that remains when the ending is removed) never changes, even if the ending changes.

We **begin** the lesson.   Consuelo **begins** the exam.
They **ask** for the answer.   David **asks** for the address.

One verb that changes spelling in the present tense is the verb **to be**.

I **am** able to play. You **are** able to work. He **is** able to sing.

A Underline the stem of each verb and circle the ending, if any. If the verb changes spelling, check the column to the right.

SPELLING CHANGE

1. Alfredo reads the comics.   _____

2. We row on the lake every summer.   _____

3. Julia is certainly in the park.   _____

4. I am a big fan of jazz.   _____

5. You skate on the weekends.   _____

6. Patrick listens to the program.   _____

7. We are crazy about apple pie.   _____

8. You collect stamps.   _____

In Spanish Verb endings change according to the subject. Some Spanish verbs also have spelling changes known as **stem changes**. Stem changes often occur in all forms except *nosotros* and *vosotros*. Review the following present tense **stem-changing verbs**.

	e ➡ ie	o ➡ ue	e ➡ i
yo	emp**ie**zo	p**ue**do	p**i**do
tú	emp**ie**zas	p**ue**des	p**i**des
él, ella, Ud.	emp**ie**za	p**ue**de	p**i**de
nosotros(as)	empezamos	podemos	pedimos
vosotros(as)	empezáis	podéis	pedís
ellos, ellas, Uds.	emp**ie**zan	p**ue**den	p**i**den

CAPÍTULO 1

Copyright © by Holt, Rinehart and Winston. All rights reserved.

B Underline the stem of each conjugated verb and circle the ending. Then check the column to the right if it is a stem-changing verb.

STEM-CHANGING

1. Yo habl(o) francés e italiano. _____

2. Ellos empiezan a las ocho. _____

3. ¿Puedes escuchar la música? _____

4. Leemos las tiras cómicas. _____

5. Carla pide un refresco. _____

6. Ricardo y su hermano tocan la guitarra. _____

7. Todos quieren ir a la playa. _____

8. Ustedes sacan muchas fotos. _____

C Complete each sentence with the correct present form of the verb in parentheses.

1. Voy al restaurante y _____ pido _____ una hamburguesa. (pedir)

2. Mi hermana _____ su clase de fotografía hoy. (empezar)

3. Nosotros _____ escalar montañas mañana. (poder)

4. Pilar y Rocío _____ una tarta en la fiesta. (servir)

5. Tú _____ después de ir en barco de vela. (dormir)

6. Ustedes _____ hacer esquí acuático. (querer)

7. El camarero nos _____ unas pastas deliciosas. (servir)

8. Nosotros le _____ un favor al profesor. (pedir)

D Conjugate the following verbs in the present tense.

	preferir	volver	vestir
yo	_____	_____	_____
tú	_____	_____	_____
él, ella, usted	_____	_____	_____
nosotros(as)	_____	_____	_____
vosotros(as)	_____	_____	_____
ellos, ellas, ustedes	_____	_____	_____

Which forms do not have a stem change? _____

CAPÍTULO 1

Copyright © by Holt, Rinehart and Winston. All rights reserved.

> **In English** The simple **past tense** is used to describe what happened in the past. For regular verbs, the past tense is formed by adding **-d or -ed** to the verb stem.
>
> I play**ed** the flute.
> We listen**ed** to the music.

A Underline the stem and circle the ending of each verb.

1. We played cards every afternoon.

2. Mary and her cousin climbed Mt. Rushmore.

3. I laughed with my friends.

4. You visited your grandparents in Florida.

5. My mother looked at photos of the new baby.

6. Ernesto practiced his saxophone.

7. They collected sea shells while on vacation.

8. Cristina and Rogelio jumped in the pool.

> **In Spanish** The **preterite tense** can be used to talk about what happened in the past. Review the preterite endings for the following **-ar**, **-er**, and **-ir** verbs.
>
> | PASAR | COMER | ESCRIBIR |
> |-------|-------|----------|
> | pas**é** | com**í** | escrib**í** |
> | pas**aste** | com**iste** | escrib**iste** |
> | pas**ó** | com**ió** | escrib**ió** |
> | pas**amos** | com**imos** | escrib**imos** |
> | pas**asteis** | com**isteis** | escrib**isteis** |
> | pas**aron** | com**ieron** | escrib**ieron** |
>
> The **yo** forms of verbs ending in **-car**, **-gar**, and **-zar** have spelling changes.
>
> TOCAR ➡ **toqué** JUGAR ➡ **jugué** COMENZAR ➡ **comencé**

B Underline the stem and circle the ending of each verb. If it has a spelling change, circle the entire verb and check the column to the right.

1. Tú tocaste tu clarinete. _____

2. Yo jugué con mis primos. _____

3. Montamos a caballo. _____

4. Mis padres comieron en un restaurante chino. _____

CAPÍTULO 1

Copyright © by Holt, Rinehart and Winston. All rights reserved.

5. Remaste en bote por el río. _____

6. Yo comencé una colección de sellos. _____

7. Jorge y su amigo vivieron en la playa. _____

8. Lourdes patinó en línea. _____

C Use the clues to tell what the following individuals did last summer.

1. Ustedes / escuchar / música latina

Ustedes escucharon música latina. _____

2. Carla y su hermanita / patinar sobre ruedas / todos los días

_____

3. Yo / sacar / fotos en el jardín

_____

4. Nosotros / practicar / ciclismo

_____

5. Mi familia / leer / muchos libros interesantes

_____

6. Laura y yo / dormir / hasta las doce del día

_____

7. Tú / vivir / en casa de la abuela

_____

8. Raquel / jugar / a los videojuegos

_____

D **1.** Look at the following sentences carefully. Notice that both use the same conjugation of the verb **bucear**. Which sentence refers to the past and which refers to the present? Explain.

El año pasado Marcos y yo **buceamos** en el mar.
Todos los días Marcos y yo **buceamos** en el mar.

_____

_____

_____

_____

2. Which type of verb has a different ending in the **nosotros** form in the present and past tense?

_____

Spanish 3 ¡Ven conmigo!, Chapter 1

Copyright © by Holt, Rinehart and Winston. All rights reserved.

CAPÍTULO 2

▮INFORMAL COMMANDS

> **In English** All commands are formed by using the infinitive form of the verb without the word *to*.
>
> **Relax**! **Stop** stressing! **Take** it easy!
>
> To make commands negative, place the word(s) **Don´t, Do not,** or **Never** before the command.
>
> **Don´t wear** yourself out! **Never get** hysterical!

A Complete each command with the correct form of the verb in parentheses.

1. Don´t _____get_____ nervous! (to get)

2. Do not _____ a hectic life. (to lead)

3. _____ your problems quickly. (to solve)

4. _____ things calmly. (to take)

5. Don´t _____ stress. (to cause)

6. _____ out your problems. (to talk)

7. _____ a lot. (to laugh)

8. Never _____ out! (to stress)

> **In Spanish** There are two types of commands, **informal** and **formal**. **Informal (tú)** commands are used to tell a peer to do something. Affirmative informal commands have the same form as the *él/ella/usted* present indicative form of the verb.
>
> **¡Come** comida sana! **Alivia** el estrés. **¡Toma** tus vitaminas!
>
> To form negative informal commands, take the **yo** form of the verb in the present indicative and drop the **-o**. Then add **-es** for **-ar** verbs, and **-as** for **-er** and **-ir** verbs.
>
> **No hables** demasiado. **¡No comas** esto! **No duermas** tanto.

B Complete each informal command with the correct form of the verb in parentheses.

1. No _____tomes_____ las cosas demasiado en serio. (tomar)

2. _____ al menos ocho horas. (dormir)

Copyright © by Holt, Rinehart and Winston. All rights reserved.

C A P Í T U L O 2

3. _____ siempre. (cuidarse)

4. No _____ el estrés. (causar)

5. _____ los problemas. (resolver)

6. No _____ demasiado. (comer)

7. _____ de tus preocupaciones. (hablar)

8. _____ ejercicio cada día. (hacer)

C It is "Healthy Living Week" at your school. Use the verbs provided to make a sign advising students and faculty what to do and what not to do in order to live well.

1. dormir ocho horas cada noche

   Duerme ocho horas cada noche. _____

2. no sufrir de tensiones

   _____

3. tomar las cosas con calma

   _____

4. no comer mucha grasa

   _____

5. aliviar el estrés

   _____

6. no llevar una vida agitada

   _____

D You have been hired to translate a promotional poster for the New York City Marathon. Write each sentence using informal Spanish commands.

Train hard.

_____

Run fast.

_____

Be positive.

_____

JUST DO IT!

_____

Copyright © by Holt, Rinehart and Winston. All rights reserved.

> **In English** **Reflexive pronouns** usually refer back to the subject of the sentence. They end in **-self** or **-selves**: **myself, yourself, himself, herself, itself, themselves, ourselves**, and **yourselves**.
>
>   I weighed **myself**.   Dora takes care of **herself**.

A   Circle the reflexive pronoun in each sentence.

1. Pilar treats (herself) to a fruit smoothie.

2. I bought myself a new car.

3. The kids dried themselves off after getting out of the pool.

4. We couldn´t believe he just invited himself to the party!

5. Do you weigh yourself every day?

6. Ricardo looked at himself in the mirror.

7. I sent myself a dozen roses for my birthday.

8. We protect ourselves from the sun by using sunscreen.

> **In Spanish** The action of **reflexive verbs** is *reflected* back on the subject. Reflexive verbs are always accompanied by a **reflexive pronoun: me, te, se, nos**, or **os**. The reflexive pronoun changes according to the subject of the sentence.
>
> | | | | |
> |---|---|---|---|
> | *yo* | **me** ducho | *nosostros (as)* | **nos** duchamos |
> | *tú* | **te** duchas | *vosotros (as)* | **os** ducháis |
> | *él, ella, usted* | **se** ducha | *ellos, ellas, ustedes* | **se** duchan |
>
> Reflexive pronouns are either placed before the verb or attached to the infinitive.
>
>   Lourdes debe cuidar **se** mejor.   OR   Lourdes **se** debe cuidar mejor.
>
> For commands, attach the reflexive pronoun to the *end* of an affirmative command and place it *before* a negative command.
>
> AFFIRMATIVE   NEGATIVE
> ¡Aliménta **te** bien!   ¡No **te** quedes frente a la tele!

B   Underline the reflexive verb and circle the reflexive pronoun in each sentence.

1. (Me) <u>alimento</u> bien y llevo una vida sana.

2. Yolanda no se cuida y por eso está enferma.

C A P Í T U L O 2

Copyright © by Holt, Rinehart and Winston. All rights reserved.

3. Felipe y Érica se mantienen en forma.

4. Nosotros no nos quemamos cuando vamos a la playa.

5. Ustedes se acuestan temprano, por lo general.

6. Te quedas frente a la tele todo el día.

7. Paloma se pesa por las mañanas.

8. Los niños se duchan antes de ir al colegio.

C Complete each sentence with the correct present form of the verb in parentheses.

1. Las chicas _____se broncean_____ en la playa. (broncearse)

2. Yo _____ frente al televisor. (dormirse)

3. Nosotros _____ crema protectora. (ponerse)

4. Tú _____ muy solo. (sentirse)

5. Ustedes no _____ cuenta de la hora. (darse)

6. Francisco _____ por la mañana. (ducharse)

7. Mis padres no _____ a la moda. (vestirse)

8. Tú y yo _____ en forma. (mantenerse)

D Some Spanish verbs are always reflexive. However, the majority of all reflexive verbs can also be non-reflexive. Read the following sentences carefully and then answer the questions.

Yo **me quemo** en la playa.
Yo **quemo** las hamburguesas.

Why does the first sentence use a reflexive pronoun and the other does not? What does this tell you about when to use reflexive pronouns?

_____

_____

_____

_____

_____

Copyright © by Holt, Rinehart and Winston. All rights reserved.

CAPÍTULO 2

CAPÍTULO 3

■ THE PRESENT PERFECT

> **In English** The **present perfect tense** is used to describe what has or has not happened in the past. The present perfect is formed by combining the present tense of the verb **to have** and the **past participle** of any other verb.
>
> Everything **has changed** a lot.
> They **have spent** three hours surfing the Internet.

A Circle the form of the verb **to have** and underline the **past participle** in each sentence.

1. We (have) made several advances.

2. The city has changed a lot in the past 20 years.

3. The situation has gotten much worse.

4. I have written my paper using the computer.

5. Have you informed them of the possible risks?

6. The area has grown a great deal.

7. The factory has improved its output.

8. The farmer has planted this year's crops.

> **In Spanish** The **present perfect tense** is also used to describe what has or has not happened in the past. The present perfect is formed by combining the present tense of the verb **haber** and the **past participle** of any verb.
>
> Past participles of *regular* verbs are formed by dropping the **-ar**, **-er**, or **-ir** ending and adding **-ado** for **-ar** verbs or **-ido** for **-er** and **-ir** verbs.
>
> | | -ar verbs (-ado) | -er/-ir verbs (-ido) |
> |---|---|---|
> | *yo* | he mejorado | he crecido |
> | *tú* | has mejorado | has crecido |
> | *él, ella, usted* | ha mejorado | ha crecido |
> | *nosotros(as)* | hemos mejorado | hemos crecido |
> | *vosotros(as)* | habéis mejorado | habéis crecido |
> | *ellos, ellas, ustedes* | han mejorado | han crecido |
>
> Some verbs have *irregular* past participles and should be memorized.
>
> | | |
> |---|---|
> | abrir: **abierto** | morir: **muerto** |
> | decir: **dicho** | poner: **puesto** |
> | descubrir: **descubierto** | romper: **roto** |
> | escribir: **escrito** | ver: **visto** |
> | hacer: **hecho** | volver: **vuelto** |

CAPÍTULO 3

Copyright © by Holt, Rinehart and Winston. All rights reserved.

B Circle the form of the verb **haber** and underline the **past participle** in each sentence.

1. Mucha gente (ha) <u>venido</u> del extranjero (abroad).

2. Han establecido una zona peatonal.

3. El gobernador ha hecho muchos cambios.

4. Nos hemos adaptado a la nueva casa.

5. ¿Has navegado por Internet?

6. ¿Has cocinado en el horno de microondas?

7. Yo he escrito un correo electrónico.

8. Los profesores han hecho fotocopias.

C How things have changed! Use the present perfect tense and the information provided to tell about the changes of the last 20 years.

1. Nosotros / navegar / por Internet

   <u>Nosotros hemos navegado por Internet.</u>

2. Las ciudades / crecer / mucho

   _____

3. La contaminación del aire / empeorar / bastante

   _____

4. Yo / escribir / correo electrónico

   _____

5. Los médicos / hacer / adelantos contra el cáncer

   _____

6. Tú / cocinar / con un horno de microondas

   _____

7. Mi abuela / ver / películas en DVD

   _____

D The present perfect and the simple past/preterite are both used to talk about the past. Review the use of each tense in the sentences below and then answer the question.

Present Perfect	Preterite
1. Ahora **he visto** todo.	**Vi** todo.
2. **Hemos bailado** tres veces.	**Bailamos** tres veces.

What is the difference in meaning between each of the pairs of sentences?

_____

_____

_____

Copyright © by Holt, Rinehart and Winston. All rights reserved.

CAPÍTULO 3

In English The **future tense** is used to talk about actions or events that are yet to take place. The future tense is formed by placing the word **will** or **shall** before the base form of the verb.

My grandchildren **will drive** electric cars.
The people of the future **will use** only solar energy.
We **shall speak** more languages.

A Underline the base form of the verb and circle the word **will** or **shall** in each sentence.

1. Someone (will) discover the cure for this disease.

2. We shall use only electric cars.

3. I shall become a millionaire.

4. Your parents will surf the Internet.

5. There will be world peace.

6. You will develop a new type of interactive telephone.

7. Solar energy will replace nuclear energy.

8. Students will learn from home and not at school.

In Spanish The **future tense** is also used to refer to events or actions that are yet to take place. The future tense is formed by taking the infinitive and adding the future endings.

verb in the infinitive + *future endings* = *future tense*

DESCUBRIR	-é	-emos	descubriré	descubriremos
	-ás	-éis	descubrirás	descubriréis
	-á	-án	descubrirá	descubrirán

Some verbs are *irregular* in the future. Add the future endings to the following stems:

decir: **dir-**	poder: **podr-**	saber: **sabr-**	valer: **valdr-**
haber: **habr-**	poner: **pondr-**	salir: **saldr-**	venir: **vendr-**
hacer: **har-**	querer: **querr-**	tener: **tendr-**	

B Underline the infinitive or stem and circle the future ending of each verb.

1. Yo visitar(é) la Luna.

2. Cada casa tendrá una computadora.

3. Hablaremos un solo idioma.

C A P Í T U L O 3

Copyright © by Holt, Rinehart and Winston. All rights reserved.

4. Habrá coches viajando por el aire.

5. Tú sabrás hablar perfectamente el español.

6. Todos vivirán 120 años.

7. Ustedes comerán únicamente plantas.

8. El mundo será más limpio.

C Write complete sentences using the future tense to tell whether or not you think the following events will take place before the year 2025.

1. Cada persona / tener / un carro eléctrico

   Cada persona tendrá un carro eléctrico.
   _____

2. El presidente / destruir / todas la bombas nucleares

   _____

3. Marcianos / venir / de Marte a la Tierra

   _____

4. Tú / descubrir / una cura para el cáncer

   _____

5. Nosotros / eliminar / la contaminación del aire

   _____

6. Los estudiantes / estudiar / en casa usando computadoras

   _____

7. Los profesores / ganar / mucho dinero

   _____

8. Yo / desarrollar / un plan para la paz mundial

   _____

D What is another way to write the following sentences in Spanish?

1. Mis nietos van a vivir en la Luna.

   _____

2. Vamos a viajar en una máquina (_machine_) del tiempo.

   _____

3. Voy a poder ir de vacaciones a Marte.

   _____

Copyright © by Holt, Rinehart and Winston. All rights reserved.

CAPÍTULO 3

CAPÍTULO 4

■ OBJECT PRONOUNS

In English Direct objects are used to tell *whom* or *what,* and **indirect objects** are used to tell *for whom* or *to whom* an action is done.

María gives Consuelo the flower.
What does María give? — the **flower** (direct object)
To whom does María give the flower? — to **Consuelo** (indirect object)

Direct and indirect objects can be replaced by the object pronouns: **me**, **you**, **him**, **her**, **it**, **us**, **you** (*plural*), and **them**.

María gives **it** to **Consuelo**. — María gives **her** the flower.

A In the following sentences, circle the direct object pronouns and underline the indirect object pronouns.

1. Who sent <u>me</u> the package? I sent (it)

2. Who gives us the assignment? Marisa gives it.

3. Their mother offers them lemonade.

4. Who writes me letters? You write them to me.

5. We bought them for Carmen.

6. Carlos offers him advice.

In Spanish Direct objects are also used to tell *whom* or *what,* and **indirect objects** are used to tell *to whom* or *for whom* an action is done.

María le da la flor a Consuelo.
¿Qué da María? — la **flor** (direct object)
¿A quién le da la flor María? — a **Consuelo** (indirect object)

• Direct objects are replaced by the pronouns: **me**, **te**, **lo**, **la**, **nos**, **os**, **los**, **las**.

• Indirect objects are replaced by the pronouns: **me**, **te**, **le**, **nos**, **os**, **les**.

• When a direct and an indirect object pronoun are used together, the indirect object pronoun always comes before the direct object pronoun.

María **me la** da.

Pronouns are *attached* to infinitives and affirmative commands and *placed before* the verb in negative commands.

Debes comprár**melo**.   Cómpra**melo**, por favor.   No **me lo** compres.

• **Le** and **les** change to **se** when followed by the direct object pronouns **lo**, **la**, **los**, and **las**.

María **les** da la flor a ellos.   María **se** la da.

CAPÍTULO 4

Copyright © by Holt, Rinehart and Winston. All rights reserved.

B In the first sentence, circle the direct object and underline the indirect object. In the second sentence, circle the direct object pronoun and underline the indirect object pronoun.

1. ¿Quién me compró el carro? Nosotros te lo compramos.

2. ¿Quién escribe una postal a tu hermano? Tú se la escribes.

3. ¿Quién les da toallas a ustedes? La mujer nos las da.

4. ¿Quién da la tarea al profesor? Yo se la doy.

5. ¿Quién nos manda los libros a nosotros? Ustedes nos los mandan.

6. ¿Quién les escribe un aviso a los clientes? Usted se lo escribe.

C Write the answer to each question using a direct and an indirect object pronoun.

1. ¿Quién pone el examen a los estudiantes? (los profesores)

   Los profesores se lo ponen.

2. ¿A quién ofreces la pizza? (a ustedes)

   _____

3. ¿A quién mandamos las maletas? (a ti)

   _____

4. ¿Quién me escribe los correos electrónicos? (Juan Miguel)

   _____

5. ¿Quién prepara la cena para nosotros? (papá)

   _____

6. ¿A quién le prestas tu bicicleta? (a Clara)

   _____

D Use the verb in parentheses to tell Marco to do or not to do something for each person.

1. Marisa quiere la cena. (preparar)   Prepárasela.

2. David no quiere la bicicleta. (comprar)   _____

3. Teresa y Marta quieren la maleta. (traer)   _____

4. Yo quiero el helado. (dar)   _____

5. Andrés no quiere más comida. (servir)   _____

6. Nosotros queremos ver las fotos. (mostrar) _____

E Why do you think Spanish speakers change **le** and **les** to **se** when followed by either **lo, la, los,** or **las?**

_____

_____

Copyright © by Holt, Rinehart and Winston. All rights reserved.

CAPÍTULO 5

■SUBJUNCTIVE TO EXPRESS WISHES ¡Ven conmigo! Level 3, pp. 142, 143

> **In English** Verbs have a **tense** (*past, present, future*) and a **mood** (*the speaker's attitude toward the event*). The most common mood is the **indicative mood**, which is used to report facts.
>
> The **subjunctive mood** is used in English only in very limited situations. One use is in expressing *wishes* that are contrary to fact. The past subjunctive is used in these constructions; **were** is the past subjunctive form of the verb **to be**. All other verb forms are identical to the indicative past tense.
>
> INDICATIVE: Virginia **is** far away.   Diego **forgot** his wallet.
> SUBJUNCTIVE: I wish Virginia **were** here.   I wish he **were** more responsible.

A Check the appropriate column to indicate whether each underlined verb is in the indicative or subjunctive mood.

	INDICATIVE	SUBJUNCTIVE
1. Mamá <u>tells</u> the children about Mexican legends.	✓	
2. Martita wishes they <u>were</u> true.		
3. The legends <u>are</u> based on real people.		
4. Pablito <u>draws</u> a picture of Quetzalcóatl.		
5. He wishes his friends <u>were</u> there to see it.		
6. Martita and Pablo <u>told</u> us about the legends.		
7. We <u>were</u> amazed!		
8. We wished the characters from the legends <u>were</u> here.		

> **In Spanish** Verbs also have a **tense** and a **mood**. The **subjunctive mood** is a lot more common in Spanish than in English. Like in English, the **subjunctive mood** is used to express *wishes*. Unlike English, all verbs have different endings in the subjunctive.
>
> To conjugate a regular verb in the **subjunctive**, start with the **yo** form of the verb in the present tense, remove the **-o**, and add the following endings:
>
> | | HABLAR | COMER | DECIR |
> |---|---|---|---|
> | yo | habl**e** | com**a** | dig**a** |
> | tú | habl**es** | com**as** | dig**as** |
> | él, ella, usted | habl**e** | com**a** | dig**a** |
> | nosotros(as) | habl**emos** | com**amos** | dig**amos** |
> | vosotros(as) | habl**éis** | com**áis** | dig**áis** |
> | ellos, ellas, ustedes | habl**en** | com**an** | dig**an** |
>
> The phrases **espero que**, **ojalá que**, and **quiero que** require the subjunctive.
> INDICATIVE: Juan **conoce** a Carmela.   **Tengo** hambre.
> SUBJUNCTIVE: Espero que Juan **hable** con ella.   Ojalá que Ana **traiga** comida.

Copyright © by Holt, Rinehart and Winston. All rights reserved.

CAPÍTULO 5

B Check the appropriate column to indicate whether each underlined verb is in the indicative or subjunctive mood.

	INDICATIVE	SUBJUNCTIVE
1. Espero que <u>salgamos</u> pronto de vacaciones.	_____	✓
2. <u>Pensamos</u> ir al Caribe.	_____	_____
3. Ojalá que mi tía <u>pueda</u> ir con nosotros.	_____	_____
4. ¡Me <u>encanta</u> la playa!	_____	_____
5. Quiero que tú <u>pasees</u> en velero.	_____	_____
6. Ignacio <u>tiene</u> un bote.	_____	_____
7. Ojalá que <u>haga</u> buen tiempo.	_____	_____
8. Espero que ustedes <u>tengan</u> tiempo para tomar el sol.	_____	_____

Some verbs, such as **ir**, **estar**, **ser**, and **dar**, are irregular in the subjunctive.

	IR	ESTAR	SER	DAR
yo	**vaya**	**esté**	**sea**	**dé**
tú	**vayas**	**estés**	**seas**	**des**
él, ella, usted	**vaya**	**esté**	**sea**	**dé**
nosotros(as)	**vayamos**	**estemos**	**seamos**	**demos**
vosotros(as)	**vayáis**	**estéis**	**seáis**	**deis**
ellos, ellas, ustedes	**vayan**	**estén**	**sean**	**den**

D Señora Vásquez is reading a story to her daughter Anita, and Anita interrupts to say what she hopes will happen. Complete Anita's sentences with the subjunctive form of each verb in parentheses.

SRA. VÁSQUEZ	Una princesa está encarcelada (*imprisoned*) en un castillo (*castle*).
ANITA	¡Espero que ___escape___! (escapar)
SRA. VÁSQUEZ	Un soldado bueno va a luchar por ella.
ANITA	¡Ojalá que _____ ayudarla! (poder)
SRA. VÁSQUEZ	El malvado del castillo se llama Héctor.
ANITA	Quiero que Héctor _____ derrotado. (ser)
SRA. VÁSQUEZ	El soldado vence a Héctor.
ANITA	Espero que al final ellos _____ una boda. (celebrar)
SRA. VÁSQUEZ	Celebran la boda y el rey está feliz.
ANITA	Ojalá los invitados les _____ muchos regalos. (dar)

D Translate each sentence into Spanish. Then check the column next to those sentences in which the subjunctive is used in Spanish, but not in English.

1. I want Rafael to go to the concert.

_____   _____

2. I hope José is happy.

_____   _____

Copyright © by Holt, Rinehart and Winston. All rights reserved.

CAPÍTULO 6

■ SUBJUNCTIVE TO EXPRESS NEED   ¡Ven conmigo! Level 3, p. 164

> **In English** The **subjunctive** mood occurs in **that** clauses used to express importance or necessity for someone to do something. The present subjunctive form is the same as the base form of the verb (the infinitive without *to*).
>
>   Dora **studies** for the exam. (*indicative*)
>   It's necessary that Dora **study** for the exam. (*subjunctive*)*
>
> With statements expressing that something needs to be done in general or by everyone, the infinitive is used.
>
>   It's necessary **to eat** well.

A Circle the verb following the expression of need in each sentence. Then write to whom the expression of need is directed: a **particular person** or **everyone**.

1. It's important (to get) enough sleep.   __everyone__

2. It's essential that Selma stop at the store.   _____

3. It's necessary that Marla give you advice.   _____

4. It's important to speak clearly.   _____

5. It's imperative that he arrive on time.   _____

6. It's necessary to work hard.   _____

7. It's necessary that Joshua take the bus.   _____

8. It's essential that the student understand the problem. _____

> **In Spanish** Expressions of the importance or need for someone to do something are also followed by the **subjunctive** mood.
>
>   Dora **estudia** para el examen. (*indicative*)
>   Es necesario que Dora **estudie** para el examen. (*subjunctive*)
>
> With statements expressing that something needs to be done in general or by everyone, the infinitive is used.
>
>   Es necesario **comer** bien.

B Circle the verb that follows the expression of need in each sentence. Then write to whom the expression of need is directed: a **particular person** or **everyone**.

1. Es necesario (hacer) ejercicio.   __everyone__

2. Es importante que vayamos a clase.   _____

* Usually, sentences like this one are rephrased to avoid the subjunctive which sounds pompous: *Dora needs to study for the exam.*

Spanish 3 ¡Ven conmigo!, Chapter 6   Grammar Tutor **139**

Copyright © by Holt, Rinehart and Winston. All rights reserved.

3. Es necesario que Pablo llegue a tiempo.   _____

4. Hace falta que nosotros hagamos la tarea.   _____

5. Es necesario que tú me ayudes con el español.   _____

6. Es necesario trabajar duro.   _____

7. Es importante que visites a tu abuela.   _____

8. Es necesario escuchar a los profesores.   _____

The subjunctive forms of verbs that end in **-car**, **-gar**, or **-zar** have spelling changes.

BUSCAR(c ➡ que)	LLEGAR (g ➡ gu)	EMPEZAR (z ➡ c)
busque	**llegues**	**empiecen**

C Roberto and Julia are preparing a cultural outing for their Spanish class. Complete their dialogue with the correct form of each verb in parentheses.

ROBERTO   Quiero que ____**organicemos**____ un viaje a Guadalajara. (organizar)

JULIA   Es necesario que _____ pasajes *(plane tickets)* baratos. (buscar)

ROBERTO   Voy a hablar con un agente de viajes hoy.

JULIA   Bien, pero es importante que _____ allí antes de las cinco. (llegar)

ROBERTO   ¿Qué vamos a hacer durante el viaje?

JULIA   Es necesario que _____ el Instituto Cultural Cabañas. (visitar)

ROBERTO   Hace falta que _____ música también. (escuchar)

JULIA   Para eso, es necesario que tú _____ a un conjunto mariachi. (contratar)

D What other verb forms have spelling changes like those listed above for the subjunctive? Explain how you can remember when the subjunctive form of a verb has a spelling change. Then list five other verbs that have spelling changes in the subjunctive.

_____

_____

_____

_____

_____

_____

Spanish 3 ¡Ven conmigo!, Chapter 6

Copyright © by Holt, Rinehart and Winston. All rights reserved.

In English The **subjunctive** mood occurs in **that** clauses used to make suggestions and recommendations, especially in formal situations. The verb form of the present subjunctive is the same as the base form of the verb.

The doctor <u>recommends</u> that Raquel **take** medicine.
Our principal <u>suggests</u> that Manolo **help** his classmates.
The governor <u>recommends</u> that the new law **be** accepted.

A Check the appropriate column to indicate whether each underlined verb is in the **indicative** (I) or **subjunctive** (S) mood.

	I	S
1. My mother recommends that my father <u>visit</u> a museum.		✓
2. My father <u>goes</u> to an art museum.		
3. Tomás <u>reads</u> about the work of Frida Kahlo.		
4. The teacher recommends that Tomás <u>finish</u> his paper.		
5. You <u>enjoy</u> Cuban music.		
6. I suggest that you <u>listen</u> to Tito Puentes.		
7. The guide recommends that Enrique <u>see</u> a dance performance.		
8. Enrique <u>sees</u> a dance performance on Friday.		

In Spanish The **subjunctive** mood also appears in **que** clauses after verbs that express suggestions and recommendations. Notice that the subjunctive appears in compound sentences with two subjects and two verbs joined by **que**.

El doctor <u>aconseja</u> que **comamos** pescado.
Nuestro director <u>sugiere</u> que Manolo **ayude** a sus compañeros.
El gobernador <u>recomienda</u> que la nueva ley **sea** aprobada.

B Check the appropriate column to indicate whether each underlined verb is in the **indicative** (I) or **subjunctive** (S) mood.

	I	S
1. Gabriela recomienda que <u>pidas</u> las enchiladas.		✓
2. Tú <u>pides</u> arroz con pollo.		
3. Yo <u>voy</u> al cine a ver una película.		
4. Mi tía me aconseja que <u>vaya</u> al teatro.		

C A P Í T U L O   6

Copyright © by Holt, Rinehart and Winston. All rights reserved.

	I	S

5. Recomiendo que ustedes <u>estudien</u> arte. _____ _____

6. Ustedes sugieren que <u>almorcemos</u> en casa. _____ _____

7. Alicia <u>canta</u> muy bien. _____ _____

8. Paco sugiere que ella <u>cante</u> canciones tradicionales. _____ _____

> Remember that the subjunctive forms of **dar**, **estar**, **ir**, and **ser** are irregular.

C David has returned from a year of study in Guadalajara. Some younger students are preparing for their own year abroad and they ask him for recommendations. Complete David's responses with the appropriate form of the verbs in parentheses.

BEATRIZ   A mí me encantan las obras de José Clemente Orozco.

DAVID   Recomiendo que _____**visites**_____ el Instituto Cultural Cabañas para ver los murales. (visitar)

GERARDO   Me interesa la historia de México.

DAVID   Recomiendo que _____ a los monumentos de la ciudad. (ir)

LAURA   Me gusta mucho la danza.

DAVID   Recomiendo que _____ el Ballet Folclórico de México. (ver)

MANUEL   Quiero ver pinturas de artistas contemporáneos.

DAVID   Recomiendo que _____ una exhibición de arte moderno. (buscar)

OLGA   Me gustaría oír cantar a los mariachis.

DAVID   Recomiendo que _____ un taxi a la Plaza Tapatía. (tomar)

D Join the two sentences with the conjunction que. Then answer the question below.

a. La profesora recomienda. Daniel estudia más.

_____

b. Yo te aconsejo. Tú lees sobre el muralismo.

_____

c. Tobías sugiere. Nosotros vamos al concierto de Maná.

_____

What happens to the second verb when it becomes part of the que clause?

_____

_____

Copyright © by Holt, Rinehart and Winston. All rights reserved.

CAPÍTULO 6

> **In English** The formula **Let's** + *base form of the verb* is used to form a **we command**. To make a negative we command, the word **not** is added.
>
> **Let's go** to a museum.   **Let's not go** to a museum.
> **Let's watch** a movie.   **Let's not watch** a movie.

A Underline the **we command** in each sentence. Then check the appropriate column to tell whether each command is affirmative or negative.

	AFFIRMATIVE	NEGATIVE
1. <u>Let's take</u> guitar lessons.	✓	
2. Let's go to the Luis Miguel concert.		
3. Let's not buy movie tickets.		
4. Let's rent a movie instead.		
5. Let's listen to the ball game on the radio.		
6. Let's buy a charango.		
7. Let's not spend too much money.		
8. Let's listen to the banjo music.		

> **In Spanish** To say *Let's…* in Spanish, the **nosotros** form of the present subjunctive or the formula **vamos a** + *infinitive* can be used.
>
> **Veamos** la escultura.   OR   **Vamos a ver** la escultura.
>
> The **nosotros** form of the present subjunctive is used to say *Let's not…*
>
> **Escuchemos** la orquesta.   No **escuchemos** la orquesta.
> **Vamos a ver** las esculturas.   No **veamos** las esculturas.

B Underline the **we command** in each sentence. Then check the appropriate column to tell whether each command is affirmative or negative.

	AFFIRMATIVE	NEGATIVE
1. <u>Aprendamos</u> a tocar un instrumento.	✓	
2. Veamos la película a las ocho.		
3. No olvidemos ir al concierto.		
4. Vamos a comprar unos libros clásicos.		
5. No bailemos ahora.		

CAPÍTULO 6

Copyright © by Holt, Rinehart and Winston. All rights reserved.

6. Cantemos esta canción.

_____ _____

7. No escuchemos la radio.

_____ _____

8. Vamos a pintar un mural.

_____ _____

C Your family is going on vacation to Spain. Everyone has ideas about what things you can do in different parts of Spain. Complete each **we command** with the appropriate form of the verb in parentheses.

1. _____ *Visitemos* _____ la Universidad de Salamanca. (visitar)

2. _____ tapas en los cafés de San Sebastián. (comer)

3. _____ a una obra de teatro en la Gran Vía de Madrid. (asistir)

4. _____ el acueducto (*aqueduct*) romano en Segovia. (ver)

5. _____ por las bonitas calles de Toledo. (pasear)

6. _____ recuerdos (*souvenirs*) en las tiendas de Barcelona. (comprar)

7. _____ el sol en las playas de Cádiz. (tomar)

8. _____ fotos en la Plaza de España de Sevilla. (sacar)

Vamos can mean either *We're going* or *Let's go*. The meaning of the phrase is determined by the context.

D Check the appropriate column to tell whether **vamos** means *we're going* or *let's go* in each sentence.

		WE'RE GOING	LET'S GO
KARINA	Lola, ¡vamos al cine hoy!	_____	✓
LOLA	Lo siento, pero no puedo. Mi madre y yo vamos a un museo.	_____	_____
KARINA	¡Qué lástima! Vamos a perdernos una buena película.	_____	_____
LOLA	¡Vamos al cine mañana!	_____	_____
KARINA	Muy bien, pero tenemos que ir después de las ocho porque mi hermano y yo vamos a la casa de mi abuela.	_____	_____
LOLA	De acuerdo, nos vemos a las ocho.		

Spanish 3 ¡Ven conmigo!, Chapter 6

Copyright © by Holt, Rinehart and Winston. All rights reserved.

CAPÍTULO 7

■ EXPRESSSIONS OF FEELINGS

¡Ven conmigo! Level 3, p. 196

> **In English** The **indicative** mood is usually used in that clauses that follow expressions of feelings such as **I'm happy**, **I fear**, **I hope**, **it's sad**.
>
> I'm happy that you **feel** better.
> Alex is afraid that he **is getting** sick.
> We hope that grandma **visits** us soon.

A Underline the expression that conveys feeling in each sentence, and circle the verb in the **that** clause.

1. It's sad that we (have) to go home.

2. I fear that Blanca will arrive very late.

3. Francisco hopes that his team will win the game.

4. I'm happy that you are going out with us!

5. I am angry that you eat all my snacks!

6. We hope that you can come.

7. Patricia is afraid that Paco has too much work to do.

> **In Spanish** The **subjunctive** mood is used with expresssions that convey feelings such as **alegrarse que**, **temer que**, **ojalá que**, and **es triste que**.
>
> Me alegro que tú **te sientas** mejor.
> Alex teme que **se enferme**.
> Esperamos que abuelita nos **visite** pronto.

B Underline the expression that conveys feeling in each sentence, and circle the verb in the **que** clause.

1. Me alegro que Carlota (quiera) visitarnos.

2. Ojalá que Ricardo pueda venir también.

3. Esperamos que haga buen tiempo.

4. Temo que vaya a llover el sábado.

5. Me frustra que no tengamos tiempo para ir a la playa.

6. Espero que todos traigan bañador.

7. Es triste que Manolo esté enfermo.

CAPÍTULO 7

Copyright © by Holt, Rinehart and Winston. All rights reserved.

C Combine the sentences to form one complete sentence in the subjunctive mood.

1. David tiene un nuevo empleo. Estoy feliz.

   Estoy feliz que David tenga un nuevo empleo.

2. Lisa habla español. Mamá está orgullosa.

   _____

3. Abuelo no se siente bien. Estamos preocupados.

   _____

4. Luis no entiende las instrucciones. Mónica está frustrada.

   _____

5. Laura puede estar mintiendo. Olga tiene miedo.

   _____

6. Isabel siempre gana. A Elena no le gusta.

   _____

7. Raquel va a lavar los platos. Yo espero.

   _____

8. Mis amigos juegan conmigo. Me alegro.

   _____

9. Anita tiene tarea. Temo.

   _____

10. Jorge no habla con su hermano. Es triste.

    _____

D Sometimes the subjunctive mood is not needed after a verb that conveys feelings. Using the following sentences as examples, write a rule to explain when the subjunctive is used with verbs that convey feelings and when it is not.

Me encanta cantar con el coro.   Me encanta que Pedro cante con el coro.

_____

_____

_____

_____

Copyright © by Holt, Rinehart and Winston. All rights reserved.

RECIPROCAL PRONOUNS

> **In English** Reciprocal pronouns express a mutual action or relationship. There are two forms: **each other** and **one another**.
>
> Vivian and Cristina aren't speaking to **each other**.
> We help **one another** with our homework.

A Underline the reciprocal pronoun in each sentence.

1. Manuel and Roberto help each other study for the test.

2. Elisa and Yolanda argue with each other.

3. Now the girls aren't speaking to one another.

4. They finally made up with each other.

5. We like each other.

6. The family members support one another.

7. Ricardo and Lucy never lie to each other.

8. The students tell one another about their homelands.

> **In Spanish** The **plural reflexive pronouns** may be used to express the idea of *each other* or *one another*. Thus, plural verbs with the reflexive pronouns **se**, **os**, or **nos** may describe reciprocal, or mutual, actions.
>
> Vivian y Cristina no **se hablan**.
> **Nos ayudamos** con nuestra tarea.

B Underline the reflexive verb forms that describe reciprocal actions in each sentence.

1. Los amigos se abrazan.

2. Teresa y Verónica se reconcilian.

3. Los niños se pelean.

4. Mi hermano y yo siempre nos apoyamos.

5. Julio y Carla no se hablan.

6. Nos vemos después de las clases los viernes.

7. Los compañeros se ven en el colegio.

8. Mi hermana y yo nos compramos regalos de Navidad.

C A P Í T U L O 7

Copyright © by Holt, Rinehart and Winston. All rights reserved.

C For each pair of sentences, write one complete sentence using a plural reflexive verb form to express the idea of *each other*.

1. Marisol ve a José en el parque. José ve a Marisol en el parque.

   <u>**Marisol y José se ven en el parque.**</u>

2. Yo siempre te cuento secretos. Tú siempre me cuentas secretos.

   _____

3. Yo escribo cartas a mi amiga de Argentina. Mi amiga de Argentina me escribe cartas.

   _____

4. Susana llama a Alfonso por teléfono. Alfonso llama a Susana por teléfono.

   _____

5. Yo te conozco muy bien. Tú me conoces muy bien.

   _____

6. El muchacho apoya a su hermana. La muchacha apoya a su hermano.

   _____

7. Irma ama a Francisco. Francisco ama a Irma.

   _____

D How do you know when a plural reflexive verb form expresses the idea of *each other*? Explain your answer using the following sentences as examples.

Paola y Virginia se escriben.   Paola y Virginia se visten.

_____

_____

_____

_____

_____

Spanish 3 ¡Ven conmigo!, Chapter 7

Copyright © by Holt, Rinehart and Winston. All rights reserved.

THE UNKNOWN OR NONEXISTENT

> **In English** When talking about someone or something that is unknown or nonexistent, the **indicative** mood is generally used.
>
> I'm looking for a class that **is** interesting. (The class is *unknown*.)
> There is nothing we **can do**. (A solution is *nonexistent*.)

A Check the appropriate column to tell whether each sentence describes something that is known (K) or unknown/nonexistent (U).

	K	U
1. I am looking for a woman who speaks Spanish.	_____	✓
2. I know someone who is in that class.	_____	_____
3. There isn't anyone in my family who plays guitar.	_____	_____
4. We want to find someone who could play piano.	_____	_____
5. Nobody here plays volleyball.	_____	_____
6. Marisa is someone who is responsible.	_____	_____
7. Sandra's pet is playful and bright.	_____	_____
8. My mom is looking for a job that would be rewarding.	_____	_____

> **In Spanish** When talking about someone or something that is unknown or nonexistent, the **subjunctive** mood is used in the **que** clause.
>
> Busco una clase que **sea** interesante.
> Necesito algo que **tenga** rayas.
>
> The subjunctive is always used in **que** clauses that follow negative words like **nada**, **nadie**, or **ninguno(a)**.
>
> No hay <u>nada</u> que **podamos** hacer.
> No veo a <u>nadie</u> que **conozca**.

B Check the appropriate column to tell whether each sentence describes something that is known (K) or unknown/nonexistent (U).

	K	U
1. Busco un novio que sea simpático.	_____	✓
2. Tengo una amiga que es muy inteligente.	_____	_____
3. No hay nadie aquí que hable inglés.	_____	_____
4. Conozco a una maestra que habla japonés.	_____	_____

CAPÍTULO 7

Copyright © by Holt, Rinehart and Winston. All rights reserved.

5. No conozco a nadie que tenga un piano.   _____   _____

6. Hay un estudiante en mi clase que es muy guapo.   _____   _____

7. No hay ningún chico que sea tan guapo como él.   _____   _____

8. Tengo una prima que juega al béisbol con los muchachos.   _____   _____

The present subjunctive of **saber** is irregular.

yo	**sepa**	*nosotros(as)*	**sepamos**
tú	**sepas**	*vosotros(as)*	**sepáis**
él, ella, usted	**sepa**	*ellos, ellas, ustedes*	**sepan**

C You are helping companies find new employees. Each person tells you what kind of employee he or she is looking for. Complete their sentences.

1. Busco un secretario que ____**sepa usar la computadora**____. (sabe usar la computadora)

2. Busco una redactora (*editor*) que _____

   _____. (hablar español)

3. Busco un abogado (*lawyer*) que _____

   _____. (ser inteligente)

4. Busco una cantante que _____

   _____. (tocar la guitarra eléctrica)

5. Busco un camarero que _____

   _____. (tener mucha energía)

6. Busco un conductor que _____

   _____. (conocer la ciudad)

7. Busco una auxiliar de vuelo que _____

   _____. (gustarle viajar)

8. Busco unos maestros que _____

   _____. (saber español)

D While Spanish uses the subjunctive to indicate that something is unknown or nonexistent, English sometimes uses helping verbs such as *will* or *could*. Translate the following sentences into Spanish.

1. I'm looking for someone who could work in the morning.

   _____

2. Marisa is looking for a friend who will write her letters.

   _____

CAPÍTULO 7

Copyright © by Holt, Rinehart and Winston. All rights reserved.

IMPERSONAL EXPRESSIONS

¡Ven conmigo! Level 3, p. 232

In English **Impersonal expressions** are so called because the subject of the phrase is not a person but *it*. These expressions usually consist of the verb *to be* and an adjective: **it's important**, **it's necessary**, **it's doubtful**, **it's true**, **it's obvious**, **it's evident**.

- The **indicative** mood is used after most impersonal expresssions.

  It's obvious that you **dislike** the food.
  It's doubtful that Pablo **will come**.

- The **subjunctive** mood is used after impersonal expresssions of need or necessity when the word *that* is used.

  It's important that he **pass** the exam.
  It's necessary that she **help** him study.

A Check the appropriate column to tell whether each sentence expresses truth (T), doubt (D), or necessity (N).

	T	D	N
1. It's true that I made a mistake.	✓		
2. It's uncertain whether Mark will come for dinner.			
3. Elisa is sure that her sister is at home.			
4. It's obvious that Mandy is in love.			
5. We doubt that we'll find cheap tickets to Spain.			
6. It's important that the students understand the rules.			

In Spanish An **impersonal expresssion** consists of a form of the verb *ser* plus an *adjective*: **es importante**, **es necesario**, **es dudoso**, **es difícil**. When it is followed by **que** and a verb, the verb is usually in the **subjunctive**.

  Es dudoso que **compremos** una computadora nueva.
  Es importante que Olga **llegue** a tiempo.

Impersonal expressions which denote truth or certainty, such as **es cierto**, **es verdad**, **es evidente**, and **no es dudoso**, are followed by the **indicative**.

  Es verdad que Pilar **sale** en las noticias.
  No es dudoso que el reportaje **fue** interesante.

When expressions of truth are made negative, the **subjunctive** follows because they then imply doubt.

  No es verdad que Carmela **sea** famosa.

C A P Í T U L O 8

Copyright © by Holt, Rinehart and Winston. All rights reserved.

B Check the appropriate column to tell whether each sentence expresses truth (T), doubt (D), or necessity (N).

	T	D	N
1. Es evidente que este periódico es el mejor.	✓	____	____
2. Es importante que leas el periódico.	____	____	____
3. No es cierto que la sección de cocina tenga la receta.	____	____	____
4. No es dudoso que la sección de ocio es interesante.	____	____	____
5. Es importante que escuches el programa de las ocho.	____	____	____
6. Es necesario que compremos esta revista.	____	____	____
7. No es verdad que Rita mire demasiado la televisión.	____	____	____
8. Es dudoso que la foto aparezca en la primera plana.	____	____	____

C Complete each sentence with the correct form of the verb in parentheses.

1. Es importante que el director _____ **compre** _____ discos compactos para las computadoras de la escuela. (comprar)

2. Es dudoso que los maestros _____ videojuegos en el salón de clases. (querer)

3. No es cierto que los estudiantes no _____ usar la tecnología. (saber)

4. Es verdad que nosotros no _____ escuchar la radio en clase. (poder)

5. Es obvio que el Sr. García no _____ tener una televisión en la biblioteca. (querer)

6. No es dudoso que Ricardo _____ muchos libros. (leer)

7. Es necesario que Rosario _____ la tarea. (hacer)

8. Es evidente que nosotros _____ mucho. (estudiar)

D Write the following sentences in Spanish. Keep in mind that sentences in the indicative mood in English are often expressed in the subjunctive in Spanish.

1. It's not true that I like math class.

   _____

2. It's doubtful that Mr. González will give us a day off.

   _____

3. It's not obvious that the answer is B.

   _____

Spanish 3 ¡Ven conmigo!, Chapter 8

Copyright © by Holt, Rinehart and Winston. All rights reserved.

CAPÍTULO 9

▦ DESCRIBING EMOTIONAL REACTIONS   *¡Ven conmigo! Level 3, p. 257*

In English The **past progressive** of verbs like **to be** and **to feel** can be used to tell how someone was feeling when something happened.

    Margaret **was feeling** sad when she woke up.

The simple **past** is used to tell how someone reacted to an event or to a piece of news.

    Margaret **felt** sad when Anthony did not call her.
    (*The feeling resulted from the event.*)

A Underline the verbs in each sentence. Then check the column to the right if the sentence describes a feeling resulting from an event.

                                                  RESULT

1. Margarita <u>was</u> happy when she <u>saw</u> her grade.   ✓ _____

2. Ignacio was feeling tired when the movie started.   _____

3. Silvia was feeling better when she left for school.   _____

4. María felt angry when Isabel yelled at her.   _____

5. Pedro was surprised when Ana showed up.   _____

6. We were feeling sleepy when Mom arrived with the movie.   _____

7. Paola was excited when she found out the final score.   _____

8. Vicente was feeling sick when his mom called the doctor.   _____

In Spanish The **imperfect** tense of verbs like **estar** and **sentirse** can be used to tell how someone was feeling at the moment something happened.

    Mariona **se sentía** mal cuando llegó Alexandra.

The **preterite** is used to tell how someone reacted to an event or to a piece of news.

    Mariona **se sintió** mal cuando Marco le dijo que cancelaron el vuelo.
    (*The feeling resulted from the event.*)

B Underline the verbs in each sentence. Then check the column to the right if the sentence describes a feeling resulting from an event.

                                                  RESULT

1. Sergio <u>estaba</u> cansado cuando su madre le <u>pidió</u> ayuda.   _____

2. Alberto se sintió feliz cuando recibió sus notas.   _____

Copyright © by Holt, Rinehart and Winston. All rights reserved.

C
A
P
Í
T
U
L
O

9

3. Carmen se sentía contenta cuando empezó a llover. _____

4. Marta estuvo enojada cuando José llegó tarde. _____

5. Tú te sentías bien cuando decidiste jugar al fútbol. _____

6. Estuve sorprendida cuando mi prima me llamó. _____

7. Nos sentimos orgullosos cuando terminamos el proyecto. _____

8. Emilio estaba confundido cuando hizo la tarea. _____

The verbs **estar**, **ponerse**, **querer**, and **saber** are irregular in the preterite.

	ESTAR	PONERSE	QUERER	SABER
yo	estuve	me puse	quise	supe
tú	estuviste	te pusiste	quisiste	supiste
él, ella, Ud.	estuvo	se puso	quiso	supo
nosotros(as)	estuvimos	nos pusimos	quisimos	supimos
vosotros(as)	estuvisteis	os pusisteis	quisiteis	supisteis
ellos, ellas, Uds.	estuvieron	se pusieron	quisieron	supieron

The verb **saber** in the preterite tense often means *found out.*

Estuve feliz cuando **supe** que el equipo ganó.
(*I was happy when I found out the team won.*)

C Complete the paragraph with the correct form of each verb in parentheses.

Sabes que Mónica va a casarse? Yo _____supe_____ (saber) la noticia el martes. Salimos con los amigos, y Mónica nos contó todo. Nosotros _____ (ponerse) muy contentos. Ella dijo que sus padres _____ (estar) sorprendidos cuando ella les contó la noticia. Cuando ellos se quedaron en silencio, ella _____ (sentirse) mal. Pero luego, cuando ellos _____ (querer) abrazarla, ella _____ (sentirse) feliz.

D Complete each sentence with the correct form of **saber** in the imperfect or the preterite.

1. Yo siempre _____ que Luis era un chico honesto.
2. Nosotros estuvimos contentos cuando _____ que Tomás se sentía mejor.
3. ¿Cuando _____ (tú) que Clara tuvo un bebé?
4. Rosa _____ cocinar muy bien y me preparaba platos deliciosos.

E Write the sentences from Activity D in English.

1. _____
2. _____
3. _____
4. _____

Spanish 3 ¡Ven conmigo!, Chapter 9

Copyright © by Holt, Rinehart and Winston. All rights reserved.

CAPÍTULO 6

> **In English** The **indicative** mood is used to express *disagreement* and *denial*, as well as *affirmation*.
>
> It is <u>not true</u> that dogs **are** better pets than cats. (*disagreement*)
> Sofía <u>denies</u> that girls only **want** to shop. (*denial*)
> <u>It is true</u> that Ricardo's brothers **are** excellent musicians. (*affirmation*)

A Underline the phrase that expresses disagreement or denial, and circle the verb that follows.

1. I <u>disagree</u> that all actors (are) arrogant.

2. It is not true that male athletes train more diligently than female athletes.

3. Teresa denies that the city is more interesting than the country.

4. It is not true that teachers are unfriendly.

5. We disagree that our employers acted unfairly.

6. It is not true that all tourists are annoying.

7. Elisa denies that musicians only think about music.

8. Eduardo disagrees that lawyers are dishonest.

> **In Spanish** The **subjunctive** mood is used to express *disagreement* and *denial*.
>
> <u>No es verdad</u> que los perros **sean** mejores mascotas que los gatos. (*disagreement*)
> Sofía <u>niega</u> que las chicas solamente **quieran** ir de compras. (*denial*)
>
> The **indicative** mood is used to express *affirmation*.
>
> <u>Es verdad</u> que los hermanos de Ricardo **son** músicos talentosos. (*affirmation*)
> <u>No niego</u> que **tienen** talento. (*affirmation*)

B Underline the phrase that expresses disagreement or denial, and circle the verb that follows.

1. Yo <u>niego</u> que los científicos no (escriban) bien.

2. No es verdad que los hombres sólo hablen de deportes.

3. No es cierto que los niños no quieran hablar con los abuelos.

4. Paco niega que los profesores sean aburridos.

5. No es verdad que los jóvenes no se preocupen por la política.

6. Verónica niega que las chicas no puedan ser matemáticas.

7. No es cierto que los hombres no sepan cocinar.

8. No es verdad que los atletas sean bobos.

CAPÍTULO 9

Copyright © by Holt, Rinehart and Winston. All rights reserved.

C Fátima is expressing opinions about education. Use the fragments to write complete sentences using the appropriate mood to express her opinions: indicative or subjunctive.

1. Es verdad / los maestros / tener un trabajo importante

   Es verdad que los maestros tienen un trabajo importante.

2. No estoy de acuerdo / las mujeres / ser mejores maestras

   _____

3. No niego / los estudiantes / trabajar duro

   _____

4. Mi maestro niega / los muchachos / sacar mejores notas

   _____

5. No es verdad / todos los estudiantes / aprender de la misma forma

   _____

6. No es cierto / todos los asiáticos / comprender las matemáticas

   _____

D The subjunctive mood is used more often in Spanish than in English. Review the following topics and tell whether the clause following each requires the **subjunctive** or the **indicative** mood in each language.

	ENGLISH	SPANISH
1. to express affirmation		
2. to express disagreement or denial		
3. to express wishes		
4. to express feelings		
5. with impersonal expresssions		
6. to make recommendations		

CAPÍTULO 9

Spanish 3 ¡Ven conmigo!, Chapter 9

Copyright © by Holt, Rinehart and Winston. All rights reserved.

In English The **conditional** verb form is used to express *what would happen if...* as opposed to what usually does happen. The conditional is formed by adding **would** to the verb.

> If I could, I **would play** all day long.
> You **would write** a letter if you missed her.

A Complete each sentence with the conditional tense of the verb in parentheses.

1. What would Luis Miguel do to relax? He _____**would sing**_____. (sing)

2. What would Julia Álvarez and Elena Quiroga do if they had free time? They _____. (write)

3. What would Juan Carlos do if he had a day off? He _____ to Mallorca. (go)

4. What would Penélope Cruz do if she won an award? She _____ the Academy. (thank)

5. What would Pedro Martínez do if he had to prepare for a game? He _____ his fast ball. (practice)

6. What would Joan Baez do if asked to perform? She _____ the guitar. (play)

7. Where would Elena Ochoa travel if she had the choice? She _____ to the Moon. (travel)

In Spanish The **conditional** verb form is also used to express *what would happen if...* as opposed to what usually does happen.

> Si pudiera, **jugaría** todo el día.
> En esa situación tú **escribirías** una carta.

The regular conditional form consists of the infinitive plus one set of endings for **-ar**, **-ir**, and **-er** verbs.

	JUGAR	ESCRIBIR	COMER
yo	jugar**ía**	escribir**ía**	comer**ía**
tú	jugar**ías**	escribir**ías**	comer**ías**
él, ella, usted	jugar**ía**	escribir**ía**	comer**ía**
nosotros(as)	jugar**íamos**	escribir**íamos**	comer**íamos**
vosotros(as)	jugar**íais**	escribir**íais**	comer**íais**
ellos, ellas, ustedes	jugar**ían**	escribir**ían**	comer**ían**

C A P Í T U L O 9

Copyright © by Holt, Rinehart and Winston. All rights reserved.

B Complete each sentence with the conditional form of the verb in parentheses.

1. ¿Qué haríamos si tuviéramos música? _____Bailaríamos_____ toda la noche. (bailar)

2. ¿Qué haría Pablo Neruda si estuviera aquí? Él _____ poesía. (escribir)

3. ¿Qué harías tú con mil dólares? _____ una computadora. (comprar)

4. ¿Qué harían los artistas si tuvieran tiempo? _____ paisajes (*landscapes*). (pintar)

5. ¿Qué harían los niños si los padres salieran? _____ helado de chocolate. (almorzar)

6. ¿Qué harían los estudiantes si no estuviera el profesor? _____ al baloncesto en el salón de clases. (jugar)

7. ¿Qué haría Henry Cisneros en una conferencia? _____ de política. (hablar)

The same verbs that have irregular stems in the future have irregular stems in the conditional.

decir: **dir-**	poder: **podr-**	saber: **sabr-**	valer: **valdr-**
haber: **habr-**	poner: **pondr-**	salir: **saldr-**	venir: **vendr-**
hacer: **har-**	querer: **querr-**	tener: **tendr-**	

C María is making a list of things that would happen if she were in charge of the household. Use each clue to write a complete sentence in Spanish telling what would happen.

1. yo / servir flan de postre cada día

_____

2. mis amigos / venir a mi casa todos los días

_____

3. nosotros / jugar todo el día y no trabajar

_____

4. yo / no tener que hacer la cama nunca

_____

5. mi madre / hacer la tarea

_____

6. el televisor / estar en la cocina

_____

Copyright © by Holt, Rinehart and Winston. All rights reserved.

CAPÍTULO 10

■ VERB MOOD AFTER CONJUNCTIONS *¡Ven conmigo! Level 3, p. 289*

> **In English** The **indicative** mood follows subordinating **conjunctions** (*adverbs that connect clauses*) such as **unless**, **before**, **in case**, **so that**, **in order that**, **after**, **until**, **as soon as**, and **when**.
>
> Unless you **have** other plans, we should make dinner.
> Pamela plans to leave as soon as Samuel **arrives**.
> After we **eat** dinner, we can play games.

A Underline the subordinating conjunction in each sentence and circle the verb that follows it.

1. Unless it (rains) we will have class outside.

2. As soon as I finish school, I leave for Venezuela.

3. When we have time, we will see the Statue of Liberty.

4. Adriana learns about Hispanic culture so that she can understand her heritage.

5. Alberto and Juan walk in Central Park until it starts to rain.

6. When you go to Costa Rica, you should explore the rainforest.

7. I have a guidebook in case we want to explore the city.

8. David will finish his work before you arrive.

> **In Spanish** Unlike English, the **subjunctive** mood is often used with subordinating **conjunctions**.
>
> • The subjunctive is always used with **a menos (de) que** (*unless*), **antes de que** (*before*), **con tal (de) que** (*provided*), **en caso de que** (*in case*), **para que** (*so, in order that*).
>
> Voy a salir antes de que Elena **llegue**.
>
> • The subjunctive follows conjunctions such as **cuando** (*when*), **en cuanto** (*as soon as*), **después de que** (*after*), **hasta que** (*until*), and **tan pronto como** (*as soon as*) when they refer to a future action that may or may not take place.
>
> En cuanto **termine** la clase, salimos a jugar.

B Underline the subordinating conjunction in each sentence and circle the verb that follows it.

1. Cuando (vayamos) a Puerto Rico, vamos a visitar a mis abuelos.

2. Traigo un paraguas en caso de que llueva.

3. Mis abuelos nos dieron un mapa para que podamos explorar la ciudad.

4. En cuanto salgas de la clase, salimos para el aeropuerto.

Copyright © by Holt, Rinehart and Winston. All rights reserved.

C
A
P
Í
T
U
L
O

1
0

5. Llámame tan pronto como llegues a San Juan.

6. Después de que visitemos a mis abuelos, vamos al campo.

7. Quiero aprender a hablar el español para que no pierda mi cultura.

8. Cuando vuelvas a Nueva York, ya hablarás mejor.

C Study the sentences in Activities A and B. Do they refer to the past, present, or future?

_____

The **indicative** mood is used after conjunctions when the action expressed happens regularly or has already happened.

Cuando **hablamos** por teléfono, siempre nos reímos.
En cuanto **llegó** Leonardo, nos fuimos al concierto.

D Translate the following sentences into Spanish, using the context to help you choose the correct mood: subjunctive or indicative.

1. As soon as class ended, we went to the movies.

   En cuanto terminó la clase, fuimos al cine.

2. When you go to Ecuador, you should visit Quito.

_____

3. I want to learn Spanish history before I study in Madrid.

_____

4. When Luis travels, he always writes me letters.

_____

5. Sergio will go to school in New York, provided he wins the scholarship (*beca*).

_____

6. Señora Álvarez speaks Spanish at home so that Rosa will be bilingual.

_____

7. When I think about my future, I always dream about being an artist.

_____

E Explain how to decide when a verb following a conjunction should be in the subjunctive.

_____

_____

_____

Spanish 3 ¡Ven conmigo!, Chapter 10

Copyright © by Holt, Rinehart and Winston. All rights reserved.

THE PAST SUBJUNCTIVE

¡Ven conmigo! Level 3, p. 327

In English The form for the **past subjunctive** is the same as the past tense except for **to be** which uses **were** for all persons: **I were, he were.**

The **past subjunctive** is used to express situations that are contrary to fact or unlikely to happen. These situations are usually introduced by the word **if**, forming an **if clause**.

> If I **were** the teacher, I would not give homework.

When a situation is considered likely to happen, the **indicative** follows **if**.

> If we **have** time, we will go to the beach.

A Underline the verb in the **if** clause. Then check the appropriate column to tell whether the verb is in the indicative (I) or subjunctive (S) mood.

	I	S
1. If I had one wish, I would wish for peace.		✓
2. If Belén lived in Spain, she would eat paella.		
3. If we go to Madrid, we will try tapas.		
4. If you were a teacher, what would you teach?		
5. If I study Spanish, I will go to South America.		
6. If they met an actor, they would be surprised.		

In Spanish The **past subjunctive** is formed by using the third person plural of the preterite. The **-on** is removed, and the following endings are added.

	HABLAR	TENER	SER/IR
yo	hablar**a**	tuvier**a**	fuer**a**
tú	hablar**as**	tuvier**as**	fuer**as**
él, ella, usted	hablar**a**	tuvier**a**	fuer**a**
nosotros(as)	hablár**amos**	tuviér**amos**	fuér**amos**
vosotros(as)	hablar**ais**	tuvier**ais**	fuer**ais**
ellos, ellas, ustedes	hablar**an**	tuvier**an**	fuer**an**

The **past subjunctive** is used to express situations that are contrary to fact or unlikely to happen. These situations are usually introduced by the word **si**.

> Si yo **fuera** el maestro, no daría tarea.

When a situation is considered likely to happen, the **indicative** follows **si**.

> Si **tenemos** tiempo, iremos a la playa.

C A P Í T U L O 1 1

Copyright © by Holt, Rinehart and Winston. All rights reserved.

B Underline the verb in the **si** clause. Then check the appropriate column to tell whether the verb is in the indicative (I) or subjunctive (S) mood.

	I	S
1. Si Paco <u>viajara</u> a Costa Rica, iría a Monteverde.		✓
2. Si hace buen tiempo, vamos a ver los volcanes.		
3. Si Mónica tuviera dinero, compraría una carreta.		
4. Si veo una iguana, sacaré una foto.		
5. Si fuera el presidente, protegería las selvas.		
6. Si pudiera, mejoraría el sistema de educación.		
7. Si luchamos, podremos hacer una diferencia.		
8. Si no haces nada, nada va a cambiar.		

C Óscar thinks that everyone else does everything wrong. Read each comment and then write a complete sentence telling what he would do in each situation.

1. Mi escuela no tiene un programa de intercambio con otros países.
   (yo / crear un intercambio con Costa Rica / ser director)

   Yo crearía un intercambio con Costa Rica si fuera el director.

2. Los políticos no cuidan el medioambiente.
   (mis amigos y yo / proteger el medioambiente / ser políticos)

   _____

3. A mis amigos mayores no les gusta viajar.
   (yo / viajar por el mundo / tener dinero)

   _____

4. El gobernador no hace nada acerca del desempleo.
   (yo / proponer un nuevo programa / conocer al gobernador)

   _____

D Why is it important to remember to add the correct accents to verbs? Think about how the meaning of the verb **hablara** in the past subjunctive would change if an accent were added.

_____

_____

_____

E Look at the second verbs in each sentence in Activities A and B. What tense follows the **if clause** in the subjunctive? What tense follows the **if clause** in the indicative?

_____

_____

_____

Copyright © by Holt, Rinehart and Winston. All rights reserved.

CAPÍTULO 12

■ THE PAST TENSE: SUMMARY

¡Ven conmigo! Level 3, p. 348

> **In English** The simple **past** tense is usually used to talk about the past.
>
> > I **talked** to Elena yesterday.
> > Marco **met** Flor last year.
> > I **found out** on Friday.
> > I **refused** to study for the exam.
> > Fernando **was** tall and handsome.
> > It **was** five-thirty.
> > Roberto **was** five years old in 1975.
>
> The formula **used** + *infinitive* is often used to describe habitual, ongoing actions in the past.
>
> > Miguel **used** *to work* in a restaurant.

A Circle the verb in each sentence.

1. Alejandro (refused) help.

2. I was ten years old in that photograph.

3. Felipe knew my grandfather.

4. It was midnight.

5. Ernesto talked on the phone until eleven o'clock.

6. My family used to go to the lake in the summertime.

7. Laura's father was athletic.

8. Mateo ate dinner early.

> **In Spanish** The **preterite** and **imperfect** tenses are often used to talk about the past.
>
> The **preterite** is used
>
> - to report completed past actions.
> - to give special meanings to verbs.
>
> > Yo **hablé** con Elena ayer.
> > Marco **conoció** a Flor el año pasado.
> > Lo **supe** el viernes.
> > No **quise** estudiar para el examen.
>
> The **imperfect** is used
>
> - for habitual, ongoing past actions.
> - to refer to mental or physical states.
> - to tell time.
> - to describe age.
>
> > Miguel **trabajaba** en un restaurante.
> > Fernando **era** alto y guapo.
> > **Eran** las cinco y media.
> > Roberto **tenía** cinco años en 1975.

CAPÍTULO 12

Copyright © by Holt, Rinehart and Winston. All rights reserved.

B Circle the verb in each sentence. Then check the appropriate column to tell whether each verb is in the preterite (P) or imperfect (I) tense.

	P	I
1. Pedro (tenía) seis años en esta foto.	_____	✓
2. Emilio estudió literatura en la Universidad.	_____	_____
3. Héctor conoció al señor Guzmán anoche.	_____	_____
4. Mi abuela era alta y rubia.	_____	_____
5. Eran las diez y cuarto.	_____	_____
6. María jugaba con sus primos los fines de semana.	_____	_____
7. El sábado supe que mi tía tuvo un bebé.	_____	_____
8. Víctor no quiso comer.	_____	_____

> When the **imperfect** and the **preterite** occur in the same sentence, the **imperfect** is used to describe what was going on (the background) when something occurred. The main action is expressed in the **preterite**.
>
> **Hacía** buen tiempo y **decidimos** pasear por el parque.
> Las niñas **miraban** la televisión cuando sus padres **entraron**.

C Complete each sentence with the correct form of the verbs in parentheses.

1. Yo _____tenía_____ (tener) veinte años cuando _____decidí_____

   (decidir) estudiar periodismo.

2. Alan _____ (estar) en la universidad cuando

   _____ (conocer) a un autor famoso.

3. Nina _____ (querer) ser enfermera y _____

   (empezar) a trabajar en un hospital.

4. Mauricio _____ (hablar) con un científico que

   _____ (vivir) en su pueblo.

D Translate the following sentences into Spanish, using the imperfect and the preterite.

1. I was crying when Rosa entered the room.

   _____

2. You knew that Raúl was at school.

   _____

3. Tina found out that José won.

   _____

Copyright © by Holt, Rinehart and Winston. All rights reserved.

CAPÍTULO 12

Answer Key

Answers: Level 1

CAPÍTULO 1

■ PUNCTUATION MARKS AND ACCENTS

A
1. Where are you from?
2. Thank you!
3. What do you like to do?
4. Hi, Mr. Núñez!
5. How are you?
6. What is your name?
7. See you tomorrow!
8. Delighted to meet you!

B
1. ¿De dónde eres?
2. ¡Gracias!
3. ¿Qué te gusta hacer?
4. ¡Hola, Sr. Núñez!
5. ¿Cómo estás?
6. ¿Cómo te llamas?
7. ¡Hasta mañana!
8. ¡Encantado de conocerte!

C Accent marks 6, Tildes 2

D Answers will vary.

E Answers will vary. Possible answer:
A question mark or exclamation point at the beginning of a sentence in Spanish adds clarity by allowing the reader to adjust intonation as necessary for different types of sentences.

■ SUBJECT PRONOUNS: *YOU* AND *I*

A
AMY	Hello. I am Amy. (Amy)
LUIS	Hi. I am Luis. (Luis)
	Where are you from? (Amy)
AMY	I am from the United States. (Amy)
	Are you from Madrid? (Luis)
LUIS	No, I am from Barcelona. (Luis)
	I am studying at the Universidad Autónoma. (Luis)
	Would you like to be pen pals? (Amy)
AMY	I think that's a great idea. (Amy)
	I could practice my Spanish! (Amy)

B
JUAN	Hola. Yo me llamo Juan. (Juan) ¿Y tú? (Pilar)
PILAR	Yo soy Pilar. ¿Qué tal? (Pilar)
JUAN	Regular. ¿Y tú? (Pilar)
PILAR	Yo estoy muy bien. (Pilar)
JUAN	Estupendo. Bueno, yo tengo que irme. (Juan)
PILAR	Sí, yo también. ¡Hasta luego! (Pilar)

C
1. Yo soy Luis Miguel.
2. ¿Y tú? ¿Cómo te llamas?
3. Yo me llamo Selena.
4. ¿Cómo estás tú?
5. Yo estoy bien, gracias.
6. Selena, ¿tú tienes clase?
7. Sí, yo tengo clase ahora.
8. Yo tengo clase también. ¡Adiós!

D In Spanish, one does not always have to use the subject pronoun because the pronoun is often implied in the verb. Most verbs in English change very little according to the subject, so the sentence would be confusing without a subject pronoun.

■ THE VERB *TO BE* TO EXPRESS ORIGIN

A
1. Juan is from Puerto Rico.
2. I am from Valencia, Spain.
3. You are from La Paz, Bolivia.
4. Anne Marie is from Boston, Massachusetts.
5. Laura is from Managua, Nicaragua.
6. You are from Los Angeles, California.
7. He is from Amarillo, Texas.
8. I am from Santiago, Chile.

B
1. Ella es de Montevideo, Uruguay.
2. Yo soy de Phoenix, Arizona.
3. Él es de San José, Costa Rica.
4. Ricardo es de Monterrey, México.
5. Tú eres de Denver, Colorado.
6. Marta es de Santafé de Bogotá, Colombia.
7. Isabel es de Quito, Ecuador.
8. Casey es de West Palm Beach, Florida.

C
1. Isabel Allende (soy/eres/es) de Chile.
2. Yo (soy/eres/es) de España.
3. Fidel Castro (soy/eres/es) de Cuba.
4. Pedro Martínez (soy/eres/es) de la República Dominicana.
5. Tú (soy/eres/es) de Estados Unidos.
6. Shakira (soy/eres/es) de Colombia.
7. Laura Esquivel (soy/eres/es) de México.
8. Jorge Luis Borges (soy/eres/es) de Argentina.

Copyright © by Holt, Rinehart and Winston. All rights reserved.

D FRIDA David, ¿de dónde **eres**? ¿De Honduras?

DAVID ¡Yo no **soy** de Honduras! **Soy** de Nicaragua.

FRIDA Mi amiga Blanca **es** de Nicaragua también. Ella **es** de Managua. ¿**Eres** tú de Managua?

DAVID No. Yo **soy** de Granada. ¿Y tú, Frida? ¿De dónde **eres**?

FRIDA Yo **soy** de Veracruz, México.

E In both English and Spanish, the verb that means *to be* is used. In both languages, the correct form of the verb is based on the subject, and the verb is followed by the preposition that means *from*.

▨ QUESTION WORDS

A 1. (Where/What) do you live?
2. (Where/How) are you feeling today?
3. (How/What) is your favorite color?
4. (How/What) language do you speak?
5. (Where/How) do you spell your name?
6. (Where/What) were you born?
7. (How/What) is your nationality?
8. (Where/How) is the nearest post office?

B 1. ¿(Cuántos/Cómo) años tienes?
2. ¿(Cuántos/De dónde) eres?
3. ¿(Cuántos/Cómo) te llamas?
4. ¿(Cuántos/De dónde) es Octavio Paz?
5. ¿(Cómo/De dónde) estás?
6. ¿(De dónde/Cuántos) años tiene Pedro?
7. ¿(Cuántos/De dónde) es la señora Martínez?
8. ¿(Cómo/Cuántos) está Miguel?

C 1. ¿De dónde eres?
2. ¿Cómo te llamas?
3. ¿Cómo estás?
4. ¿De dónde es ella/tu amiga?
5. ¿Cuántos años tienes?

D Answers may vary. Possible answer: Question words in Spanish have accents to let the reader know it is a question and perhaps to differentiate them from **como**, **donde**, and **cuantos**, which have another meaning.

▨ DEFINITE ARTICLES AND GENDER

A 1. The musician plays jazz.
2. My brother took the football.
3. She ate all the pizza.
4. The homework was easy.
5. We won the volleyball game.

6. My mom dropped the salad.
7. The CD is scratched.
8. The soccer ball is missing.

B 1. Me gusta el fútbol norteamericano. (M)
2. ¿Te gusta la música pop? (F)
3. No me gusta la natación. (F)
4. A mí me gusta el baloncesto. (M)
5. Te gusta mucho la comida italiana. (F)
6. No, no me gusta la pizza. (F)
7. Te gusta la clase de español. (F)
8. ¿Te gusta el jazz? (M)

C 1. ¿Te gusta **el** fútbol?
2. Me gusta **la** pizza.
3. Te gusta mucho **la** música clásica.
4. **La** fruta me gusta mucho.
5. A ti te gusta **el** tenis.
6. No, no me gusta mucho **el** tenis.
7. Me gusta **el** español.
8. Te gusta **el** baloncesto.

D Answers will vary.

E All of the masculine nouns end in *o* and all of the feminine nouns end in *a*. Therefore, I can often determine the gender of a noun by the ending, and this will tell me which definite article to use.

CAPÍTULO 2

▨ PLURAL NOUNS

A 1. boxes
2. calculators
3. libraries
4. bushes
5. binders
6. textbooks
7. parties
8. supplies

B 1. marcadores
2. pinturas
3. lápices
4. cuadernos
5. pinceles
6. luces
7. papeles
8. clases

C 1. Yo necesito dos cuadernos.
2. Yo necesito dos mochilas.
3. Yo necesito dos lápices.
4. Yo necesito dos calculadoras.
5. Yo necesito dos papeles.
6. Yo necesito dos luces.
7. Yo necesito dos pinceles.
8. Yo necesito dos bolígrafos.

Copyright © by Holt, Rinehart and Winston. All rights reserved.

ANSWERS

D clubs, clubes
radios, radios
conductors, conductores
buses, buses
faxes, faxes

Nouns that end in vowels or that end in *-s,*
-x, or *-sh* are made plural the same way.

■ INDEFINITE ARTICLES

A 1. Ricardo has (a) colored <u>pencil.</u>
2. Ana María needs (a) new <u>backpack.</u>
3. Lisa wants (a) black <u>marker.</u>
4. Andy has (an) <u>eraser</u> on his desk.
5. Isabel wants (a) fancy <u>notebook.</u>
6. Sheila needs (a) <u>folder</u> for each class.
7. Rachel has (an) <u>exam</u> tomorrow.
8. Miguel wants (a) <u>set</u> of paintbrushes.

B 1. Marta necesita (una) calculadora. (S, F)
2. Brigid quiere (unos) cuadernos azules. (P, M)
3. Jimena tiene (unas) carpetas nuevas. (P, F)
4. Fabiola quiere (una) regla. (S, F)
5. Paulina necesita (unos) lápices de colores. (P, M)
6. Ricardo tiene (unas) gomas de borrar. (P, F)
7. Ángel no quiere (una) mochila verde. (S, F)
8. Juan Manuel necesita (un) libro de gramática. (S, M)

C 1. Ana tiene **unos** marcadores para la clase de arte.
2. Yo quiero **un** libro bueno.
3. Clarisa necesita **unos** cuadernos de actividades.
4. Fernando tiene **un** diccionario para la clase de inglés.
5. Margarita quiere **unas** carpetas para su clase.
6. Elvira necesita **unos** lápices de colores.
7. Tú tienes **unas** reglas para la clase de matemáticas.
8. Marcos quiere **una** lección fácil.

D **El bolígrafo** refers to a specific pen. In the second sentence, the speaker needs a pen, any pen. If it said **Necesito el bolígrafo,** the speaker would have a specific pen in mind.

■ SUBJECT PRONOUNS: *HE* AND *SHE*

A 1. <u>Francisco</u> has to buy a math book. (He)
2. <u>Juana</u> needs two pencils for her class. (She)

3. <u>Patricio</u> wants to buy a new backpack. (He)
4. <u>Miguel</u> needs a binder and two folders. (He)
5. <u>Donald</u> has three Spanish dictionaries. (He)
6. <u>María</u> wants a new computer. (She)
7. <u>Ana María</u> has to borrow a book from the library. (She)
8. <u>Brian</u> needs to buy school supplies. (He)

B 1. <u>Paco</u> es mi amigo. (Él)
2. <u>Luisa</u> necesita estudiar. (Ella)
3. <u>Carmen</u> tiene que ir a clase. (Ella)
4. <u>Manolo</u> quiere comprar el libro. (Él)
5. <u>Sergio</u> es inteligente. (Él)
6. <u>María</u> es profesora de historia. (Ella)
7. <u>Roberto</u> tiene seis cuadernos. (Él)
8. <u>Eugenia</u> necesita la goma de borrar. (Ella)

C 1. Ella necesita una calculadora.
2. Él quiere un diccionario.
3. Ella necesita un pincel.
4. Ella necesita una calculadora.
5. Él quiere unos cuadernos.
6. Él necesita una goma de borrar.
7. Él necesita un libro.
8. Ella quiere una mochila.

D Repeating the subject would be redundant and boring.

■ QUANTITY

A 1. How <u>many</u> books are on the shelf? (P)
2. There is <u>a lot of</u> noise in the hallway. (S)
3. How <u>much</u> paper is left in the copy machine? (S)
4. There are <u>many</u> students in this class. (P)
5. There is too <u>much</u> material to study. (S)
6. How <u>much</u> time will it take to complete the exam? (S)
7. How <u>many</u> workbooks are from last year? (P)
8. I learned <u>a lot of</u> new words in Spanish class. (P)

B 1. ¿<u>Cuántas</u> clases tienes? (P, F)
2. Alejandro tiene <u>muchos</u> amigos. (P, M)
3. No tengo <u>mucho</u> papel. (S, M)
4. ¿<u>Cuánta</u> pizza hay? (S, F)
5. ¿<u>Cuánto</u> papel hay en tu cuaderno? (S, M)
6. ¿Tienes <u>mucha</u> tarea? (S, F)
7. ¿<u>Cuántos</u> profesores están aquí? (P, M)
8. Hay <u>muchas</u> revistas en la mesa. (P, F)

C 1. ¿**Cuántas** camas tienes en tu cuarto?

Copyright © by Holt, Rinehart and Winston. All rights reserved.

2. Hay **muchas** computadoras en mi escuela.
3. Tienes **muchos** libros en tu estante.
4. ¿**Cuántos** carteles hay en el cuarto de tu amigo?
5. Hay **muchas** plantas en el cuarto de Miguel.
6. ¿**Cuántos** discos compactos tienes?
7. Hay **mucho** espacio en tu cuarto.

D Both words are followed immediately by a noun and they both agree in number and gender with the noun. However, **cuánta** begins the question, whereas **mucha** follows the verb. Also, **cuánta** has an accent and **mucha** doesn't. **Cuánta** can only be used in questions; **mucha** can be used in both statements and questions.

■ INFINITIVES

A 1. I have to buy school supplies.
2. We are trying to find colored pencils.
3. I like to study Spanish.
4. Luisa hopes to learn about new places.
5. Manolo wants to be a professor.
6. The students decide to eat lunch.
7. Elena agrees to help me with my homework.
8. Rosa and Teresa sign up to play soccer.

B 1. Necesito comprar una mochila.
2. ¿Quieres conocer a mi amiga?
3. ¿Dónde quieres poner los lápices?
4. Quiero comprar papel.
5. Eduardo necesita ir a la escuela.
6. ¿Quieres hacer la tarea?
7. Virginia necesita encontrar la goma de borrar.
8. Nosotros necesitamos organizar la clase.

C
-AR Verbs	-ER Verbs	-IR Verbs
comprar	conocer	ir
encontrar	poner	
organizar	hacer	

D 1. Yo quiero **conocer** a la nueva chica.
2. Ella no puede **encontrar** sus libros. ¿Dónde están?
3. La chica necesita **organizar** su cuarto.
4. Nosotros queremos **ir** a la librería.
5. Vamos a **comprar** un libro nuevo.
6. Yo necesito **hacer** la tarea.
7. Elena necesita **poner** el libro en su mochila.
8. Quiero **encontrar** el dinero.

E other verbs that are not in the infinitive

F Answers will vary.

CAPÍTULO 3

■ DEFINITE ARTICLES

A 1. Constance has the first class. (S)
2. The students always arrive on time. (P)
3. The art class meets at 9A.M. (S)
4. Vanesa brings the calculators to geometry class. (P)
5. I think the teachers at my school are nice. (P)
6. We have the history exam tomorrow. (S)
7. At 7:30A.M. the school bus arrives. (S)
8. Manuel always gets the highest grades. (P)

B 1. Sí, tengo la clase de biología. (S, F)
2. ¿Tienes los libros de ciencias? (P, M)
3. Quiero conocer a los profesores. (P, M)
4. Me gusta el arte. (S, M)
5. Quiero ir a la pizzería. (S, F)
6. ¿Estudias las ciencias? (P, F)
7. Los estudiantes son excelentes. (P, M)
8. Tengo que hacer las tareas. (P, F)

C 1. **La** clase de español es estupenda.
2. No me gusta **la** tarea de español.
3. ¿Tienes **los** libros para la clase de geografía?
4. ¿Qué hay en **el** armario?
5. Necesito **el** dinero.
6. **Los** diccionarios están en la librería.
7. El profesor tiene **las** gomas de borrar.
8. **Las** calculadoras son para la clase de matemáticas.

D The definite article in Spanish lets you know whether the noun refers to a group of females when the noun itself doesn't convey that information.

■ POSSESSION

A 1. The **student's** grades are excellent.
2. **Paco´s** French lesson ends at 7 o'clock.
3. The **bus driver's** hat is black.
4. My **classmates'** homework is difficult.
5. **Gabriella's** class starts at one o'clock.
6. The **books'** bindings are breaking.

B 1. Los libros son **de Rebecca**.
2. La guitarra es **de la profesora**.
3. La goma de borrar es **de Sara**.
4. El lápiz es **del señor**.
5. Las calculadoras son **de Luis**.
6. El marcador es **del profesor**.

C 1. El libro es de Ángela.
2. Los pinceles son de Alfonso.

Copyright © by Holt, Rinehart and Winston. All rights reserved.

ANSWERS

3. Las revistas son del profesor Ruiz.
4. La calculadora nueva es de Miguel.
5. El cuaderno es del estudiante nuevo.
6. Los papeles son de los señores.

D Answers will vary. Possible answer: Contractions are used to make the sentence flow more smoothly. These sentences sound choppy when the contraction is removed.

■ ADJECTIVE AGREEMENT

A 1. Larry is (handsome) (S)
2. Math exams are not (difficult) (P)
3. The teacher is (dark-haired) (S)
4. The topics are (interesting) (P)
5. The boys are (funny) (P)
6. My classmate is (short) (S)
7. The school lunches are (bad) (P)
8. She is (beautiful) (S)

B 1. El libro de historia es (nuevo) (S, M)
2. Los conciertos son (divertidos) (P, M)
3. Miguel es (alto) (S, M)
4. Susana es (bonita) (S, F)
5. Las ventanas son (pequeñas) (P, F)
6. Mis amigos son (cómicos) (P, M)
7. La compañera de clase es (buena) (S, F)
8. Las señoritas son (guapas) (P, F)

C 1. Ellos son **bajos**.
2. Marisa es **alta**.
3. Los libros son **interesantes**.
4. Paco es **rubio**.
5. Mis amigas son **simpáticas**.
6. Los exámenes son **difíciles**.
7. Mi profesora es **buena**.
8. El compañero de clase es **divertido**.

D 1. a. The rooms are big.
b. Los cuartos son grandes.

2. Only the noun and verb changed in the English sentence. In the Spanish sentence, all the words —the definite article, the noun, the verb, and the adjective— changed. Unlike in English, Spanish articles and adjectives change forms according to the number and gender of the noun.

■ TAG QUESTIONS

A 1. Your birthday party is next week, (isn't it?)
2. Our Spanish exam is this Friday, (right?)
3. You have a date for the dance, (right?)
4. The video game is yours, (isn't it?)
5. You like the novel, (don't you?)
6. The film festival is next month, (isn't it?)

7. That's the truth, (right?)
8. You have tickets for the game, (don't you?)

B 1. Te gusta la novela, (¿verdad?)
2. La fiesta es divertida, (¿no?)
3. Los videojuegos son interesantes, (¿no?)
4. Tienes la clase a la una, (¿verdad?)
5. El perro es feo, (¿no?)
6. Tienes la clase de historia, (¿verdad?)
7. Te gustan las mochilas grandes, (¿verdad?)
8. El cuaderno es nuevo, (¿no?)

C Answers will vary.

D Tag questions can change the tone of a question by adding more certainty. The addition of a tag question often conveys that the speaker simply wants confirmation of something he or she believes to be true, whereas a simple question often conveys the idea that the speaker has no idea of the answer.

CAPÍTULO 4

■ VERB ENDINGS

A 1. Carlos (sings) well.
2. They (walk) home.
3. Sara (listens) to music.
4. I (dance) at parties.
5. You (talk) to Juan.
6. Luis (plays) every day.
7. We (work) hard.
8. Claudia (rides) her bicycle.

B 1. Carlos (canta) bien.
2. Ellos (caminan) a casa.
3. Sara (escucha) la música.
4. Yo (bailo) en las fiestas.
5. Tú (hablas) con Juan.
6. Luis (estudia) computación.
7. Nosotros (trabajamos) mucho.
8. Claudia (monta) en bicicleta.

C 1. Ellos **hablan** y descansan.
2. José **habla** inglés.
3. Yo **hablo** español.
4. Nosotros **hablamos** por teléfono.
5. Ellos **hablan** en clase.
6. Tú **hablas** muy bien.
7. El profesor **habla** mucho.
8. Sergio y Berta **hablan** con sus amigos.

D 1.

	ACTIVITY A		ACTIVITY B	
1. to sing	s	cantar		a
2. to walk		caminar		an
3. to listen	s	escuchar		a

Copyright © by Holt, Rinehart and Winston. All rights reserved.

4. to dance		bailar	o
5. to talk		hablar	as
6. to play	s	estudiar	a
7. to work		trabajar	amos
8. to ride	s	montar	a

2. Answers will vary. Possible answer: In English, usually the only ending is -s, in the third person singular. In Spanish, each subject has a different ending. So for an -ar verb, like *escuchar*, I know that for the third person singular I must take off the -ar ending and add -a.

■ THE VERB *TO BE* TO STATE LOCATION

A 1. They (are) at home. (They)
2. The dog (is) outside. (dog)
3. We (are) in class. (We)
4. I (am) in the bookstore. (I)
5. You (are) with your family. (You)
6. She (is) in the kitchen. (She)
7. Ana (is) at the supermarket. (Ana)
8. Geraldo (is) at the gym. (Geraldo)

B 1. (Estoy) en el cine. (Yo)
2. María (está) en casa de Pilar. (María)
3. (Estás) en la tienda de deportes. (Tú)
4. (Estamos) en la ciudad de México. (Nosotros)
5. El correo (está) en la calle principal. (el correo)
6. Elena y Ricardo (están) en la plaza. (Elena y Ricardo)
7. Lucía (está) en la piscina. (Lucía)
8. Mi papá (está) en casa. (mi papá)

C 1. **Estoy** en la clase.
2. **Está** en el centro.
3. **Estamos** en la ciudad.
4. **Están** en la librería.
5. **Está** en la calle ocho.
6. **Está** en la Universidad.
7. **Estás** en el Museo de Bellas Artes.
8. **Está** en casa.

D 1. **yo**   5. **ella**
2. **él**   6. **él**
3. **nosotros**   7. **tú**
4. **ellos**   8. **él**

E Answers will vary. Possible answer: In Spanish, when the subject of a verb is not mentioned in a sentence I can tell what the subject pronoun is by looking at the verb ending. I can then look at other sentences to figure out the exact subject noun. In English the subject must be included in each sentence because in most cases the

ending of the verb does not tell us the subject pronoun.

■ MORE SUBJECT PRONOUNS

A 1. (I) walk to school.
2. (You) buy lunch.
3. (He) dances well.
4. (We) sing in class.
5. (They) need books.
6. (It) scurried across the floor.
7. (She) found a penny.
8. (You) are my favorite students.

B 1. Soy de Texas. (yo)
2. ¿Dónde está (usted)?
3. ¿(Ella) canta contigo?
4. Tienes un examen hoy. (tú)
5. (Él) quiere ser artista.
6. Pintamos un mural. (nosotros)
7. Hablo con mi amigo en clase. (yo)
8. (Él) compra revistas en español.

C Answers will vary.

D Answers will vary. Possible answer: In Spanish, it would be useful to use the subject pronoun when a verb is used in the third person. *Está en clase*, for instance, could refer to *usted*, *él*, or *ella*. To clarify who is the subject, one would say, *Ella está en clase*. The use of the subject pronoun also gives special emphasis. For example, in the sentence *Yo no soy Joaquín*, the speaker emphasizes the fact that he is not someone else.

■ THE IRREGULAR VERB *TO GO*

A Answers will vary.

B 1. **Yo** voy a clase.
2. **Tú** vas al gimnasio.
3. **Ella** (**Sr. Navarro**) va al baile.
4. **Nosotros** vamos al cine.
5. **Vosotros** vais al centro.
6. **Claudia y Luis** (**Mis hermanos**) van a casa.
7. **Sr. Navarro** (**Ella**) va a una conferencia.
8. **Mis hermanos** (**Claudia y Luis**) van al concierto.

C 1. ¿Adónde va Luis?
2. ¿Adónde va Celia?
3. ¿Adónde vas tú?
4. ¿Adónde van ellos?
5. ¿Adónde vamos nosotros?
6. ¿Adónde voy (yo)?

Copyright © by Holt, Rinehart and Winston. All rights reserved.

7. ¿Adónde van ustedes?
8. ¿Adónde van mis padres?

D Answers will vary. Possible answer: Even though the verb **ir** is irregular, the endings are the same as regular **-ar** verbs, with the exception of the **yo** form. I can use these endings to determine the hidden subject pronoun.

CAPÍTULO 5

■ NEGATIVE WORDS

A 1. I never watch television in the morning.
2. Yesterday nobody wanted to play tennis with me.
3. I do not want to arrive late to class.
4. I am so tired I am not going to do anything.
5. Samuel is never late.
6. Sundays are boring becasuse there is nothing to do.
7. Nobody expected Aunt Ana to come to visit.
8. Manolito will not eat his string beans.

B 1. David nunca va a la playa.
2. Andrés no conoce a nadie en la fiesta.
3. No quiero comer nada.
4. Marta no baila nunca en las fiestas.
5. ¿Nunca vas a la Fiesta de la Calle Ocho?
6. Nadie quiere ir conmigo a Miami.
7. No desayuno cereal nunca.
8. Alejandro no ve a nadie alto y moreno.

C 1. No ayudo nunca en casa.
2. No va nadie a la biblioteca para estudiar.
3. No descansamos nunca después de clases.
4. No necesito nada para la clase de inglés.
5. No quiere nadie más pizza.
6. José no va nunca al centro comercial.
7. No sabe nadie tocar el saxofón.
8. No quiero nada para el postre.

D You can't combine two negatives in English because two negatives make a positive.

■ THE VERB *TO LIKE*

A 1. Benito likes surfing. (noun)
2. Adolfo likes fishing. (noun)
3. Rita likes riding her bike. (noun)
4. They like eating at the Cuban restaurant. (pronoun)
5. My friends like to ski. (noun)
6. You like to play the guitar. (pronoun)
7. I like to play in the park. (pronoun)

8. Margarita likes to play volleyball at the beach. (noun)

B 1. A Benito le gusta hacer *surfing*. (Benito, le)
2. A Adolfo le gusta pescar. (Adolfo, le)
3. A Rita le gusta montar en bicicleta. (Rita, le)
4. Les gusta comer en el restaurante cubano. (-, les)
5. A mis amigos les gusta esquiar. (amigos, les)
6. Te gusta tocar la guitarra. (-, te)
7. Me gusta jugar en el parque. (-, me)
8. A Margarita le gusta jugar al voleibol en la playa. (Margarita, le)

C Answers will vary.

D The second sentence could refer to **them** or **you plural**. It needs a phrase like **A ellos** or **A ustedes** for clarification.

■ MORE VERB ENDINGS

A 1. Alligators **live** in the Everglades wetlands.
2. A scuba diver **explores** Biscayne Bay.
3. People **dance** to Caribbean music at the festival.
4. Several men **play** chess at a park in Little Havana.
5. Raúl **listens** to music under the bright sun.
6. The girls **swim** at the neighborhood pool.
7. Artists **sell** paintings near Miami Beach.
8. Many people **speak** Spanish in southern Florida.

B 1. Los turistas **comen** pizza en el café.
2. Mi amiga **escribe** una carta de amor.
3. Yo **corro** por la playa.
4. Gustavo **asiste** a una escuela secundaria en Miami.
5. Gloria **ve** a su madre en el jardín.
6. Tú **recibes** muchas cartas de tu familia.
7. Nosotros **bebemos** refrescos.
8. Mimi **lee** el periódico en el patio.

C Answers will vary.

D The **nosotros** endings are not identical.

CAPÍTULO 6

■ POSSESSIVE ADJECTIVES

A 1. Elena and Isabel, your dog is very friendly! (S)

Copyright © by Holt, Rinehart and Winston. All rights reserved.

2. Have you ever seen my kittens? (P)
3. Their mother is very protective. (S)
4. Our neighbors want two kittens. (P)
5. Their parents will only let them have one. (P)
6. Will your parents let you take one? (P)
7. Rita will give you directions to our house. (S)
8. You are going to love your new kitten! (S)

B
1. Vamos a la boda de nuestra prima. (S, F)
2. Rafael y Manuel bailan con sus amigas. (P, F)
3. Nuestros hermanos son altos. (P, M)
4. ¿Ustedes ven a sus abuelos? (P, M)
5. Los abuelos hablan con sus nietos. (P, M)
6. Hay mucha comida en nuestra mesa. (S, F)
7. Los padres encuentran a sus hijos. (P, M)
8. ¿Preparan ustedes su desayuno? (S, M)

C Answers will vary. Sentences will begin:

1. Su esposa es...
2. Su padrastro es...
3. Nuestros padres son...
4. Su nieta es...
5. Nuestro abuelo es...

D In English, you might have to clarify whether **your** refers to one person or a group of people. In Spanish, you might have to clarify whether **su** refers to one person or a group of people and whether it means *your* or *their*.

CAPÍTULO 7

■ SPELLING OF VERB STEMS

A
1. She prefers tennis. (prefer)
2. You want to dance with your friend. (want)
3. We start the course in August. (start)
4. My friend prefers to watch thrillers. (prefer)
5. I want to visit my grandmother. (want)
6. The movie starts at seven o'clock. (start)
7. They want to have dinner at their place. (want)
8. Luisa prefers to invite them to the restaurant. (prefer)

B
1. Yo tengo un libro en casa. (ten-)
2. Tú prefieres ir a la playa este verano. (prefer-)

3. La película empieza a las cinco y media. (empez-)
4. Cristina no quiere invitar a Diego a su fiesta. (quer-)
5. Sus amigos prefieren ir a un concierto de guitarra. (prefer-)
6. Ellos vienen a mi fiesta. (ven-)
7. Ellos quieren bailar con sus amigos. (quer-)
8. Tú tienes dos hermanos. (ten-)

C
1. Hoy yo quiero ir al cine.
2. Esta tarde tú prefieres mirar la televisión.
3. Mi madre quiere salir al campo.
4. Mis amigos y yo queremos ir a la playa.
5. Los domingos mis abuelos prefieren cenar en casa.
6. Mi familia y yo preferimos la comida italiana.

D DIFFERENCES: This class of stem-changing verbs is different from the regular -ar, -er, and –ir verbs in the fact that it has a change in the stem (except in the nosotros and vosotros forms).
SIMILARITIES: The similarities between stem-changing verbs and regular verbs are that the *nosotros* and *vosotros* form follow the same pattern in both classes of verbs (i.e. no stem-change) and that stem-changing verbs add the same endings to the stem as regular verbs.

■ REFLEXIVE VERBS AND PRONOUNS

A
1. I clean myself up before dinner. (myself)
2. Luisa dresses herself quickly. (herself)
3. You buy yourself a razor at the store. (yourself)
4. We admire ourselves in the mirror. (ourselves)
5. You prepare yourself to go out. (yourself)
6. I make myself a new dress. (myself)
7. The babies cannot feed themselves. (themselves)
8. The dog finds itself a new stick. (itself)

B
1. Yo voy a lavarme la cara. (me)
2. Luisa necesita peinarse el pelo. (se)
3. Tú necesitas afeitarte la barba. (te)
4. Paco va a lavarse los dientes antes de salir. (se)
5. Tú vas a prepararte para salir. (te)
6. Yo voy a maquillarme la cara. (me)
7. Ana va a lavarse el pelo antes de la fiesta. (se)
8. Él necesita afeitarse antes de salir. (se)

ANSWERS

C 1. ¿Vas a afeitarte hoy?
2. Necesito lavarme los dientes cada día.
3. ¿Vas a maquillarte para la fiesta?
4. ¿Él necesita ducharse por la mañana?
5. A veces necesito bañarme por la tarde.
6. ¿Vas a lavarte las manos?

D The reflexive pronoun is sometimes implied in English, but not in Spanish. For example, *Amy showers before dinner* (*herself* is implied). *Joe bathes in the morning* (*himself* is implied).

CAPÍTULO 8

■ INDIRECT OBJECT PRONOUNS

A 1. My sister sent me a recipe for paella. (S)
2. My grandmother used to make us seafood paella. (P)
3. Juan served him flan for dessert. (S)
4. You told them your secret ingredient. (P)
5. Lisa, I would like to make you dinner tonight. (S)
6. Could you give me directions to your house? (S)
7. I will tell you my secret when I arrive. (S)
8. Then you can make them dessert! (P)

B 1. Me encantan las uvas. (S)
2. ¿Te gusta la piña? (S)
3. A mis padres les encantan las frutas del Caribe. (P)
4. A Luisa y a mí nos encanta el café con leche. (P)
5. A mi hermano le gusta el jugo de manzana. (S)
6. A Susana le encantan las ensaladas. (S)
7. Me gusta el helado de chocolate. (S)
8. A Ricardo y a Juan les encantan los plátanos. (P)

C 1. A mi abuela le encantan las papitas.
2. A ti te encanta la crema de maní.
3. A mi me encanta la sopa.
4. A Laura y a mí nos encanta el pollo.
5. A los niños les encantan los pasteles.
6. A Olga y a Luisa les encanta el pescado.

■ STEM-CHANGING VERBS

A 1. I eat a sandwich for lunch.
2. José eats tamales at his grandmother's house.
3. We eat lunch in the school cafeteria during the week.
4. The cooks eat lunch later.
5. You eat chicken tacos at the Mexican restaurant.
6. Luisa eats a salad with her meal.
7. Our parents eat dinner early.
8. The professors eat Spanish custard.

B 1. Diana almuerza una sopa de pollo.
2. Cristina y yo almorzamos quesadillas.
3. Yo almuerzo en mi casa los miércoles.
4. Tú puedes comer conmigo.
5. ¿Almuerza Carmen con nosotros hoy?
6. Juan y Mario almuerzan perros calientes.
7. Ellos pueden comer el postre.
8. Nosotros almorzamos huevos con tocino.

C Answers will vary.

D The stem changes from **o** to **ue** only when that syllable is stressed.

■ THE VERB *TO BE* TO DESCRIBE THINGS

A 1. Gazpacho is a cold soup served in Spain. (G)
2. Maria's gazpacho is chunky. (S)
3. Plantains are a traditional side dish in Latin America. (G)
4. These plantains are ripe. (S)
5. Red snapper is my favorite fish. (G)
6. Red snapper is a mild fish. (G)
7. Arepas are like pancakes. (G)
8. These arepas are warm. (S)

B 1. La sopa es mi comida favorita. (G)
2. Tu sopa está caliente. (S)
3. La limonada de Ana está fría. (S)
4. La limonada no es un refresco. (G)
5. El arroz con frijoles es un plato popular. (G)
6. El arroz con frijoles está picante. (S)
7. La toronja es una fruta. (G)
8. Mi toronja está muy dulce. (S)

C 1. La comida mexicana es picante.
2. ¡El pan dulce está delicioso!
3. Lorco es un plato del Ecuador.
4. ¡La sopa está caliente!
5. Mi jamón está muy salado.

D 1. es / *picante* is an inherent quality
2. está / you are speaking of a specific sweet roll
3. es / describes where the dish is from, which is a permanent characteristic
4. está / *caliente* is a variable quality
5. está / you are describing the quality of a specific piece of ham, not all ham is that salty

Copyright © by Holt, Rinehart and Winston. All rights reserved.

A N S W E R S

CAPÍTULO 9

■ MORE INDIRECT OBJECT PRONOUNS

A
1. Alexandra showed them her first film yesterday.
2. Tim cooked him some cheeseburgers.
3. He wrote her a letter about the party.
4. Give him his lucky charm immediately!
5. Their grandmother gave them the country house.
6. Did Jaime tell her the story?
7. We should give her the ring.
8. Did you give them the present?

B
1. Le regalo un disco compacto a Miguel.
2. Les quiere regalar juguetes a sus niños.
3. Quiere regalarte un collar.
4. Tienes que regalarnos camisas.
5. Le doy una cartera a mi abuelo.
6. Les quiero dar dulces a mis hermanas.
7. Vamos a darle un libro a Juan.
8. Ustedes nos dan regalos a nosotros.

C
1. A Juana le voy a regalar una planta.
2. Les quiero dar refrescos a mis primos.
3. A usted yo le voy a dar el libro de matemáticas.
4. A ustedes voy a darles mis zapatos viejos.
5. Tienes que darle las llaves a Mauricio.
6. Les voy a regalar mis discos a Julia y Lourdes.
7. Yo le doy a usted la tarea.
8. Tengo que darles papel a mis estudiantes.

D It would be useful to have both the indirect object and the pronoun in one sentence in order to clarify for whom or to whom. For example, if you haven't mentioned the person who is going to receive the action, it would be helpful to mention it along with the pronoun: *Le voy a dar estas guayabas a Lizette.* If you have been talking about the person and it is fairly obvious who you mean, then it is all right to just use the pronoun:
-¿Vas a ver a Lizette hoy?
-Sí, le voy a dar estas guayabas.

■ MAKING COMPARISONS

A
1. Raúl is heavier than Reynaldo.
2. Your grass is greener than mine.
3. Tito is as talented as his brother.
4. Her second movie was less interesting than her first.
5. Your speech was less boring than mine.
6. The dessert was as delicious as the main course.
7. That poem is more inspiring than this one.
8. My dog is prettier than any other.

B
1. Lupe es más divertida que Francisca.
2. Eva es más alta que Gabriela.
3. La falda es menos cara que el vestido.
4. Tus hijas son tan simpáticas como mis hijos.
5. La blusa es más barata que los pantalones.
6. Mi libro es más interesante que tu libro.
7. Ramón es más grande que Rosita.
8. Las sandalias son tan baratas como los zapatos.

C Answers will vary.

D Answers will vary. A possible mnemonic "song" is: "More or less than as-as is Más o menos que tan-como". Give it the rhythm you prefer, and repeat it many times until you memorize it.

■ DEMONSTRATIVE ADJECTIVES

A
1. Myrna prefers this dress to the one I gave her. (S)
2. Johanna selected these ties for her husband. (P)
3. What did Inés say about those flowers? (P)
4. I gave him one dollar for this mango. (S)
5. That tree looks quite old. (S)
6. I love this beach more than any other. (S)
7. Would you rather have these decorations? (P)
8. This car is very clean. (S)

B
1. Esta casa es bonita. (S, F)
2. Me gusta esa cartera. (S, F)
3. Voy a comprar ese diccionario.
4. Esos chicos son simpáticos. (S, M)
5. ¿Te gusta este plato rojo? (P, M)
6. Estas niñas son muy inteligentes. (P, F)
7. Estos discos compactos son mis favoritos. (P, M)
8. Julián me va a regalar este libro. (S, M)

C Answers will vary.

D *Este zapato* refers to a shoe that is close by, probably a shoe that the speaker is holding or at least can reach. *Ese zapato* refers to a shoe that is farther away. It can even refer to a shoe that is not present but that the

Copyright © by Holt, Rinehart and Winston. All rights reserved.

speaker recalls.

CAPÍTULO 10

■ PRESENT PROGRESSIVE

A 1. I am writing.
2. Luis is eating.
3. We are singing.
4. You are watching the birds.
5. The sun is shining.
6. They are telling stories.
7. It is snowing.
8. He is playing guitar.

B 1. Yo estoy escribiendo.
2. Luis está comiendo.
3. Nosotros estamos cantando.
4. Tú estás saliendo.
5. Yolanda está pintando.
6. Ellos están nadando.
7. Está nevando.
8. ¿Qué está haciendo él?

C Answers will vary.

D Answers will vary. Possible answer: The present progressive describes what is happening right now (Yo estoy comiendo carne *ahora*.), whereas the present tense can describe a general action that occurs in the present, but may not be occurring right now (Yo como carne *a veces*).

■ COMMANDS

A 1. Read the directions carefully.
2. He listens to his parents.
3. Speak clearly when you give a presentation.
4. Smell the roses!
5. I go to my appointment.
6. Take some medicine.
7. They drink plenty of orange juice.
8. Please mow the lawn.

B 1. Come todo el arroz.
2. Dibujas muy bien.
3. Bebes mucha agua.
4. Corta el césped.
5. Limpia la sala.
6. Escuchas con atención.
7. Pon la mesa.
8. Haz la tarea.

C 1. Llama a los invitados.
2. Pon la mesa.
3. Prepara la cena.
4. Haz un postre.

5. Lava los platos.
6. Manda las invitaciones.
7. Infla los globos.

D gives instructions
expresses an order
requests a favor
An order often only consists of the verb, while a request often uses request words such as *please*. This is true in both English and Spanish. *Hazlo* (Do it) is an order while *Por favor, hazlo* (Please do it) is a request.

■ THE PAST TENSE

A 1. Yolanda worked at the ice cream stand. (PAST)
2. They talk all night. (PRESENT)
3. You play tennis. (PRESENT)
4. Ana lived in Boston for two years. (PAST)
5. Luisa and Juan visited your grandmother. (PAST)
6. I finished the book on Monday. (PAST)
7. He cleans his room. (PRESENT)
8. They planted a lot of pretty flowers. (PAST)

B 1. María habló mucho en la reunión. (PRETERITE)
2. Pedro y Luis cantan bien. (PRESENT)
3. Ustedes bailaron con gracia. (PRETERITE)
4. Rolando lavó la ropa ayer. (PRETERITE)
5. Tú inflaste los globos, ¿no? (PRETERITE)
6. Ellas organizan los papeles. (PRESENT)
7. Preparo la cena. (PRESENT)
8. Nosotros pasamos la aspiradora ayer. (PRETERITE)

C 1. No, caminé a casa ayer.
2. No, María planchó la ropa ayer.
3. No, Elena montó en bicicleta ayer.
4. No, ellos hablaron por teléfono ayer.
5. No, organizamos la casa ayer.
6. No, Isabel cortó el césped ayer.
7. No, Alejandra preparó la cena ayer.
8. No, trabajaste ayer.

D The *nosotros* form of the verb requires more information to tell whether it is in the present or preterite tense because the ending is the same for both. For example, if we say *Escribimos una carta,* the listener does not know whether this was in the past or the present. Words such as *ahora*, *ayer* and *anoche* must be added for clarification.

Copyright © by Holt, Rinehart and Winston. All rights reserved.

■ DIRECT OBJECT PRONOUNS

A 1. I saw the <u>film</u> and enjoyed (it) immensely.
2. David thought the <u>cake</u> was delicious, so he ate (it)
3. I met <u>Liliana</u> at the party, but I knew (her) from before.
4. You want to meet <u>Julián</u>, so I will introduce (him) to you.
5. They finished their <u>mural</u>, and they love (it)
6. If you are interested in Nick's <u>game</u>, I can lend (it) to you.
7. We knew <u>Raquel</u> was going to come, but we didn't think we would see (her) here.
8. I saw <u>José</u> at the beach yesterday and gave (him) my phone number.

B 1. Tengo que hablar con <u>María</u>. (La) llamo por teléfono.
2. La <u>torta</u> está deliciosa. (La) quiero comer.
3. Quiero <u>jamón</u>. (Lo) necesito para hacer un sándwich.
4. ¿Cuándo compró el <u>regalo</u> Eva? (Lo) compró ayer.
5. <u>Juan</u> está en la playa. (Lo) veo nadando.
6. ¿Me puede traer un <u>cuchillo</u>? (Lo) necesito para cortar la carne.
7. ¿Tienes la <u>tarea</u>? (La) necesito hoy.
8. ¡Ese <u>libro</u> es de Nacho! ¿Dónde (lo) encontraste?

C 1. Sí (or No, no) la quiero ver.
2. Sí (or No, no) lo leo.
3. Sí (or No, no) lo toma.
4. Sí (or No, no) lo va a cuidar.
5. La compro en...
6. Sí (or No, no) lo tengo.
7. Sí (or No, no) lo quiero leer.

D

ENGLISH	SPANISH
him	lo
her	la
it	lo
it	la

The main difference is that the pronoun for an object in English is always *it*, while in Spanish it can be *lo* or *la*. In Spanish you have to know the gender of the noun being replaced and you must write the correct pronoun based on the gender.

CAPÍTULO 11

■ THE VERB *TO PLAY* IN THE PAST

A 1. (He) <u>played</u> racquetball yesterday. (PAST)
2. (Emma) <u>plays</u> with her friends in the yard.

(PRESENT)
3. (Lucía and Jaime) <u>played</u> dominoes last night. (PAST)
4. (We) <u>played</u> basketball this morning. (PAST)
5. (They) <u>play</u> volleyball at the beach. (PRESENT)
6. (You) <u>played</u> water polo the night before last. (PAST)
7. (I) <u>play</u> tennis with my brother. (PRESENT)
8. (You) <u>played</u> soccer with the champions. (PAST)

B 1. (Elías) <u>jugó</u> al tenis conmigo. (PRETERITE)
2. (Emilia y Modesto) <u>juegan</u> en la casa. (PRESENT)
3. (Nosotros) <u>jugamos</u> al béisbol ayer por la tarde. (PRETERITE)
4. ¿(Tú) <u>jugaste</u> al jai alai con Reinaldo? (PRETERITE)
5. (Yo) <u>juego</u> al voleibol en la escuela. (PRESENT)
6. (Ellos) <u>jugaron</u> al baloncesto muy bien anoche. (PRETERITE)
7. (Ustedes) <u>juegan</u> al dominó con Inés y Nico. (PRESENT)
8. (Elena) <u>jugó</u> con Pepe ayer. (PRETERITE)

C The ending of the verb tells me the tense except in the *nosotros* form because the ending is the same in both the present and in the preterite tense. Clue words such as *ayer* indicate that the verb is in the preterite.

D 1. Yo **jugué** al tenis ayer.
2. Mario **jugó** al golf con sus amigos la semana pasada.
3. Nosotros **jugamos** con el perro anoche.
4. Tú **jugaste** al baloncesto.
5. Julia y Francisco **jugaron** a las cartas anteanoche.
6. Rigo y yo **jugamos** con los niños.
7. Nancy y Kristen **jugaron** al dominó con los chicos.

E A **u** is added to the **yo** form of **jugar** in the preterite because **g** is pronounced like **h** before the letter **e.** The **u** is added to maintain the hard **g** sound. When verbs end in **-gar**, a **u** is added before the ending in the **yo** form of the preterite tense.

■ THE VERB *TO GO* IN THE PAST

A 1. (I) <u>went</u> to the theater yesterday. (PAST)
2. (You) <u>go</u> to the movies with Roger. (PRESENT)

Copyright © by Holt, Rinehart and Winston. All rights reserved.

3. We went to a restaurant for dinner last night. (PAST)
4. You went to yoga class this morning. (PAST)
5. Rogelio went to the concert with his friends. (PAST)
6. Mimi and Rolando go to a writing workshop. (PRESENT)
7. Sylma goes to San Juan to see the soccer game. (PRESENT)
8. You go to New York to study. (PRESENT)

B 1. Antonia va a la Puerta de San Juan. (PRESENT)
2. Pedro y Benjamín fueron al Viejo San Juan. (PRETERITE)
3. Carmela va a la playa. (PRESENT)
4. Ignacio y yo fuimos al Castillo del Morro. (PRETERITE)
5. Tú fuiste al Museo de Pablo Casals. (PRETERITE)
6. Usted fue a la Plaza de Hostos. (PRETERITE)
7. Yo fui a casa de mis amigos. (PRETERITE)
8. El profesor va a la universidad. (PRESENT)

C 1. Yo **fui** a la Plaza de Hostos ayer.
2. ¿Tú **fuiste** a la universidad ayer?
3. Nosotros **fuimos** al concierto el jueves por la noche.
4. Ellos **fueron** a la casa de Sergio para jugar al dominó.
5. ¿Sabes si Julián **fue** al estadio de fútbol?
6. ¿Ustedes **fueron** al partido de béisbol el sábado?
7. María **fue** al mercado ayer.

D 1. No, fui anoche.
2. No, fueron anoche.
3. No, fuiste anoche.
4. No, fuimos anoche.
5. No, fui anoche.
6. No, fue anoche.

E Answers will vary.

CAPÍTULO 12

■ VERBS + INFINITIVES

A Answers will vary, but the verb must be in the infinitive.

B Answers will vary, but the verb must be in the infinitive.

C Answers will vary.

D The verb **ir** means *to go* and **ir a** can mean to *be going to*. The verb **tener** means *to have* while **tener que** means *to have to*. **Ir a** and **tener que** can be followed by an infinitive.

E should, to think, to hope

■ THE VERB *TO BE*: SUMMARY

A 1. María is Luisa's sister. (3)
2. The books are in bad condition. (6)
3. Julio and José are quite tall. (1)
4. I am calmer than yesterday. (6)
5. It is five o'clock. (5)
6. Ruth is from Santiago, Chile. (2)
7. They are dancing the merengue. (8)
8. My pants are wool. (4)

B 1. ¿Dónde está Héctor ahora? (7)
2. Yolanda es muy guapa. (1)
3. Hoy es el 7 de septiembre. (5)
4. Abuela está cansada. (6)
5. El señor Ruiz es un profesor. (3)
6. Tu chaqueta es de cuero. (4)
7. Jaime está preparando la cena. (8)
8. Rita es de Buenos Aires. (2)

C 1. Ema **es** una mujer elegante. (PERMANENT)
2. Juan Luis **es** un excelente cantante. (PERMANENT)
3. Las toallas **están** en el baño. (IMPERMANENT)
4. María Elena **está** un poco enferma. (IMPERMANENT)
5. Nosotros **somos** hermanos. (PERMANENT)
6. Ustedes **están** muy equivocados. (IMPERMANENT)

D **Ser aburrida/o** means to be *boring*, while **estar aburrida/o** means to be *bored*. **Ser delgada** means *to be thin*, while **estar delgada** means *to have become thin*.

Copyright © by Holt, Rinehart and Winston. All rights reserved.

Answers: Level 2

CAPÍTULO 1

ADJECTIVES

A
1. My sister is extroverted. (S, F)
2. My nephews are athletic. (P, M)
3. Claudia is smart. (S, F)
4. Your brother is shy. (S, M)
5. Luis is Mexican. (S, M)
6. My grandmother is gray-haired. (S, F)
7. María is intelligent. (S, F)
8. Tanya is very tall. (S, F)

B
1. El muchacho es rubio. (S, M)
2. Tu compañera está deprimida. (S, F)
3. La materia es difícil. (S, F)
4. Las casas son bonitas. (P, F)
5. Luis es argentino. (S, M)
6. Los chicos están enfadados. (P, M)
7. Me gusta la comida china. (S, F)
8. Los libros son interesantes. (P, M)

C
1. Las chicas **jóvenes** bailan sevillanas.
2. Una anciana **canosa** camina por la Plaza de España.
3. Los turistas **costarricenses** visitan la Plaza del Triunfo.
4. Un hombre **delgado** pasea por el Parque de María Luisa.
5. La Giralda es una torre **vieja**
6. Vivo en Sevilla, pero mis padres son **venezolanos**
7. Cenamos en un café **pequeño**

D
1. Valeria Mazza es una modelo argentina.
2. Frida Kahlo y Diego Rivera son artistas mexicanos.
3. David Torres es un cantante cubano.
4. Pedro Martínez y Sammy Sosa son atletas dominicanos.
5. Rita Moreno es una actriz puertorriqueña.

PRESENT TENSE OF REGULAR VERBS

A
1. Raúl returns from Andalucía.
2. His family throws a party.
3. Friends and neighbors help with the preparations.
4. Julia makes a cake.
5. After dinner, Raúl shows pictures of Sevilla.
6. He describes the beautiful buildings.
7. Then he tells about his adventures.

8. The guests listen intently.

B
1. Eduardo vive en Sevilla.
2. Nosotros estudiamos juntos todos los días.
3. Yo visito a su familia.
4. Ellos leen libros españoles.
5. Su madre me presta (*lends me*) un libro de Lorca.
6. Luego, nosotros comemos paella y ensalada de frutas.
7. Eduardo y su hermano aprenden inglés en la escuela.
8. Ellos practican conmigo.

C
1. vivir   -ir
2. estudiar   -ar
3. visitar   -ar
4. leer   -er
5. prestar   -ar
6. comer   -er
7. aprender   -er
8. practicar   -ar

D
1. Ellos **hablan** todo el día.
2. ¿Ustedes **leen** español?
3. ¿A qué hora **limpias** tú el cuarto?
4. Andrés **nada** perfectamente.
5. Nosotros **practicamos** el baloncesto los viernes.
6. Yo no **toco** el piano.
7. Ustedes **compran** mucho en el mercado.
8. El coro **canta** música clásica.

E The ending of a verb often allows you to eliminate the subject because the subject is implied in the verb ending. For example, the subject of *vamos* must be *nosotros*. In some cases such as the third person singular (*corre*) the subject could be *él* or *ella* and therefore may be needed for clarification.

CAPÍTULO 2

PAST TENSE OF REGULAR VERBS

A
1. He looked for his hat everywhere. (He)
2. They worked hard all day. (They)
3. We sailed all the way to Costa Rica. (We)
4. I passed the exam. (I)
5. You all expected to see him there. (You)
6. Luisa talked on the phone. (Luisa)
7. Carlos scolded his little sister. (Carlos)

Copyright © by Holt, Rinehart and Winston. All rights reserved.

8. The teacher assigned three pages. (The teacher)

B 1. Compré fresas ayer. (yo)
2. Estudiamos ciencias la semana pasada. (nosotros)
3. Mis amigos tomaron café por la tarde. (Mis amigos)
4. Les gustó la película anoche. (la película)
5. María Luisa me regaló una blusa anteayer. (María Luisa)
6. Todos los chicos regresaron a la escuela. (Todos los chicos)
7. Luis y Teo jugaron al fútbol esta mañana. (Luis y Teo)
8. Las muchachas cantaron en el coro. (Las muchachas)

C 1. ¿Qué **compraron** Andrés y Juana en el mercado?
2. Ayer Luisa **cantó** canciones mexicanas.
3. ¿Por qué tú **tomaste** café después de cenar?
4. La semana pasada nosotros **estudiamos** la cultura de Andalucía.
5. Todas las chicas **regresaron** a clase a la una.
6. ¿Quién **estudió** la lección ayer?
7. Carlos **nadó** en la piscina de su amigo.
8. Anoche yo **preparé** la comida.

D hablamos
hablamos

You must use the context to determine whether the action is in the present or in the past when the *-ar* verb is in the *nosotros* form.

CAPÍTULO 3

■ REFLEXIVE VERBS AND PRONOUNS

A 1. I dry myself after leaving the shower. (to dry)
2. The little bird bathes himself in the pond. (to bathe)
3. You call yourself an exceptional student? (to call)
4. They prepare themselves before entering the library. (to prepare)
5. Marta admires herself in the mirror. (to admire)
6. The athletes treat themselves to ice cream after the big win. (to treat)
7. Paola dresses herself before eating breakfast. (to dress)
8. The raccoon cleans itself in the stream. (to clean)

B 1. María se pone la ropa. (ponerse)
2. Te cepillas los dientes con pasta de dientes. (cepillarse)
3. Se miran en el espejo. (mirarse)
4. Nos acostamos a las diez de la noche. (acostarse)
5. Me lavo el pelo con champú. (lavarse)
6. Los hermanos se levantan a las seis de la mañana. (levantarse)
7. Mi amiga se viste de amarillo todos los días. (vestirse)
8. Nos despertamos con el despertador. (despertarse)

C 1. Normalmente José **se levanta** a las once los fines de semana.
2. Yo siempre **me miro** en el espejo antes de ir al colegio.
3. Iván siempre **se cepilla** los dientes después de comer.
4. Nosotros **nos vestimos** de ropa formal para la fiesta.
5. Tú **te secas** el pelo después de bañarte.
6. Los estudiantes **se despiertan** a las seis por lo general.
7. Nosotros **nos acostamos** a la medianoche casi todos los días.
8. Yo **me pongo** la ropa que me gusta.

D Answers will vary. Possible answers:

Sam takes a shower.	Sam se ducha.
Ana brushes her teeth.	Ana se cepilla los dientes.
Tomás wakes up at nine.	Tomás se despierta a las nueve.
Laura dries her hair.	Laura se seca el pelo.

■ ADVERBS

A 1. Mary showers quickly. (how)
2. The child looked shyly at the guests. (how)
3. Guadalupe sat here. (where)
4. I will buy new clothes tomorrow. (when)
5. Generally I get dressed after breakfast. (when)
6. The alarm clock rings softly. (how)
7. Dad bathes the baby carefully. (how)
8. Please put your toothbrush there. (where)

B 1. Yo me baño rápidamente. (how)
2. Ella normalmente se mira en el espejo antes de ir al colegio. (when)
3. Nosotros nos vestimos elegantemente para la fiesta. (how)
4. Tú te secas el pelo lentamente. (how)

Copyright © by Holt, Rinehart and Winston. All rights reserved.

5. Mi abuela baila allí. (where)
6. La modelo se viste estupendamente. (how)
7. Ustedes típicamente se levantan a las ocho y cuarto. (when)
8. Mi tía viene mañana. (when)

C
1. Plácido Domingo canta **estupendamente**.
2. Mi amigo Tomás se viste **rápidamente**.
3. **Típicamente** voy a la escuela en bicicleta.
4. Mi hermana menor canta **dulcemente**.
5. Magda se despierta siempre **fácilmente**.
6. No me gusta bailar con Jorge porque baila **cómicamente**.
7. El estudiante contestó la pregunta **inteligentemente**.
8. Como siempre, tía Meches nos habló **cariñosamente**.

D
1. Ella habla lentamente.
2. La fiesta es linda.
3. Debemos caminar cuidadosamente.
4. Comimos rápidamente.
5. El nuevo estudiante es simpático.

The words that end in -*mente* in the Spanish sentences are adverbs in the English sentences.

■ DIRECT OBJECT PRONOUNS

A
1. Fernando mops the floor. (it)
2. Maricarmen vacuums the rugs. (them)
3. My mom pays the mechanic. (him or her)
4. Guadalupe clears the tables. (them)
5. Manuela cleans the basement. (it)
6. Lorenzo´s dad calls the cleaning lady. (her)
7. Mateo does the chores. (them)
8. The homeowner hires the gardener. (him or her)

B
1. Yo riego las flores. (las)
2. Su padre barre el cuarto de baño. (lo)
3. Tú llamas al jardinero. (lo)
4. Mi hermano tiende la cama. (la)
5. Los niños sacuden el polvo. (lo)
6. Mi madre ordena los libros. (los)
7. Ustedes lavan las toallas. (las)
8. El abuelo ayuda a la abuela. (la)

C Answers will vary, but the following fragments must be used:

1. ...la quita.
2. ...las tiende.
3. ...lo limpia.
4. ...los hace.

5. ...lo barre.
6. ...los cuida.
7. ...la limpia.

D If the direct object has not already been stated, it is unclear what the pronoun refers to.

CAPÍTULO 4

■ THE VERB *TO BE*

A
1. My little brother is sick today. (a state or condition)
2. The students are responsible. (characteristics)
3. My aunt is Ecuadorian. (nationality)
4. The exam is on your desk. (location)
5. The books are heavy and old. (characteristics)
6. Guadalupe is tired. (how someone feels)
7. The computer is in the basement. (location)
8. Mary's sisters are tall and blond. (characteristics)

B
1. Estoy en la cocina. (location)
2. Susana es rubia y delgada. (characteristics)
3. Emilio y Eva son españoles. (nationality)
4. Ustedes están de mal humor. (how someone feels)
5. Tu padre es estricto. (personality)
6. El café está caliente. (a state or condition)
7. Mi abuela es generosa. (personality)
8. Alejandro y yo estamos contentos. (how someone feels)

C Me llamo Andrew. Tengo quince años. **Soy** estadounidense pero mis padres **son** italianos. Vivo en Nueva York. Mi casa **está** en la avenida Washington. **Es** una casa grande, de color amarillo. Yo también **soy** grande. Mido 6' 4" y peso 230 lbs. **Soy** jugador de baloncesto. Hoy **estoy** alegre porque no tengo clase. Mis clases **son** interesantes pero yo no **soy** un estudiante muy aplicado. Mi hermana menor se llama Matilda. Ella **está** en su clase de baile. Yo **soy** muy torpe y no bailo. Bueno, **estoy** aburrido, así que me voy a practicar baloncesto.

D Answers will vary.

■ MORE DIRECT OBJECT PRONOUNS

A
1. Elizabeth invites us to the party.

Copyright © by Holt, Rinehart and Winston. All rights reserved.

2. David's brothers ask (you) for the address.
3. Carol calls (me) in the morning.
4. We invite (you) to the show.
5. Gabriela asks (you) for the homework.
6. Lauren believes (me).
7. Felipe calls (us) every weekend.
8. I see (you) jogging every morning.

B 1. (Me) llama una amiga.
2. Roberto tiene que invitarnos.
3. Elena (te) ayuda a cocinar.
4. La profesora (nos) cree.
5. Voy a invitarte a mi fiesta.
6. ¿(Me) necesitas, mamá?
7. (Nos) mira el vecino.
8. Tengo que llamarlos.

C FRANCISCO Hola Silvia. Mira, quiero
invitarte a mi fiesta el viernes.
SILVIA ¿**Me** invitas a tu fiesta?
FRANCISCO ¡Claro que sí! Y a tu hermano
también.
SILVIA ¡Qué bien! Yo **te** llamo el martes.
FRANCISCO Tengo clase el martes. **Los** llamo
yo el miércoles.
SILVIA Bueno, **te** veo el viernes. Gracias
por invitar**nos**.
FRANCISCO Adiós.

D 1. Joaquín te ve en el café Mayapán.
2. Ustedes me pueden llamar por teléfono.
3. Marisol nos ayuda a hacer la tarea.
4. Eulalio te visita en el hospital.
5. Nosotros los esperamos por una hora.
6. El profesor los presenta a la clase.

E 1. Estamos ayudándolos.
Los estamos ayudando.
2. Quiero verte.
Te quiero ver.
In English the direct object pronoun is placed
after the verb, whereas in Spanish it can be
placed before the conjugated verb or attached
to the end of the infinitive.

CAPÍTULO 5

■ MORE PAST TENSE VERBS

A 1. (They) attended the soccer game last
Thursday.
2. (He) played on the hockey team.
3. (You) jumped rope last night at the gym.
4. (We) competed in the martial arts competition last fall.
5. (Gregorio) performed with the band in
college.
6. (Amelia and Pilar) missed their aerobics
class this afternoon.

7. (I) rowed in the regatta every September.
8. (She) lifted weights for an hour.

B 1. (Javier) corrió el maratón de Boston.
2. Asistimos al partido de voleibol ayer.
(subject implied)
3. ¿Diste la pelota a Hermán? (subject
implied)
4. (Margarita y Cristina) asistieron a la competición de natación.
5. Di la receta a mi amiga. (subject implied)
6. Corriste con un equipo en el colegio.
(subject implied)
7. (Eric) se inscribió al nuevo gimnasio.
8. (Mi tía Teresa) me dio la bicicleta.

C 1. Yo **corrí** a la casa de Marcos ayer.
2. Gustavo y Pedro **asistieron** al partido
de golf.
3. El hermano de Sara **dio** la pelota al
jugador.
4. Nosotros **corrimos** la carrera de
ochocientos metros.
5. Tú me **diste** la bicicleta a mí.
6. Ustedes **asistieron** al gimnasio.
7. Elisa **corrió** cien metros.
8. Nosotros **salimos** a dar un paseo.

D You cannot tell from the verb whether these
sentences are in the preterite or the present
tense. Context clues such as *ayer, anoche,
esta mañana,* etc. could be added to show
the tense.

■ INFORMAL COMMANDS

A 1. You're so nervous. (Calm) down! (positive)
2. (Be quiet!) The teacher is talking. (positive)
3. I'm bored. Please (take) me home. (positive)
4. It is raining. (Drive) carefully! (positive)
5. You are going to the gym? (Don't forget)
your ID! (negative)
6. I'm really hot. Please (give) me that fan.
(positive)
7. What a racket. Please (turn) off the television! (positive)
8. You're friends. (Don't fight!) (negative)

B 1. Te duelen los pies. (Deja) de correr! (positive)
2. Eres antipático. ¡No me (hables) así! (negative)
3. Mañana tenemos examen. (Estudia)
mucho. (positive)
4. Es muy tarde. (Duerme!) (positive)
5. ¡No (escales) montañas! Es peligroso.

Copyright © by Holt, Rinehart and Winston. All rights reserved.

6. ¡No levantes pesas! Te puedes lastimar la espalda. (negative)
7. Come bien. Te vas a sentir mejor. (positive)
8. ¡No juegues en la cocina! Papá está trabajando allí. (negative)

C
1. No fumes.
2. Saca la basura.
3. Paga el alquiler.
4. No comas en la cama.
5. Corta el césped.
6. No escuches música muy fuerte.

D I knew which sentences expressed commands because of the verb and the context. In English both negative and positive commands use the same verb form, but in Spanish the verb form is different for each type of command.

■ IRREGULAR INFORMAL COMMANDS

A
1. We finished school. Celebrate! (positive)
2. Don't steal. Stealing is wrong. (negative)
3. Tomás is studying. Don't make noise. (negative)
4. I'm trying to sleep. Don't disturb me, please. (negative)
5. Biking can be dangerous. Always wear your helmet. (positive)
6. Don't be grumpy! It is Friday. (negative)
7. It is snowing. Bring your gloves. (positive)
8. You're on my foot. Please move! (positive)

B
1. Tu cuarto es un desastre. ¡Haz la cama! (positive)
2. Quiero hablar contigo. ¡Ven aquí! (positive)
3. ¿Te gusta fumar? ¡No seas tonto! (negative)
4. La ropa está en el piso. ¡Pon la ropa en el armario! (positive)
5. Te quiero. ¡No te vayas! (negative)
6. Es tarde. ¡Sal de prisa! (positive)
7. Es un secreto. ¡No digas nada! (negative)
8. Es un regalo. ¡Ten! (positive)

C
1. Ven aquí. No vengas aquí.
2. Sé estudioso. No seas estudioso.
3. Pon la mesa. No pongas la mesa.
4. Ten calma. No tengas calma.
5. Haz eso. No hagas eso.
6. Di mentiras. No digas mentiras.
7. Sal del cuarto. No salgas del cuarto.
8. Ve por la leche. No vayas por la leche.

D Answers will vary.

CAPÍTULO 6

■ THE VERB *TO KNOW*

A
1. The sisters know the dance. (activity)
2. I know his cousin. (person)
3. We know how to get to the town. (information)
4. The guide knows the work of art. (information)
5. You know the neighborhood. (place)
6. They know my grandmother. (person)
7. Clarisa knows the lesson. (information)
8. Bobby and Marc know the restaurant. (place)

B
1. Ana sabe usar la computadora. (activity)
2. Ellos saben tocar la guitarra. (activity)
3. Mi primo conoce a Britney Spears. (person)
4. Nosotros sabemos escribir la fecha en español. (information)
5. Su hermana mayor conoce la discoteca. (place)
6. Yo sé escribir en chino. (activity)
7. ¿Ustedes conocen a mi madre? (person)
8. ¿Conoces este lugar? (place)

C
1. Leann **sabe** cantar muy bien.
2. Yo **conozco** a la hermana de José.
3. Nosotros **conocemos** la casa de la profesora.
4. Emilia y Jacobo **saben** su número de teléfono.
5. Tú **conoces** a la secretaria.
6. Ustedes **saben** escribir poemas.
7. Rodrigo **conoce** el parque de atracciones.
8. Ellas **saben** cocinar pasteles de chocolate.

D
1. ¿Conoces un buen restaurante cerca de aquí?
2. ¿Sabes dónde está el restaurante?
3. ¿Conoce usted al nuevo estudiante?
4. ¿Sabe el nombre del nuevo estudiante?
5. ¿Saben llegar a la biblioteca?
6. ¿Conocen a mis compañeros de clase?

■ IRREGULAR VERBS IN THE PAST

A Subjects will vary.
1. **Harold** brought two notebooks.
2. ...served ice cream to everybody.
3. ...asked for some water.
4. ...brought the boys to the park.
5. ...served dessert on the patio.

Copyright © by Holt, Rinehart and Winston. All rights reserved.

ANSWERS

6. ...brought a camera and film.
7. ...asked for paper and pencils.
8. ...brought nothing.

B Subjects may vary.
1. **Juan** trajo el menú.
2. **Ustedes/Tim y Jimmy/Ellas** sirvieron la comida.
3. **Tim y Jimmy/Ustedes/Ellas** pidieron la cuenta.
4. **Yo** traje la ensalada.
5. **Alicia** trajo la propina.
6. **Nosotros** pedimos el postre.
7. **Ellas/Ustedes/Tim y Jimmy** sirvieron pastas.
8. **Tú** trajiste un refresco.

C 1. Tú trajiste el pastel de cumpleaños.
2. Elisa trajo un radio.
3. Nosotros trajimos una pelota para jugar.
4. Yo traje refrescos.
5. Los amigos trajeron regalos.
6. Tú trajiste música salsa.

D To conjugate the verb *pedir* in the preterite, remove the ending and add the regular -*ir* endings. For the third person singular and the third person plural, change the *e* to *i* in the stem.

CAPÍTULO 7

▇ THE PAST TENSE: *USED TO*

A 1. We used to share an apartment. (We)
2. Teresa used to get scared at night. (Teresa)
3. I used to hate beets. (I)
4. You guys used to climb trees. (You)
5. My brother used to play tricks on me. (brother)
6. María used to write poetry. (María)
7. Ivan and Guy used to dream about being stars. (Ivan and Guy)
8. Bernadette used to build snowmen. (Bernadette)

B 1. Amy peleaba con su hermanito. (Amy)
2. Trepábamos a los árboles. (nosotros)
3. Ellos tenían dos gatos. (ellos)
4. Yo hacía travesuras. (yo)
5. Odiabas los exámenes. (tú)
6. Mi padre contaba chistes. (mi padre)
7. Encontrabas genial las tiras cómicas. (tú)
8. Elí y Dana fastidiaban al profesor. (Elí y Dana)

C Cuando yo era niña siempre **jugaba** en el parque. **Venía** también mi hermano.

Nosotros **trepábamos** a los árboles y **construíamos** castillos de arena. A mi hermano le **gustaba** molestar a los pájaros en el lago del parque. Mis padres también **venían** al parque con nosotros. Ellos **traían** la comida y todos nosotros **comíamos** juntos. Yo siempre **estaba** muy contenta con mi familia en el parque. ¿Y tú? ¿**Visitabas** el parque con tu familia?

D 1. Escribí una carta a mi abuela ayer.
describes a completed action in the past
2. Escribía cartas a mi abuela cada semana.
describes something I used to do in the past
3. Jugué al fútbol hoy.
describes a completed action in the past
4. Jugaba al fútbol cuando era joven.
describes something I used to do in the past

▇ COMPARISONS OF EQUALITY

A 1. Your mother talks as loud as our teacher. (quality)
2. Sheila has as much money as Bill Gates. (quantity)
3. Hillary is as friendly as Carmen. (quality)
4. He is as stubborn as my brother. (quality)
5. Michael is as strong as my father. (quality)
6. Mary has as many gray hairs as her grandmother. (quantity)
7. My backpack is as big as the desk. (quality)
8. We have as much work as the seniors. (quantity)

B 1. Soy tan alta como Linda. (quality)
2. Ella tiene tantos vestidos como su hermana. (quantity)
3. Los científicos son tan interesantes como los autores. (quality)
4. Tenemos tanto tiempo como para ir y regresar. (quantity)
5. Mi hermano es tan fuerte como tu hermano. (quality)
6. Escribes tan bien como un poeta. (quality)
7. Tengo tantos zapatos como la tía de Ana. (quantity)
8. Eres tan noble como el rey. (quality)

C 1. Pablo tenía tantos libros como Pedro.
2. Teresa era tan delgada como Marisol.

Copyright © by Holt, Rinehart and Winston. All rights reserved.

3. Mi abuela tomaba tantas clases de pintura como mi abuelo.
4. Juan tiene tantas hermanas como Manolo.
5. Rosa practica tantos deportes como Paola.
6. Mi hermano toca tantos instrumentos como yo.

D Answers will vary.

CAPÍTULO 8

■ SUPERLATIVES

A 1. The snake is the least attractive animal I can imagine.
2. The Ferris wheel is the slowest ride in the park.
3. The zoo is the funniest place in the city.
4. This is the biggest roller coaster we have ever seen.
5. We saw the longest movie in the history of Hollywood.
6. Tom Hanks is the most famous actor of his generation.
7. Julia Roberts is the prettiest actress I know.
8. The monkey is the silliest animal in the zoo.

B 1. Harrison Ford es el hombre más inteligente de la película.
2. La tortuga y la serpiente son los animales menos activos de todos.
3. La montaña rusa es la atracción más divertida del parque.
4. Son las estrellas de cine menos simpáticas del mundo.
5. Jackie Chan es el mejor actor de películas de acción.
6. Ésta es la peor película de Almodóvar.
5. Penélope Cruz es la actriz más guapa de la película.
6. Los días en el parque son los mejores días de mi vida.

C 1. Carolina es la estudiante más inteligente del colegio.
2. Mateo y Juan son los chicos más traviesos del colegio.
3. Patricio es el estudiante menos estudioso del colegio.
4. Daniel es el mejor estudiante del colegio.
5. Laura es la estudiante menos atlética del colegio.
6. María es la estudiante menos chismosa del colegio.

D The noun can be omitted when it is already

clear what the speaker is talking about.

■ *TO SAY/TO TELL* IN THE PAST

A 1. I said that I hated parades.
2. We told them that the festival fascinated us.
3. The children said that they loved the costumes.
4. Josephine told me that you liked the floats.
5. You told us that you enjoyed everything.
6. Mathew and Andy said that the decorations bored them.
7. They said that the masks impressed them.
8. You told her that you disliked the festival.

B 1. Elisa dijo que le interesaba el desfile.
2. Dijimos que nos gustaban los disfraces.
3. Yo les dije que me fastidiaba el festival.
4. Ellos nos dijeron que les gustaba la carroza.
5. Dijeron que no les interesaban las máscaras.
6. Tú le dijiste que te chocaba decorar para la fiesta.
7. Yo te dije que me interesaba diseñar disfraces.
8. Farola y Marí dijeron que todo les parecía bonito.

C 1. Yo **dije** que a mí me **gustaban** las máscaras.
2. Antonia **dijo** que a ella le **fastidiaba** desfilar.
3. Ellos **dijeron** que a ellos no les **gustaban** los diseños.
4. Nosotros **dijimos** que no nos **interesaba** el festival.
5. Tú **dijiste** que a ti te **chocaban** los disfraces.
6. Los padres **dijeron** que les **encantaban** las carrozas.
7. Yo **dije** que me **fascinaba** el carnaval.
8. Pablo **dijo** que él **pensaba** disfrutar del día.

D 1. Yo **dije** que a mí me **gustaba** el juego.
2. Elizabeth nos **dijo** que **estaba** cansada.
3. Nosotros **dijimos** que la película nos **aburría**.
4. Mi hermano **dijo** que la idea le **interesaba**.

E Answers will vary. Possible answer:
When used with an indirect object pronoun, **decir** means *to tell*.

Copyright © by Holt, Rinehart and Winston. All rights reserved.

CAPÍTULO 9

■ FORMAL COMMANDS

A 1. (Be) nice! (to be)
2. Laura, (stop) that bus! (to stop)
3. (Walk) in the hallways! (to walk)
4. Professor Ayala, (show) me the new library! (to show)
5. (Feed) the dogs in the morning. (to feed)
6. Honey, (bring) me my slippers please! (to bring)
7. (Write) me! (to write)
8. Please (close) the door, Mr. López. (to close)

B 1. ¡(Estudie)! (estudiar)
2. ¡(Sigan) las instrucciones! (seguir)
3. ¡(Duerma) ya! (dormir)
4. ¡(Suban) al coche! (subir)
5. ¡(Lávese) la cara! (lavarse)
6. ¡(Tenga) cuidado! (tener)
7. ¡(Cierre) las ventanas antes de irse! (cerrar)
8. ¡(Asistan) a las clases! (asistir)

C 1. ¡**Cruce** la avenida La Paz!
2. ¡**Dé** el nombre a su profesor!
3. ¡**Sean** inteligentes!
4. ¡**Empiecen** el examen ahora!
5. ¡**Juegue** limpio!
6. ¡**Esté** tranquilo!
7. ¡**Vayan** dos cuadras más al norte!
8. ¡**Sepan** protegerse de los criminales!

D In Spanish there are two forms of you, *tú* and *usted*, so there must also be two command forms in order to indicate who is being addressed.

CAPÍTULO 10

■ PAST TENSE FORMS

A 1. The sun was shining when the women (fainted).
2. I was watching TV when the phone (rang).
3. They were eating dinner when they (heard) the noise.
4. She was crying when they (said) goodbye.
5. It was snowing when the heater (broke).
6. The crowd was panicking when the police (arrived).
7. The guard was napping when the robbery (occurred).
8. We were surfing when I (saw) the shark.

B 1. Hacía buen tiempo cuando (se casaron).

2. Estaban en el valle cuando (vieron) el rayo.
3. Hablabas con los amigos cuando (llegó) el profesor.
4. Había una tormenta cuando (ocurrió) el accidente.
5. Había niebla cuando (se perdieron) en la montaña.
6. Miguel estaba en el sofá cuando (entré) en la casa.
7. Estábamos contentos cuando (recibimos) las notas.
8. Yo jugaba con mi hermano cuando me (caí).

C **Era** una noche nublada y misteriosa. El príncipe Pier **estaba** en su cuarto cuando, de repente, **oyó** un ruido espantoso. **Había** un monstruo en su armario. El príncipe **tenía** mucho miedo y por eso, **empezó** a llorar. En seguida **llegó** su hermana pequeña, la princesa Francesca. La pequeña **tenía** mucha valentía. **Venció** al monstruo y **salvó** a su hermano mayor. Y todos **vivieron** felizmente.

CAPÍTULO 11

■ WE COMMANDS

A 1. Let's protect the environment. (we)
2. Conserve energy. (you)
3. Exercise daily. (you)
4. Let's go home. (we)
5. Let's finish the project. (we)
6. Let's be friends. (we)
7. Respect your teachers. (you)
8. Follow your dreams. (you)

B 1. Hagamos un viaje juntos. (we)
2. Pida ayuda de los empleados. (you formal)
3. Limpia el cuarto. (you familiar)
4. Conservemos energía. (we)
5. Usemos pocos recursos. (we)
6. Habla con tus padres. (you familiar)
7. Pongamos los libros aquí. (we)
8. Explica la respuesta. (you familiar)

C 1. Reciclemos los periódicos.
2. Conservemos los recursos naturales.
3. Respetemos la naturaleza.
4. Protejamos las especies en peligro de extinción.
5. Llevemos el vidrio al centro de reciclaje.
6. Apaguemos la luz al salir de un cuarto.
7. No pongamos las latas de aluminio en la basura.

Spanish 2 ¡Ven conmigo!, Answer Key

Copyright © by Holt, Rinehart and Winston. All rights reserved.

A
N
S
W
E
R
S

D In English, the formula *let's + base form of the verb* is used. In Spanish, the *you formal* command is used, with *-mos* added to the end.

CAPÍTULO 12

■ SUBJUNCTIVE MOOD

A 1. I wish we <u>were</u> finished with the work. (SUB)
2. We <u>are</u> finished with the work. (IND)
3. She wished they <u>were</u> done. (SUB)
4. <u>Finish</u> the work! (IMP)
5. Elena <u>rides</u> her bicycle. (IND)
6. Eduardo wishes he <u>had</u> a bicycle. (SUB)
7. Please <u>leave</u> all bicycles outside. (IND)
8. I wish you <u>were</u> there. (SUB)

B 1. Cuando <u>llegue</u> a casa, voy a comer. (SUB)
2. Lorenzo y Natalia <u>nadan</u> en la piscina. (IND)
3. ¡<u>Mira</u> las estrellas! (IMP)
4. Quiero comprar un carro cuando <u>tenga</u> dinero. (SUB)
5. Cuando <u>termine</u> la clase, jugamos al fútbol. (SUB)
6. <u>Ayúdame</u> con la tarea. (IMP)
7. Cuando <u>tenga</u> tiempo, vamos a salir. (SUB)
8. <u>Quiero</u> ir a un restaurante cubano. (IND)
9. <u>Pide</u> el arroz con pollo. (IMP)
10. Cuando <u>vuelva</u> a casa, voy a estudiar. (SUB)

C 1. Cuando Teresa **llegue** a casa, va a dormir.
2. Cuando **encuentre** un empleo, voy a comprar un carro nuevo.
3. Cuando **terminen** las clases, todos vamos a la fiesta.
4. Cuando **tenga** más dinero, voy a visitar España.
5. Cuando **llegue** mi primo, vamos a ver un partido de béisbol.
6. Cuando mi tío **tenga** un nuevo empleo, va a estar muy contento.
7. Cuando **vuelva** a México, voy a ir a un concierto de mariachis.
8. Cuando **encuentre** mi tarea, la voy a entregar.

D Verb forms in the subjunctive are like formal commands.

Copyright © by Holt, Rinehart and Winston. All rights reserved.

Answers: Level 3

CAPÍTULO 1

■ MORE STEM-CHANGING VERBS

A 1. Alfredo reads the comics.
2. We row on the lake every summer.
3. Julia is certainly in the park. (spelling change)
4. I am a big fan of jazz. (spelling change)
5. You skate on the weekends.
6. Patrick listens to the program.
7. We are crazy about apple pie. (spelling change)
8. You collect stamps.

B 1. Yo hablo francés e italiano.
2. Ellos empiezan a las ocho. (stem-changing)
3. ¿Puedes escuchar la música? (stem-changing)
4. Leemos las tiras cómicas.
5. Carla pide un refresco. (stem-changing)
6. Ricardo y su hermano tocan la guitarra.
7. Todos quieren ir a la playa. (stem-changing)
8. Ustedes sacan muchas fotos.

C 1. Voy al restaurante y **pido** una hamburguesa.
2. Mi hermana **empieza** su clase de fotografía hoy.
3. Nosotros **podemos** escalar montañas mañana.
4. Pilar y Rocío **sirven** una tarta en la fiesta.
5. Tú **duermes** después de ir en barco de vela.
6. Ustedes **quieren** hacer esquí acuático.
7. El camarero nos **sirve** unas pastas deliciosas.
8. Nosotros le **pedimos** un favor al profesor.

D

preferir	volver	vestir
prefiero	vuelvo	visto
prefieres	vuelves	vistes
prefiere	vuelve	viste
preferimos	volvemos	vestimos
preferís	volvéis	vestís
prefieren	vuelven	visten

The *nosotros* and *vosotros* forms do not have a stem change.

■ THE PAST TENSE: REVIEW

A 1. We played cards every afternoon.
2. Mary and her cousin climbed Mt. Rushmore.
3. I laughed with my friends.
4. You visited your grandparents in Florida.
5. My mother looked at photos of the new baby.
6. Ernesto practiced his saxophone.
7. They collected sea shells while on vacation.
8. Cristina and Rogelio jumped in the pool.

B 1. Tú tocaste tu clarinete.
2. Yo jugué con mis primos.
3. Montamos a caballo.
4. Mis padres comieron en un restaurante chino.
5. Remaste en bote por el río.
6. Yo comencé una colección de sellos.
7. Jorge y su amigo vivieron en la playa.
8. Lourdes patinó en línea.

C 1. Ustedes escucharon música latina.
2. Carla y su hermanita patinan sobre ruedas todos los días.
3. Yo saco fotos en el jardín.
4. Nosotros practicamos ciclismo.
5. Mi familia lee muchos libros interesantes.
6. Laura y yo dormimos hasta las doce del día.
7. Tú vives en casa de la abuela.
8. Raquel juega a los videojuegos.

D 1. The phrase *el año pasado* in the first sentence indicates that the action refers to the past. The phrase *todos los días* in the second sentence refers to a habitual action in the present.
2. Irregular verbs, such as *ser*, have a different ending in the *nosotros* form in the present and past tense: *somos* and *fuimos*.

CAPÍTULO 2

■ INFORMAL COMMANDS

A 1. Don´t **get** nervous!
2. Do not **lead** a hectic life.
3. **Solve** your problems quickly.
4. **Take** things calmly.
5. Don´t **cause** stress.

Copyright © by Holt, Rinehart and Winston. All rights reserved.

6. **Work** out your problems.
7. **Laugh** a lot.
8. Never **stress** out!

B 1. No **tomes** las cosas demasiado en serio.
2. **Duerme** al menos ocho horas.
3. **Cuídate** siempre.
4. No **causes** el estrés.
5. **Resuelve** los problemas.
6. No **comas** demasiado.
7. **Habla** de tus preocupaciones.
8. **Haz** ejercicio cada día.

C 1. Duerme ocho horas cada noche.
2. No sufras de tensiones.
3. Toma las cosas con calma.
4. No comas mucha grasa.
5. Alivia el estrés.
6. No lleves una vida agitada.

D Entrena mucho.
Corre rápido.
Sé positivo.
¡Simplemente hazlo!

■ REFLEXIVE CONSTRUCTION

A 1. Pilar treats herself to a fruit smoothie.
2. I bought myself a new car.
3. The kids dried themselves off after getting out of the pool.
4. We couldn´t believe he just invited himself to the party!
5. Do you weigh yourself every day?
6. Ricardo looked at himself in the mirror.
7. I sent myself a dozen roses for my birthday.
8. We protect ourselves from the sun by using sunscreen.

B 1. Me alimento bien y llevo una vida sana.
2. Yolanda no se cuida y por eso está enferma.
3. Felipe y Érica se mantienen en forma.
4. Nosotros no nos quemamos cuando vamos a la playa.
5. Ustedes se acuestan temprano, por lo general.
6. Te quedas frente a la tele todo el día.
7. Paloma se pesa por las mañanas.
8. Los niños se duchan antes de ir al colegio.

C 1. Las chicas **se broncean** en la playa.
2. Yo **me duermo** frente al televisor.
3. Nosotros **nos ponemos** crema protectora.
4. Tú **te sientes** muy solo.
5. Ustedes no **se dan** cuenta de la hora.

6. Francisco **se ducha** por la mañana.
7. Mis padres no **se visten** a la moda.
8. Tú y yo **nos mantenemos** en forma.

D The first sentence uses a reflexive pronoun because the action is reflected back on the subject: I burn *myself*. In the second sentence, the action is not reflected back on the subject.

CAPÍTULO 3

■ THE PRESENT PERFECT

A 1. We have made several advances.
2. The city has changed a lot in the past 20 years.
3. The situation has gotten much worse.
4. I have written my paper using the computer.
5. Have you informed them of the possible risks?
6. The area has grown a great deal.
7. The factory has improved its output.
8. The farmer has planted this year's crops.

B 1. Mucha gente ha venido del extranjero.
2. Han establecido una zona peatonal.
3. El gobernador ha hecho muchos cambios.
4. Nos hemos adaptado a la nueva casa.
5. ¿Has navegado por Internet?
6. ¿Has cocinado en el horno de microondas?
7. Yo he escrito un correo electrónico.
8. Los profesores han hecho fotocopias.

C 1. Nosotros hemos navegado por Internet.
2. Las ciudades han crecido mucho.
3. La contaminación del aire ha empeorado bastante.
4. Yo he escrito correo electrónico.
5. Los médicos han hecho adelantos contra el cáncer.
6. Tú has cocinado con un horno de microondas.
7. Mi abuela ha visto películas en DVD.

D The first pair of sentences refers to the general past, while the second sentences refer to a specific moment in the past.

■ THE FUTURE TENSE

A 1. Someone will discover the cure for this disease.
2. We shall use only electric cars.
3. I shall become a millionaire.
4. Your parents will surf the Internet.

Copyright © by Holt, Rinehart and Winston. All rights reserved.

5. There will be world peace.
6. You will develop a new type of interactive telephone.
7. Solar energy will replace nuclear energy.
8. Students will learn from home and not at school.

B 1. Yo visitaré la Luna.
2. Cada casa tendrá una computadora.
3. Hablaremos un solo idioma.
4. Habrá coches en el aire.
5. Tú sabrás hablar perfectamente el español.
6. Todos vivirán 120 años.
7. Ustedes comerán únicamente plantas.
8. El mundo será más limpio.

C 1. Cada persona tendrá un carro eléctrico.
2. El presidente destruirá todas las bombas nucleares.
3. Marcianos vendrán de Marte a la Tierra.
4. Tú descubrirás una cura para el cáncer.
5. Nosotros eliminaremos la contaminación del aire.
6. Los estudiantes estudiarán en casa usando computadoras.
7. Los profesores ganarán mucho dinero.
8. Yo desarrollaré un plan para la paz mundial.

D 1. Mis nietos vivirán en la Luna.
2. Viajaremos en una máquina del tiempo.
3. Podré ir de vacaciones a Marte.

CAPÍTULO 4

■ OBJECT PRONOUNS

A 1. Who sent me the package? I sent it.
2. Who gives us the assignment? Marisa gives it.
3. Their mother offers them lemonade.
4. Who writes me letters? You write them to me.
5. We bought them for Carmen.
6. Carlos offers him advice.

B 1. ¿Quién me compró el carro? Nosotros te lo compramos.
2. ¿Quién le escribe una postal a tu hermano? Tú se la escribes.
3. ¿Quién les da toallas a ustedes? La mujer nos las da.
4. ¿Quién da la tarea al profesor? Yo se la doy.
5. ¿Quién nos manda los libros a nosotros? Ustedes nos los mandan.
6. ¿Quién les escribe un aviso a los clientes? Usted se lo escribe.

C 1. Los profesores se lo ponen.
2. Se la ofrezco a ustedes.
3. Te las mandamos.
4. Juan Miguel me los escribe.
5. Papá nos la prepara.
6. Se la presto a Clara.

D 1. Prepárasela.
2. No se la compres.
3. Tráigasela.
4. Dámelo.
5. No se la sirvas.
6. Muéstranoslas.

E The sentence would not flow smoothly with two pronouns beginning with "l" right next to each other.

CAPÍTULO 5

■ SUBJUNCTIVE TO EXPRESS WISHES

A 1. Mamá tells the children about Mexican legends. (indicative)
2. Martita wishes they were true. (subjunctive)
3. The legends are based on real people. (indicative)
4. Pablito draws a picture of Quetzalcóatl. (indicative)
5. He wishes his friends were there to see it. (subjunctive)
6. Martita and Pablo told us about the legends. (indicative)
7. We were amazed! (indicative)
8. We wished the characters from the legends were here. (subjunctive)

B 1. Espero que salgamos pronto de vacaciones. (subjunctive)
2. Pensamos ir al Caribe. (indicative)
3. Ojalá que mi tía pueda ir con nosotros. (subjunctive)
4. ¡Me encanta la playa! (indicative)
5. Quiero que tú pasees en velero. (subjunctive)
6. Ignacio tiene un bote. (indicative)
7. Ojalá que haga buen tiempo. (subjunctive)
8. Espero que ustedes tengan tiempo para tomar el sol. (subjunctive)

C SRA. VÁSQUEZ Una princesa está encarcelada (*imprisoned*) en un castillo (*castle*).
ANITA ¡Espero que **escape**!
SRA. VÁSQUEZ Un soldado bueno va a luchar por ella.
ANITA ¡Ojalá que **pueda** ayudarla!

Copyright © by Holt, Rinehart and Winston. All rights reserved.

Sra. Vásquez	El malvado del castillo se llama Héctor.		Roberto	¿Qué vamos a hacer durante el viaje?
Anita	Quiero que Héctor **sea** derrotado.		Julia	Es necesario que **visitemos** el Instituto Cultural Cabañas.
Sra. Vásquez	El soldado vence a Héctor.		Roberto	Hace falta que **escuchemos** música también.
Anita	Espero que al final ellos **celebren** una boda.		Julia	Para eso, es necesario que tú **contrates** a un conjunto mariachi.
Sra. Vásquez	Celebran la boda y el rey está feliz.			
Anita	Ojalá los invitados les **den** muchos regalos.			

D 1. Quiero que Rafael vaya al concierto. ✓
   2. Espero que José esté feliz. ✓

CAPÍTULO 6

■ SUBJUNCTIVE TO EXPRESS NEED

A 1. It's important to get enough sleep. (everyone)
   2. It's essential that Selma stop at the store. (particular person)
   3. It's necessary that Marla give you advice. (particular person)
   4. It's important to speak clearly. (everyone)
   5. It's imperative that he arrive on time. (particular person)
   6. It's necessary to work hard. (everyone)
   7. It's necessary that Joshua take the bus. (particular person)
   8. It's essential that the student understand the problem. (particular person)

B 1. Es necesario hacer ejercicio. (everyone)
   2. Es importante que vayamos a clase. (particular person)
   3. Es necesario que Pablo llegue a tiempo. (particular person)
   4. Hace falta que nosotros hagamos la tarea. (particular person)
   5. Es necesario que tú me ayudes con el español. (particular person)
   6. Es necesario trabajar duro. (everyone)
   7. Es importante que visites a tu abuela. (particular person)
   8. Es necesario escuchar a los profesores. (everyone)

C

Roberto	Quiero que **organicemos** un viaje a Guadalajara.
Julia	Es necesario que **busques** pasajes *(plane tickets)* baratos.
Roberto	Voy a hablar con un agente de viajes hoy.
Julia	Bien, pero es importante que **llegues** allí antes de las cinco.

D Formal commands and negative *you* commands have a similar spelling change. Verbs that end in *-car*, *-gar*, or *-zar* have spelling changes in the subjunctive. I can remember this by looking at how the verb would be pronounced without the spelling change. (Verbs listed will vary.)

■ SUBJUNCTIVE FOR RECOMMENDATIONS

A 1. My mother recommends that my father visit a museum. (S)
   2. My father goes to an art museum. (I)
   3. Tomás reads about the work of Frida Kahlo. (I)
   4. The teacher recommends that Tomás finish his paper. (S)
   5. You enjoy Cuban music. (I)
   6. I suggest that you listen to Tito Puentes. (S)
   7. The guide recommends that Enrique see a dance performance. (S)
   8. Enrique sees a dance performance on Friday. (I)

B 1. Gabriela recomienda que pidas las enchiladas. (S)
   2. Tú pides arroz con pollo (I).
   3. Yo voy al cine a ver una película. (I)
   4. Mi tía me aconseja que vaya al teatro. (S)
   5. Recomiendo que ustedes estudien arte. (S)
   6. Ustedes sugieren que almorcemos en casa. (S)
   7. Alicia canta muy bien. (I)
   8. Paco sugiere que ella cante canciones tradicionales. (S)

C

Beatriz	A mí me encantan las obras de José Clemente Orozco.
David	Recomiendo que **visites** el Instituto Cultural Cabañas para ver los murales.
Gerardo	Me interesa la historia de México.
David	Recomiendo que **vayas** a los monumentos de la ciudad.
Laura	Me gusta mucho la danza.
David	Recomiendo que **veas** el Ballet

Copyright © by Holt, Rinehart and Winston. All rights reserved.

Folclórico de México.

MANUEL Quiero ver pinturas de artistas contemporáneos.

DAVID Recomiendo que **busques** una exhibición de arte moderno.

OLGA Me gustaría oír cantar a los mariachis.

DAVID Recomiendo que **tomes** un taxi a la Plaza Tapatía.

D a. La profesora recomienda que Daniel estudie más.
b. Yo te aconsejo que leas sobre el muralismo.
c. Tobías sugiere que vayamos al concierto de Maná.

The second verb changes to the subjunctive when it becomes part of the **que** clause.

■ WE COMMANDS: REVIEW

A 1. Let's take guitar lessons. (affirmative)
2. Let's go to the Luis Miguel concert. (affirmative)
3. Let's not buy movie tickets. (negative)
4. Let's rent a movie instead. (affirmative)
5. Let's listen to the ball game on the radio. (affirmative)
6. Let's buy a charango. (affirmative)
7. Let's not spend too much money. (negative)
8. Let's listen to the banjo music. (affirmative)

B 1. **Aprendamos** a tocar un instrumento. (affirmative)
2. **Veamos** la película a las ocho. (affirmative)
3. **No olvidemos** ir al concierto. (negative)
4. **Vamos a comprar** unos libros clásicos. (affirmative)
5. **No bailemos** ahora. (negative)
6. **Cantemos** esta canción. (affirmative)
7. **No escuchemos** la radio. (negative)
8. **Vamos a pintar** un mural. (affirmative)

C 1. **Visitemos** la Universidad de Salamanca.
2. **Comamos** tapas en los cafés de San Sebastián.
3. **Asistamos** a una obra de teatro en la Gran Vía de Madrid.
4. **Veamos** el acueducto (*aqueduct*) romano en Segovia.
5. **Paseemos** por las bonitas calles de Toledo.
6. **Compremos** recuerdos (*souvenirs*) en las tiendas de Barcelona.

7. **Tomemos** el sol en las playas de Cádiz.
8. **Saquemos** fotos en la Plaza de España de Sevilla.

D KARINA LET'S GO
LOLA WE'RE GOING
KARINA WE'RE GOING
LOLA LET'S GO
KARINA WE'RE GOING

CAPÍTULO 7

■ EXPRESSIONS OF FEELINGS

A 1. It's sad that we have to go home.
2. I fear that Blanca will arrive very late.
3. Francisco hopes that his team will win the game.
4. I'm happy that you are going out with us!
5. I am angry that you are eating my snacks!
6. We hope that you can come.
7. Patricia is afraid that Paco has too much work to do.

B 1. Me alegro que Carlota quiera visitarnos.
2. Ojalá que Ricardo pueda venir también.
3. Esperamos que haga buen tiempo.
4. Temo que vaya a llover el sábado.
5. Me frustra que no tengamos tiempo para ir a la playa.
6. Espero que todos traigan bañador.
7. Es triste que Manolo esté enfermo.

C 1. Estoy feliz que David tenga un nuevo empleo.
2. Mamá está orgullosa que Lisa hable español.
3. Estamos preocupados que Abuelo no se sienta bien.
4. Mónica está frustrada que Luis no entienda las instrucciones.
5. Olga tiene miedo que Laura pueda estar mintiendo.
6. A Elena no le gusta que Isabel siempre gane.
7. Yo espero que Raquel vaya a lavar los platos.
8. Me alegro que mis amigos jueguen conmigo.
9. Temo que Anita tenga tarea.
10. Es triste que Jorge no hable con su hermano.

D The subjunctive is used with verbs that convey feelings when the verbs are followed by a **que** clause. This usually means that the person is expressing feelings about

Copyright © by Holt, Rinehart and Winston. All rights reserved.

someone else's actions. When expressing feelings about one's own actions, the infinitive usually follows.

■ RECIPROCAL PRONOUNS

A 1. Manuel and Roberto help <u>each other</u> study for the test.
2. Elisa and Yolanda argue with <u>each other</u>.
3. Now the girls aren't speaking to <u>one another</u>.
4. They finally made up with <u>each other</u>.
5. We like <u>each other</u>.
6. The family members support <u>one another</u>.
7. Ricardo and Lucy never lie to <u>each other</u>.
8. The students tell <u>one another</u> about their homelands.

B 1. Los amigos <u>se abrazan</u>.
2. Teresa y Verónica <u>se reconcilian</u>.
3. Los niños <u>se pelean</u>.
4. Mi hermano y yo siempre <u>nos apoyamos</u>.
5. Julio y Carla no <u>se hablan</u>.
6. <u>Nos vemos</u> después de las clases los viernes.
7. Los compañeros <u>se ven</u> en el colegio.
8. Mi hermana y yo <u>nos compramos</u> regalos de Navidad.

C 1. Marisol y José se ven en el parque.
2. Nosotros siempre nos contamos secretos.
3. Nos escribimos cartas.
4. Susana y Alfonso se llaman por teléfono.
5. Nosotros nos conocemos muy bien.
6. Los hermanos se apoyan.
7. Irma y Francisco se aman.

D You can use the context to determine when the plural reflexive verb form expresses the idea of *each other*. In the first sentence, it doesn't make sense to say *Paola and Virginia write themselves*, and in the second sentence it does not make sense to say *Paola and Virgina dress each other*.

■ THE UNKNOWN OR NONEXISTENT

A 1. I am looking for a woman who speaks Spanish. (U)
2. I know someone who is in that class. (K)
3. There isn't anyone in my family who plays guitar. (U)
4. We want to find someone who could play piano. (U)
5. Nobody here plays volleyball. (U)
6. Marisa is someone who is responsible. (K)
7. Sandra's pet is playful and bright. (K)

8. My mom is looking for a job that would be rewarding. (U)

B 1. Busco un novio que sea simpático. (U)
2. Tengo una amiga que es muy inteligente. (K)
3. No hay nadie aquí que hable inglés. (U)
4. Conozco a una maestra que habla japonés. (K)
5. No conozco a nadie que tenga un piano. (U)
6. Hay un estudiante en mi clase que es muy guapo. (K)
7. No hay ningún chico que sea tan guapo como él. (U)
8. Tengo una prima que juega al béisbol con los muchachos. (K)

C 1. Busco un secretario que sepa usar la computadora.
2. Busco una redactora que hable español.
3. Busco un abogado que sea inteligente.
4. Busco una cantante que toque la guitarra eléctrica.
5. Busco un camarero que tenga mucha energía.
6. Busco un conductor que conozca la ciudad.
7. Busco un auxiliar de vuelo que le guste viajar.
8. Busco unos maestros que sepan español.

D 1. Busco una persona que trabaje por la mañana.
2. Marisa busca a una amiga que le escriba cartas.

CAPÍTULO 8

■ IMPERSONAL EXPRESSIONS

A 1. It's true that I made a mistake. (T)
2. It's uncertain whether Mark will come for dinner. (D)
3. Elisa is sure that her sister is at home. (T)
4. It's obvious that Mandy is in love. (T)
5. We doubt that we'll find cheap tickets to Spain. (D)
6. It's important that the students understand the rules. (N)

B 1. Es evidente que este periódico es el mejor. (T)
2. Es importante que leas el periódico. (N)
3. No es cierto que la sección de cocina tenga la receta. (D)
4. No es dudoso que la sección de ocio es interesante. (T)

Copyright © by Holt, Rinehart and Winston. All rights reserved.

5. Es importante que escuches el programa de las ocho. (N)
6. Es necesario que compremos esta revista. (N)
7. No es verdad que Rita mire demasiado la televisión. (D)
8. Es dudoso que la foto aparezca en la primera plana. (D)

C 1. Es importante que el director **compre** discos compactos para las computadoras de la escuela.
2. Es dudoso que los maestros **quieran** videojuegos en el salón de clases.
3. No es cierto que los estudiantes no **sepan** usar la tecnología.
4. Es verdad que nosotros no **podemos** escuchar la radio en clase.
5. Es obvio que el Sr. García no **quiere** tener una televisión en la biblioteca.
6. No es dudoso que Ricardo **lee** muchos libros.
7. Es necesario que Rosario **haga** la tarea.
8. Es evidente que nosotros **leemos** mucho.

D 1. No es verdad que me guste la clase de matemáticas.
2. Es dudoso que el Sr. González nos dé un día libre.
3. No es obvio que la respuesta sea B.

CAPÍTULO 9

▇ DESCRIBING EMOTIONAL REACTIONS

A 1. Margarita <u>was</u> happy when she <u>saw</u> her grade. (result)
2. Ignacio <u>was feeling</u> tired when the movie <u>started</u>.
3. Silvia <u>was feeling</u> better when she <u>left</u> for school.
4. María <u>felt</u> angry when Isabel <u>yelled</u> at her. (result)
5. Pedro <u>was</u> surprised when Ana <u>showed</u> up. (result)
6. We <u>were feeling</u> sleepy when Mom <u>arrived</u> with the movie.
7. Paola <u>was</u> excited when she <u>found out</u> the final score. (result)
8. Vicente <u>was feeling</u> sick when his mom called the doctor.

B 1. Sergio <u>estaba</u> cansado cuando su madre le <u>pidió</u> ayuda.
2. Alberto <u>se sintió</u> feliz cuando <u>recibió</u> sus notas. (result)
3. Carmen <u>se sentía</u> contenta cuando <u>empezó</u> a llover.

4. Marta <u>estuvo</u> enojada cuando José <u>llegó</u> tarde. (result)
5. Tú <u>te sentías</u> bien cuando <u>decidiste</u> jugar al fútbol.
6. <u>Estuve</u> sorprendida cuando mi prima me <u>llamó</u>. (result)
7. <u>Nos sentimos</u> orgullosos cuando <u>terminamos</u> el proyecto. (result)
8. Emilio <u>estaba</u> confundido cuando <u>hizo</u> la tarea.

C Sabes que Mónica va a casarse? Yo **supe** la noticia el martes. Salimos con los amigos, y Mónica nos contó todo. Nosotros **nos pusimos** muy contentos. Ella dijo que sus padres **estuvieron** sorprendidos cuando ella les contó la noticia. Cuando ellos se quedaron en silencio, ella **se sintió** mal. Pero luego, cuando ellos **quisieron** abrazarla, ella **se sintió** feliz.

D 1. Yo siempre **sabía** que Luis era un chico honesto.
2. Nosotros estuvimos contentos cuando **supimos** que Tomás se sentía mejor.
3. ¿Cuando **supiste** (tú) que Clara tuvo un bebé?
4. Rosa **sabía** cocinar muy bien y me preparaba platos deliciosos.

E 1. I always knew that Luis was an honest boy.
2. We were happy when we found out that Tomás was feeling better.
3. When did you find out that Clara had a baby?
4. Rosa knew how to cook very well, and she always made me delicious meals.

▇ VERB MOOD TO EXPRESS DENIAL

A 1. I <u>disagree</u> that all actors are arrogant.
2. It is not true that men are more diligent athletes than women.
3. Teresa <u>denies</u> that the city is more interesting than the country.
4. It is not true that teachers are unfriendly.
5. We <u>disagree</u> that our employers acted unfairly.
6. It is not true that all tourists are annoying.
7. Elisa <u>denies</u> that musicians only think about music.
8. Eduardo <u>disagrees</u> that lawyers are dishonest.

B 1. Yo <u>niego</u> que los científicos no escriban bien.
2. <u>No es verdad</u> que los hombres sólo

Copyright © by Holt, Rinehart and Winston. All rights reserved.

hablen de deportes.

3. No es cierto que los niños no (quieran) hablar con los abuelos.
4. Paco niega que los profesores (sean) aburridos.
5. No es verdad que los jóvenes no se preocupen por la política.
6. Verónica niega que las chicas no (puedan) ser matemáticos.
7. No es cierto que los hombres no (sepan) cocinar.
8. No es verdad que los atletas (sean) bobos.

C 1. Es verdad que los maestros tienen un trabajo importante.
2. No estoy de acuerdo que las mujeres sean mejores maestras.
3. No niego que los estudiantes trabajan duro.
4. Mi maestro niega que los muchachos saquen mejores notas.
5. No es verdad que todos los estudiantes aprendan de la misma forma.
6. No es cierto que todos los asiáticos comprendan las matemáticas.

D

ENGLISH	SPANISH
1. indicative	indicative
2. indicative	subjunctive
3. subjunctive	subjunctive
4. indicative	subjunctive
5. both	both
6. subjunctive	subjunctive

■ THE CONDITIONAL

A 1. What would Luis Miguel do to relax? He **would sing** .
2. What would Julia Álvarez and Elena Quiroga do if they had free time? They **would write** .
3. What would Juan Carlos do if he had a day off? He **would go** to Mallorca.
4. What would Penélope Cruz do if she won an award? She **would thank** the Academy.
5. What would Pedro Martínez do if he had to prepare for a game? He **would practice** his fast ball.
6. What would Joan Baez do if asked to perform? She **would practice** the guitar.
7. Where would Elena Ochoa travel if she had the choice? She **would travel** to the Moon.

B 1. ¿Qué haríamos si tuviéramos música? **Bailaríamos** toda la noche.

2. ¿Qué haría Pablo Neruda si estuviera aquí? Él **escribiría** poesía.
3. ¿Qué harías tú con mil dólares? **Compraría** una computadora.
4. ¿Qué harían los artistas si tuvieran tiempo? **Pintarían** paisajes.
5. ¿Qué harían los niños si los padres salieran? **Almorzarían** helado de chocolate.
6. ¿Qué harían los estudiantes si no estuviera el profesor? **Jugarían** al baloncesto en el salón de clases.
7. ¿Qué haría Henry Cisneros en una conferencia? **Hablaría** de política.

C 1. Yo serviría flan de postre cada día.
2. Mis amigos vendrían a mi casa todos los días.
3. Nosotros jugaríamos todo el día y no trabajaríamos.
4. Yo no tendría que hacer la cama nunca.
5. Mi madre haría la tarea.
6. El televisor estaría en la cocina.

CAPÍTULO 10

■ VERB MOOD AFTER CONJUNCTIONS

A 1. Unless it rains, we will have class outside.
2. As soon as I finish school, I leave for Venezuela.
3. Provided we have time, we will see the Statue of Liberty.
4. Adriana learns about Hispanic culture so that she can understand her heritage.
5. Alberto and Juan walk in Central Park until it starts to rain.
6. When you go to Costa Rica, you should explore the rainforest.
7. I have a guidebook in case we want to explore the city.
8. David will finish his work before you arrive.

B 1. Cuando vayamos a Puerto Rico, vamos a visitar a mis abuelos.
2. Traigo un paraguas en caso de que llueva.
3. Mis abuelos nos dieron un mapa para que podamos explorar la ciudad.
4. En cuanto salgas de la clase, salimos para el aeropuerto.
5. Llámame tan pronto como llegues a San Juan.
6. Después de que visitemos a mis abuelos, vamos al campo.
7. Quiero aprender a hablar el español para

Copyright © by Holt, Rinehart and Winston. All rights reserved.

que no pierda mi cultura.
8. Cuando vuelvas a Nueva York, ya hablarás mejor.

C future

D
1. En cuanto terminó la clase, fuimos al cine.
2. Cuando vayas a Ecuador, debes visitar Quito.
3. Quiero aprender el español antes de que estudie en Madrid.
4. Cuando Luis viaja, siempre me escribe cartas.
5. Sergio irá a la escuela en Nueva York, con tal de que gane la beca.
6. Señora Álvarez habla español en casa para que Rosa sea bilingüe.
7. Cuando pienso en mi futuro, siempre sueño con ser artista.

E A verb following a conjunction should be in the subjunctive when it refers to a future event that may or may not occur.

CAPÍTULO 11

■ THE PAST SUBJUNCTIVE

A
1. If I had one wish, I would wish for peace. (S)
2. If Belén lived in Spain, she would eat paella. (S)
3. If we go to Madrid, we will try tapas. (I)
4. If you were a teacher, what would you teach? (S)
5. If I study Spanish, I will go to South America. (I)
6. If they met an actor, they would be surprised. (S)

B
1. Si Paco viajara a Costa Rica, iría a Monteverde. (S)
2. Si hace buen tiempo, vamos a ver los volcanes. (I)
3. Si Mónica tuviera dinero, compraría una carreta. (S)
4. Si veo una iguana, sacaré una foto. (I)
5. Si fuera el presidente, protegería las selvas. (S)
6. Si pudiera, mejoraría el sistema de educación. (S)
7. Si luchamos, podremos hacer una diferencia. (I)
8. Si no haces nada, nada va a cambiar. (I)

C
1. Yo crearía un intercambio con Costa Rica si fuera el director.
2. Mis amigos y yo protegeríamos el

medioambiente si fuéramos políticos.
3. Yo viajaría por el mundo si tuviera dinero.
4. Yo propondría un nuevo programa si conociera al gobernador.

D It is important to add the correct accents to verbs because the accent can change the tense. For example, *hablara* is the past subjunctive, but *hablará* is the future tense.

E The future tense follows the *if clause* if the verb is in the present tense. The conditional follows if the verb is in the subjunctive.

CAPÍTULO 12

■ THE PAST TENSE: SUMMARY

A
1. Alejandro refused help.
2. I was ten years old in that photograph.
3. Felipe knew my grandfather.
4. It was midnight.
5. Ernesto talked on the phone until eleven o'clock.
6. My family used to go to the lake in the summertime.
7. Laura's father was athletic.
8. Mateo ate dinner early.

B
1. Pedro tenía seis años en esta foto. (I)
2. Emilio estudió literatura en la Universidad. (P)
3. Héctor conoció al señor Guzmán anoche. (P)
4. Mi abuela era alta y rubia. (I)
5. Eran las diez y cuarto. (I)
6. María jugaba con sus primos los fines de semana. (I)
7. El sábado supe que mi tía tuvo un bebé. (P)
8. Víctor no quiso comer. (P)

C
1. Yo **tenía** veinte años cuando **decidí** estudiar periodismo.
2. Alan **estaba** en la universidad cuando **conoció** a un autor famoso.
3. Nina **quería** ser enfermera y **empezó** a trabajar en un hospital.
4. Mauricio **habló** con un científico que **vivía** en su pueblo.

D
1. Yo lloraba cuando entró Rosa en el cuarto.
2. Tú sabías que Raúl estaba en la escuela.
3. Tina supo que José ganó.

Copyright © by Holt, Rinehart and Winston. All rights reserved.